Midnight at the Barrelhouse

MIDNIGHT AT THE BARRELHOUSE

The Johnny Otis Story

George Lipsitz

University of Minnesota Press
Minneapolis
London

Visit Johnny Otis's web site at http://www.johnnyotisworld.com to view
some of his artworks and vintage photographs.

All quotations from interviews in this book are reproduced with the permission of
interview subjects.

All photographs are from the personal collection of Johnny Otis and are reproduced here with
permission of Johnny Otis, with the exception of Tom Reed's photograph of Johnny Otis
with Joe Louis at the Club Alabam, which is reproduced with permission from Tom Reed.

Portions of chapter 2 were previously published as "How Johnny Veliotes Became Johnny Otis,"
Journal of the Hellenic Diaspora 22, nos. 1–2 (2007): 81–104.

Published by the University of Minnesota Press
111 Third Avenue South, Suite 290
Minneapolis, MN 55401-2520
http://www.upress.umn.edu

Library of Congress Cataloging-in-Publication Data

Lipsitz, George.
Midnight at the Barrelhouse : the Johnny Otis story / George Lipsitz.
p.   cm.
Includes bibliographical references and index.
ISBN 978-0-8166-6678-2 (hc : alk. paper) — ISBN 978-0-8166-6679-9 (pb : alk. paper)
1. Otis, Johnny, 1921– 2. Rhythm and blues musicians—United States—Biography.
I. Title.
ML419.O85L56   2010
781.643092—dc22
[B]
2009012628

Printed in the United States of America on acid-free paper

The University of Minnesota is an equal-opportunity educator and employer.

17 16 15 14 13   10 9 8 7 6 5 4 3

Contents

Introduction THERE'S A RIOT GOIN' ON

 As he drove home from work late in the afternoon on Friday the 13th in August 1965, Johnny Otis could see black smoke rising in the sky and orange flames flickering from the rooftops of distant buildings. Rioters in the Watts ghetto were looting stores, setting buildings on fire, and pelting police officers and firefighters with bricks, bottles, and stones. It started with a seemingly routine traffic stop on Wednesday night near the intersection of 116th and Avalon in Watts. Some pushing and shoving between white California Highway Patrol officers and a small group of spectators who had witnessed the officers' arrest of a black motorist escalated rapidly. Over the next five days, rioters set a major part of the city ablaze. Eventually fourteen thousand National Guard soldiers and fifteen hundred police officers occupied South Central Los Angeles and Watts in an attempt to quell the uprising. They made close to four thousand arrests, shot and wounded more than nine hundred people, and killed thirty-four looters and bystanders. By the time the smoke cleared, authorities estimated that more than two hundred million dollars worth of property and six hundred buildings had been either damaged or destroyed.[1] The death toll in Watts over five days exceeded the number of Americans killed in Vietnam during the same period of time; the number of Blacks killed during the insurrection exceeded the combined number of people killed in all of the civil disturbances that had convulsed the nation in the previous year.[2]

Although stunned by the force and fury of the riots, Otis felt that he had known for a long time that this day would come. During his long and successful career as a musician, bandleader, singer, radio disc jockey, television show host, and music producer, he had witnessed mounting frustration and rage in the Black community in Los Angeles. Rebellion had been in the air and on his mind. A few months before the riots broke out, he had completed an oil painting and entered it into a competition celebrating works of art about Black history. His entry won first prize. Otis's painting depicted the 1831 Virginia slave rebel Nat Turner, a visionary preacher who took up arms against the slave system and struck fear into the hearts of slave owners everywhere.[3]

In Otis's weekly column in the *Sentinel,* one of the newspapers serving the local African American community, he had called attention over and over again to the anger that pervaded the ghetto: anger about stores that charged customers high prices for inferior goods yet refused to hire neighborhood residents as workers, anger about the city's segregated Black residential areas and the exorbitant profits that slumlords extracted from dwellings unfit for human habitation, and anger about the largely segregated, poorly funded, and culturally insensitive schools that Black children found themselves forced to attend.

Most of all, Otis knew that inner-city residents deeply resented the policies and practices of local law enforcement agencies. Los Angeles Police Department officers and Los Angeles County Sheriff's deputies routinely provoked citizens with confrontational tactics, subjecting them to arbitrary traffic stops and detentions on dubious charges. The police were nowhere to be found, however, when asked to respond to actual crimes against Black people. The ghetto was thus both overpoliced and underpoliced. In a *Sentinel* column in May 1962, Otis complained, "The police department approaches our community like a military arm of occupation."[4] A little more than a month later he noted, "The detestable attitude of many Los Angeles policemen toward Negro citizens continues to boil as a major issue in the community. Almost every letter received by this column now deals with the problem."[5]

The Black executive director of the Los Angeles World Trade Center reported that police officers had stopped him twelve times in the previous six years while driving his car. They treated him roughly every time, even though they found no crime for which he could be detained or charged.[6] Journalist, attorney, and activist Loren Miller had warned that Los Angeles was ripe for a riot in May 1964.[7] Roy Wilkins, the leader of the National Association for the Advancement of Colored People, had singled out the

Los Angeles Police Department for unusually strong criticism for years. The generally moderate and temperate leader spoke with unusual fervor when he informed participants in a rally on October 1, 1961, that his organization had received frequent complaints from Blacks in Los Angeles about police officers stopping and detaining people on their way home from work. In many cases, the officers made Blacks raise their hands and lean against walls while the police interrogated them, often when no crimes had even been reported in the area. When Wilkins protested against these practices in a letter to the LAPD early in 1962, the Police Commission's president, John Kenney, dismissed the complaint as "libelous and provocative in tone." He condemned Wilkins's letter as filled with content designed to "stimulate inordinate emotional responses" that would create "unwarranted divisions in the country" and impede "progress toward improved race relations."[8] Yet the facts were on Wilkins's side. Local police officers had killed more than sixty Black suspects between 1963 and 1965. Twenty-seven of them were shot in the back. Twenty-five of them were unarmed.[9]

Ignoring the problem had not made it go away, Otis thought. It only guaranteed that the day of reckoning would be all that much more violent when it finally came. As he drove into the riot area, Otis remembered when the neighborhoods now convulsed by violence had been thriving entertainment and shopping districts. He recalled a time when the Dunbar Hotel, the Club Alabam, and the Lincoln Theatre had been focal points of a rich musical, artistic, social, and political culture in Black Los Angeles. Even when the city's bar curfew took effect at two in the morning, the fun did not stop. Revelers moved to "after-hours" joints such as Johnny Cornish's Double V or the Casablanca Club. Menus at these establishments featured fried chicken with biscuits and honey, but these places also served up impromptu jam sessions, dancing to hot rhythm and blues, and saxophone duels between the likes of Wardell Gray and Dexter Gordon. The Brownskin Café served the best chili in town. Alex Lovejoy's Breakfast Club advertised itself as the home of the Big Leg Chicken. Even people who had never visited Lovejoy's club knew its slogan: "If you haven't tried Lovejoy's Big Leg Chicken, then, Jack, you just ain't been stickin'." Jack's Basket Room at Thirty-second and Central offered "Bird in a Basket" from midnight until dawn and advertised its specialty with the slogan "Chicken Ain't Nuten but a Bird." Musicians playing at the Harlem Hot Spot nightclub in San Pedro looked forward to intermissions between sets, because they could wander over to a nearby Filipino restaurant that served plates of delicious chicken adobo. Black Dot McGee's experiences paying off police officers while he ran a small illegal horse race betting parlor on Central Avenue prepared him perfectly to become the proprietor of a series of after-hours cafés, barbecue cafés, and grills including the Bar-B-Q Café on Western Avenue.[10]

Customers came to Central Avenue from all over the metropolitan area by catching the U or the V Red Car streetcar line downtown. A passenger on those cars or a motorist driving along Central Avenue on Wednesday nights could hear the sounds of gospel choirs rehearsing in churches mixed with the sounds of blues singers performing in nightclubs. Sometimes their styles were so similar that it was hard to tell which was which until the lyrics gave them away. If the singers said, "Ooh Baby," the song came from a nightclub, but if they said, "Ooh Jesus," the song came from a church.

Saxophonist Clifford Solomon remembers how Central Avenue and adjoining streets vibrated with the musical culture of Los Angeles. This vibrant culture was felt not just on the avenue itself but also in the bustling business atmosphere and street life on Washington Boulevard, San Pedro Street, Santa Barbara Boulevard, Western Avenue, Avalon Boulevard, and Jefferson Boulevard. Blocks away in Watts, Central Avenue's culture spread out along Wilmington Avenue, Imperial Highway, and 103rd Street.[11] These beautiful places owed their existence to ugly realities. Housing segregation and aggressive policing confined African Americans to a geographically small sector of the metropolitan area. That concentration produced a strong sense of community. Solomon recalls how the mere sight of other saxophonists on the streets challenged and inspired him. "Walk down Central Avenue any afternoon and you might see Lucky Thompson in a barbershop getting his hair cut. You might see Ben Webster arguing with Don Byas in a bar and Johnny Hodges getting on the streetcar."[12]

For more than two decades prior to the Watts Riots, Black Los Angeles had been very good to Johnny Otis. It had given him the chance to meet and play music with some of the musicians he admired most. At one time or another, he had accompanied jazz virtuosos Lester Young, Charlie Parker, Ben Webster, Lionel Hampton, Illinois Jacquet, and Art Tatum. His bands featured performances by blues singers T-Bone Walker, Pee Wee Crayton, and Big Joe Turner. In the neighborhood nightclubs, restaurants, and after-hours joints along Central Avenue, Otis encountered an impressive succession of intellectuals, artists, activists, and entrepreneurs. He helped the multitalented Maya Angelou raise money to send greatly needed educational and health supplies to people in newly independent African nations. He routinely exchanged ideas with local black newspaper publishers and journalists who crusaded for civil rights, especially Charlotta Bass of the *California Eagle* and Leon Washington of the *Los Angeles Sentinel.* Johnny Otis found himself drawn to religious life in Los Angeles as well, especially to the preaching and teaching of the dynamic reverend Clayton Russell of the People's Independent Church. During the 1930s and 1940s, the charismatic young minister routinely told his congregation and radio listeners that he felt he would be sinning if he preached to hungry people from the pulpit but failed to work to help them get jobs and food. Russell's church sponsored a performance by the Duke Ellington Orchestra in 1941, because the pastor wanted to demonstrate that the Holy Spirit was at work in the secular world as well as in the sanctuary. He employed a jazz musician to play the organ for Sunday morning services, knowing full well that the keyboardist played swing music on Saturday nights at clubs until 2 AM, coming to church after having gotten only four hours' sleep. Yet despite his exhaustion, the keyboardist would make Reverend Russell's services "swing" in a unique way. At a time when African Americans were frequently excluded from welfare and relief programs run by local, state, and federal governments, Russell mobilized his parishioners to provide housing, job training, and education for young people in the neighborhood. He promoted self-help projects incessantly, raising capital for a chain of grocery stores to be owned and managed by Blacks so that customers could shop for high-quality food in their own neighborhoods, while their neighbors acquired important managerial and job skills.

Russell also organized public political campaigns against discrimination, protesting against the Los Angeles streetcar system because it confined its Black workers to janitorial jobs. He organized Black women to flood the offices of the U.S. Employment Services agency with job applications when agency spokespersons argued that the absence of Black women from wartime assembly-line jobs was caused by the women's lack of interest in obtaining such jobs. Otis listened regularly to Reverend Russell's Sunday morning radio program, *The Visitor,* and admired the flair and fervor of his ministry. Later in his life, Otis would become a preacher himself, and he modeled the activities of his ministry along the lines established by the People's Independent Church.[13]

The Central Avenue scene in the 1940s and early 1950s attracted visitors from all over the nation and all over the world. During one nightclub engagement, lawyer and future Supreme Court justice Thurgood Marshall came up to the bandstand to introduce himself to Otis. Author and playwright Langston Hughes often said hello when he dropped in to hear the music. Otis joined with community activists and musicians to found Attack, a black political activist organization dedicated to fair hiring and electing Blacks to public office. Attack organized study groups to help people learn more about social issues. Its members profited from long and intense discussions with visiting notables. Otis attended talks delivered to the group by famed author James Baldwin and by a man whom Otis had known back in the 1940s as a street hustler named Detroit Red. By the time he spoke to the group though, he had become known to the world as the Muslim minister and activist Malcolm X.[14]

From the moment Johnny Otis first arrived in Los Angeles in 1943, every day seemed to offer a marvelous new experience. He led the House Band at the Club Alabam and later opened his own nightclub, the Barrelhouse, in Watts. As a recording artist, he succeeded in placing fifteen songs on the best-seller charts from 1950 to 1952. Otis had one of the biggest pop music hits of all time with "Willie and the Hand Jive" in 1958. He composed top-selling songs that became successes for other artists as well, including "Every Beat of My Heart" for Gladys Knight and the Pips, "So Fine" for the Fiestas, "Roll with Me Henry," which became "The Wallflower" for Etta James, and "Dance with Me Henry" for Georgia Gibbs. As a promoter, producer, and talent scout for Savoy, King, Duke, and other independent record labels, Otis discovered and launched the careers of Etta James, Hank Ballard, Esther Phillips, Jackie Wilson, Big Mama Thornton, Sugar Pie DeSanto, Linda Hopkins, and Little Willie John, among others. He produced big hits for Little Esther, Etta James, and Johnny Ace, as well as less commercially successful but even more artistically triumphant recordings by Charles Williams, Barbara Morrison, and Don "Sugarcane" Harris.

As a musician, Otis played the drums on Big Mama Thornton's original recording of "Hound Dog," on Illinois Jacquet's "Flying Home," and on Lester Young's "Jammin' with Lester." Otis provided the hauntingly beautiful vibraphone accompaniment to Johnny Ace's "Pledging My Love," played vibes on his own recording of "Stardust," featuring Ben Webster on tenor saxophone, and he played piano and tambourine on Frank Zappa's

Hot Rats album. When the occasion demanded it, Otis could also play harpsichord, celesta, and timpani.

As an artist, promoter, disc jockey, and television host, he brought Black music to new audiences, in the process inspiring some of his listeners to become performers themselves. Youthful customers at his Watts rhythm and blues nightclub, the Barrelhouse, included future activist and poet Jayne Cortez and world champion surfer Miki Dora.[15] Brian Wilson, who later formed the Beach Boys, felt inspired to take up the electric guitar after his cousins introduced him to Otis's radio show on KFOX.[16] Legendary producer Phil Spector was also a fan of the show when he was a youth.[17] As teenagers, John Stewart (later of the Kingston Trio) and Frank Zappa (later of the Mothers of Invention) hung around Otis's recording studio to learn about music.[18] Zappa even grew a mustache in imitation of—and in tribute to—Johnny Otis.[19] Dave Alvin, who later formed the Blasters with his brother Phil, discovered what he wanted to do with his life one night at the Ash Grove nightclub when he heard his first live music show, a performance that featured Johnny Otis, Joe Turner, and T-Bone Walker.[20] Roy Buchanan learned his distinctive guitar playing as part of the Johnny Otis Orchestra, drawing directly on the sixteenth-note patterns played by Otis's guitarist Jimmy Nolen, who later played with James Brown.[21] Eric Clapton enjoyed one of his biggest commercial successes with a cover version of "Willie and the Hand Jive." Bob Dylan bought an artwork that Johnny Otis created. When Dylan had difficulty with one number he was trying to record in New Orleans in the 1980s, he imagined himself singing the song with the Johnny Otis Orchestra.[22] Colonel Tom Parker's decision to have his client Elvis Presley do a cover version of the Jerry Leiber and Mike Stoller composition "Hound Dog," which Johnny Otis had produced for Big Mama Thornton, enabled Presley to secure one of his biggest hits.

Yet even more precious to Johnny Otis than his commercial successes were the personal, social, intellectual, and cultural opportunities that opened up to him in the Black community. His life in music had enabled him to meet people he deeply respected and loved. It allowed him to witness the wonderful personal qualities of Willie Mae "Big Mama" Thornton. She sang, played drums and harmonica, and wrote songs while frequently taking sips from a concoction of her own invention: grape juice mixed with embalming fluid. Big Mama was so strong that she sometimes picked up a large standing stage microphone in one hand, singing through the microphone end while holding the stand airborne and pointing its large iron bottom at the audience.[23] One night at a dance in Florida, a drunk came out of the crowd and slapped Johnny Otis in the face. Before Johnny himself had a chance to respond, Big Mama picked up the drunk and threw him across the floor, bellowing, "Don't nobody mess with my buddy!"[24] It pained Otis to see how little recognition and reward Thornton derived from her artistry and how justifiably bitter it made her. She told one interviewer that her recording of "Hound Dog" had sold more than two million copies but that she had received only five hundred dollars for her efforts.[25]

Otis played drums on eight recordings by Lester Young. The tenor saxophonist dazzled Otis with his virtuosity. Young's conversational tone on the instrument and his extraordinarily long, original, and carefully conceived solos, coupled with his sensitivity to all that was being played by the other musicians, set a high standard for others to follow. Otis knew that Young's influence went far beyond jazz, that an entire generation of blues and rhythm and blues artists played the way they did because of Young. Blues great B. B. King derived much of his style on the guitar from Young's phrasing, and Otis himself imitated Young every time he played a solo on the vibraphone.[26]

Young was even more impressive to Otis, however, as a person. The saxophonist's personal eccentricities often prevented people from seeing the serious individual underneath. Young smoked marijuana constantly, sang to himself on the bandstand, and dressed distinctively in a signature porkpie hat. He held his saxophone high in the air when he performed, sometimes holding it above his head, turning the mouthpiece around, and playing the instrument as if he were smoking a pipe. Young had his own unique way of speaking as well. He added endings like *-o-reenie* and *-o-roonie* to nouns. He made up new words such as *evonce,* a term he deployed to punctuate conversations solemnly, although Otis never found anyone who knew exactly what Young meant by the word. Young's slang expressions "you dig?" and "cool" influenced generations of musicians and their followers. Other phrases, however, remained his own. Young would say, "I feel a draft," to express his perception of hostility in the room, "letter A" to represent the beginning of things, and "doom" to say good-bye or to end a conversation.[27]

Otis saw Young as a man who loved his people and his culture deeply, perhaps too deeply for a racist society to tolerate. Young's eccentric behavior worked to protect the tenor saxophonist's privacy, to insulate him from mistreatment and discrimination, to build bridges with others through speech in the same way that he did with his playing, which reminded many people of a human voice singing. Most important, Otis viewed Young's speech, dress, and flamboyant stage performances as responses to the demeaning minstrel show antics that Black musicians characteristically had to enact in order to perform before white audiences. Otis experienced some of this humiliation himself while playing in swing bands in the early 1940s. He perceived Young's many inventions as carefully crafted alternatives to minstrelsy rather than as mere personal eccentricities.[28] Deeply offended by racism, Young found few role models in U.S. society. "Everybody's so chickenshit," he once complained. "They want everybody who is a Negro to be an Uncle Tom, or Uncle Remus, or Uncle Sam, and I can't make it."[29]

Los Angeles seemed to have come a long way from the days of Lester Young when Johnny Otis started his drive home on August 13, 1965. He wondered what had happened to the world he had shared with Young and others in the 1940s and 1950s. It seemed to him that more was being destroyed in the riots than businesses and homes. The community that had nurtured and sustained him for most of his adult life seemed on the verge of destruction. When Otis reached the intersection of Manchester and Broadway, he felt that he had to see for himself close up what was happening. Earlier that day he had had his first argument ever with his longtime friend Preston Love. Johnny said he wanted to witness what was happening in the riot area. Worried about his friend's safety, Love had implored him to stay away from the danger. Yet instead of taking the freeway to his home, Otis turned east on Manchester Boulevard and drove right toward the disturbance. "I know it was stupid. I know it was foolish," he admitted later, "but I had to go! Nothing naïve like wanting to help or get into the mess, but I wanted to see. SEE WITH MY OWN EYES . . . even if I got the hell kicked out of me or worse."[30]

As he thought about the encounter between citizens and police officers near Avalon and 116th, which had sparked the riots, Otis recalled his own violent impulses in response to police mistreatment. He had been part of a group picketing a ghetto store owned by whites in the mid-1950s. The owners would not hire any Blacks, and the demonstrators demanded that they do so. At one demonstration, a police officer grabbed Otis's picket sign out of his hands and asked, "What the fuck do you think you're doing?" As Otis started to explain carefully that Black people were being treated unfairly and that he was trying to make things better, the officer circled behind him and kicked him in the rear, "so hard I saw stars!" Enraged, Otis turned around to hit the officer, but *Sentinel* publisher Leon Washington grabbed him first and pulled him away, whispering, "No fighting back, son . . . no fighting back, we can't win that way, they'll kill us baby." Just about every time Otis encountered Washington after that, the publisher would chuckle and say, "I saved your life, didn't I?"[31]

Three years before the riots, Otis had attended a mass community meeting at the Second Baptist Church. People assembled there to protest the actions of police officers who had killed a member of the Nation of Islam, Ronald Stokes, and severely wounded four others, including one man paralyzed for life by a police bullet that shattered his spine.[32] Malcolm X spoke to the crowd that night, and he impressed Johnny tremendously. Otis discovered that the man whom he had known casually back in the 1940s as Detroit Red had become a different person. It amazed Otis to see him speak with such dignity, commitment, and eloquence. After Minister Malcolm spoke, the crowd demonstrated its enthusiastic agreement with his remarks, hugging one another and cheering. Tears of happiness flowed down people's faces because they were so grateful for Malcolm's ability to express their frustration, anger, and grief so precisely. Johnny felt that, like many of the people who were present at that meeting, he would never be the same person he had been before it, that he had been permanently transformed by Malcolm X's words.[33]

Other memories flashed through Johnny Otis's mind as he traveled past familiar landmarks. He thought about the Largo Theater, where he had discovered Little Esther Phillips at a talent show, and about Helen's on Hooper, a private house converted into a club where Art Tatum used to hold forth on the piano. He remembered broadcasting his radio show live from the front window of Dolphin's of Hollywood Record Store, at Vernon and Central, and from Conley's Record Rack, at 110th and Wilmington. He recalled Little Willie John performing at the Normandie Theatre and stopping the show with an eight-minute version of the song "CC Rider." He remembered the Barrelhouse Club that he used to run at 107th and Wilmington and the song he wrote in its honor, "Midnight at the Barrelhouse." Yet in the midst of all this remembering, as he drove right into the heart of one of the most violent outbreaks of Black rage in U.S. history, Otis seemed to forget one important thing, at least for the moment.

He was white.

For all his immersion in African American life and culture, Johnny Otis was not actually Black. He was a white man born as John Alexander Veliotes into an immigrant Greek family. He had grown up among Blacks and had lived much of his life as if he were Black. Yet rioters who encountered him on the street might not know about his complex personal history or his deep commitments to the Black community. His skin color and phenotype matched those of people who insulted and plundered the community—the slumlords, store owners, bill collectors, police officers, and con artists who got away with things in the ghetto they could not do in more prosperous parts of town. Otis shared the rage of the rioters, but when they saw his face, he would likely bear the brunt of their rage as well. As Malcolm X once said, when a racial powder keg explodes, it doesn't care who it hits. It takes the innocent along with the guilty.[34]

Born in Vallejo, in northern California, in 1921, Otis grew up in the city of Berkeley with his Greek immigrant parents and a younger sister and brother. The Veliotes family lived upstairs from the small grocery store they ran at 2725 Dohr Street in a racially mixed neighborhood.[35] At an early age Johnny felt captivated by Black culture, by the spiritual, moral, and intellectual richness he encountered in the sanctified churches that he attended with his Black playmates, by the music of gospel choirs, jazz bands, and blues singers, by the way Black people dressed, danced, and talked. "Everybody I came into contact with as a kid, all my playmates were black," he recalls. His friendship circle sometimes disturbed authority figures. "I was around thirteen when the ugly head of racism really reared up," he recalls. "I was told very diplomatically at school by a counselor that I should associate more with whites. After that I left and never came back to school. I never felt white. I wouldn't leave black culture to go to heaven. It's richer, more rewarding and fulfilling for me."[36]

Otis moved to Los Angeles in the summer of 1943 as the drummer in Harlan Leonard's "territory" band. The ensemble played to enthusiastic crowds at Central Avenue's premier night spot, the Club Alabam. When that engagement ended, Otis stayed in the city, joining Bardu Ali's band for performances at the Lincoln Theatre. Curtis Mosby, the Club Alabam's manager and the self-proclaimed "mayor" of Central Avenue, asked Otis to form and lead the house band at his club. Drawing from a rich pool of available local musicians, Otis created the sixteen-piece Johnny Otis Orchestra, featuring the talents of Paul Quinchette, James Von Streeter, Teddy Buckner, and Art Farmer.[37]

Otis knew he was white, of course, but thought of himself as "Black by persuasion."[38] When he started playing music for a living as a teenager, he entered a virtually all-Black world. First with Count Otis Matthews's West Oakland House Stompers, and later in the bands of George Morrison, Lloyd Hunter, and Harlan Leonard, Otis embraced the cultural values, musical codes, and political stances of his fellow musicians. "I was never viewed as a white kid," he explains. "It was unheard of. There wouldn't be such a thing, a white kid wouldn't be playing with black bands. Besides, there were lighter skinned black youngsters than myself playing in the bands."[39] He changed his last name from Veliotes to Otis and started dying his reddish brown hair black. Otis's wife and children were African American. He attended Black churches, wrote for a Black newspaper, and on several occasions worked as an aide to Mervyn Dymally, an extremely successful Black politician who served in the California legislature, in the House of Representatives, and as the state's lieutenant governor. Otis threw himself into the forefront of civil rights activism, marching in picket lines and speaking at rallies. The Ku Klux Klan threatened him and his family. They burned a cross on the lawn in front of his house in 1960. Yet Otis remained undaunted in his activism.[40]

Now, in 1965, he faced another kind of fire. As Otis drove his car east on Manchester and then south on Central, he entered the center of the riots. He saw looters breaking into stores. Young men threw bricks, bottles, and stones at passing cars. Buildings erupted in flames. When rioters approached Otis's car, he gave them the hand signal devised by light-skinned Blacks to indicate their race and that they were local: three fingers held up with the arm out the window and positioned as if signaling a right turn.[41] The crowd in the street let him pass without incident. Just past 103rd Street and Central, near Will Rogers Park, however, three men rushed right at his car. The first paid no heed to the hand signal, but the second stopped to look inside the vehicle. Startled, he shrieked, "Johnny Otis, are you out of your goddam mind? Get the hell out of here before you get killed!"[42]

Otis knew the man was right, that he should get out of there, but he felt torn. At that moment, his phenotype and physiognomy made it dangerous for him to remain in the ghetto, but in his mind and his heart he felt he did not belong anywhere else. The three men cleared a path for Otis's car, moving rioters away from the vehicle. One of them shouted, "It's Johnny Otis, let him back up here." Another yelled, "Blood brother, blood brother, let him through."[43] In the act of being told to leave, Otis found himself protected by Black men to whom his commitments and his culture meant something. Yet they knew full well that to many other people on the street that day, Johnny Otis would seem to be just another outsider in the ghetto.

The fact that he had been risking his life needlessly dawned on Otis for the first time. He heaved a sigh of relief now that he started to make his escape. Just as he began to pull away, however, a heavy-set Black woman flagged down his car and leaned in the driver's window. Otis didn't know if she saw him as friend or foe. He was eager to drive away and afraid of physical harm, but he simply did not want to view Black people as his enemies. Amid the frightening sounds of windows breaking, objects striking automobiles, and police car and fire engine sirens wailing, he stopped to hear what the woman had to say. Smiling in the midst of the chaos around her, she leaned against his car. Speaking calmly as if they were in the middle of a picnic, she said, "Hi, Johnny Otis." The woman asked Johnny if Pete Lewis still played with his band and if he was scheduled to play anywhere that night, because she sure liked Pete's playing. Otis answered her questions cordially (and quickly). Then he drove away as the woman turned her attentions back to the melee.[44]

As he drove away, Otis was overcome by mixed emotions. He felt his whiteness that day in a way that he had not been forced to feel it in decades. He wondered if the life he had chosen for himself as a white man living as if he were Black would still be possible in this deeply polarized country. Yet he also believed that he understood the frustration and rage that led to the riots. He knew full well how the ghetto had been created, isolated, and abandoned by the local power structure.

In just one three-block area radiating from the intersection of 103rd Street and Central Avenue, rioters burned down forty-one buildings. Johnny drove right past that intersection on August 13. As he watched buildings burn he felt a strange mixture of fear and elation. He did not enjoy seeing property destroyed or contemplating the human costs of businesses ruined. Yet he felt that the destruction reflected justified rage generated by unbearable human misery. "I thought, burn, you son of a bitch, burn!" he recalled later.[45] Otis saw the Largo Theater consumed in flames. The store where he used to buy feed for the chickens he kept in his backyard was also ablaze. He felt nostalgia for all that was being erased by the riots. But he also thought to himself, "Burn down you raggedy, funky image of Watts.... burn anyhow, DAMMIT BURN!"[46] Convulsed with emotion, Otis found himself singing the gospel song "Listen to the Lambs." "Listen, listen, listen to the lambs. / They're crying for the Lord to come by." Nobody listened, Otis thought. "They wouldn't listen to the lambs. . . . The lambs cried and finally one day the lambs turned into lions."[47]

The fears and frustrations that Johnny Otis experienced on August 13, 1965, have never left him. Everything that he had been able to accomplish up to that point, and everything he would subsequently do, depended on his appreciation of the aesthetic, moral, intellectual, and spiritual power of the Black community. But he lived in a country that seemed to despise that community and its culture. He wondered why. "That's been the big question in my life," he muses. "I've got to figure that one out. Instead of thanking God for the African presence, because they've been a great gift to this country. . . and they constantly attempted to share this gift, . . . they were always rebuffed and always used and abused and not accepted."[48]

Otis mourned the Watts world that had been destroyed even before the riots, destroyed by police harassment, housing segregation, urban renewal, disinvestment, and racist practices in education, employment, and environmental protection. He grieved over the loss of life and the damage to property that took place during the uprising, but still cherished the Watts that survived as a place "where the human spirit refuses to yield."[49] In the hearts, minds, and everyday life of its residents, Otis saw what he had come to describe as the surging glory of the African character: an indomitable and indefatigable insistence on resistance and survival that spanned centuries and held firm in the present.

Yet the Watts Riots presented Johnny Otis with another particularly personal crisis. The insurrection marked the end of the era that began for him in 1943 when he first appeared at the Club Alabam. He came to a community that quickly coalesced around its shared sense of political purpose and its lively and creative cultural life. His personal confidence grew significantly as he imbibed the optimism of that era. Otis learned to survive and thrive in Black Los Angeles. But the riots made clear that Watts would never again be what it was in the 1940s. Black Los Angeles permanently lost the places, networks, and institutions that had sustained it over the previous two decades. Johnny had felt this coming for a long time. He saw with his own eyes how city officials and private citizens conspired to close down Central Avenue in the late 1940s and early 1950s, how federal highway construction and urban renewal programs subsidized white flight from the city and destroyed the social ecology of the Black community, how housing discrimination, educational inequality, and police brutality stacked the deck against Black people. The riots seemed to place a final nail in the coffin of the social world that he knew best.

Otis had long communicated his feelings about these changes through melancholy expressions of loss. In a 1960 column for the *Sentinel,* he expressed his desire for a time machine that would enable him to take his readers back in history so that they could experience firsthand things that he had seen and done. He fantasized about showing them the jam session at Scott's Theatre Restaurant in Kansas City in 1942, where he first met Charlie Parker. He expressed his wish to travel back to the early 1950s, when stage mothers brought their children to compete in his talent shows and when he first laid eyes on young Little Willie John in his bow tie and too-tight tuxedo and an adolescent Sallie Blair in a Cinderella gown. He pined for the day when he first saw Ray Charles play in Lowell Fulson's band, for the moments when he discovered Etta James, Marie Adams, Big Mama Thornton, and Floyd Dixon.[50] The metaphor of time travel expressed his feelings of betrayal by the passage of time, feelings of displacement and dispossession by history.

These feelings started before the Watts rebellion. For much of his life Otis felt situated between a past that would not die and a future that had not yet arrived. He had witnessed the death of several social worlds during the first four decades of his life, years of dramatic political upheaval, technological innovation, and economic transformation. The transition from the 1950s to the 1960s was especially hard on him. The rising commercial appeal of guitar-based rock 'n' roll music made rhythm and blues ensembles like the ones he first created and managed in the 1940s seem obsolete. The emergence of the "baby boom" demographic transformed popular music into an endeavor in which young musicians played for young audiences. Guitar players and singers of varying abilities became stars right away, without the kinds of tutelage, apprenticeship, and acculturation that Otis and other young musicians went through in the 1930s and 1940s. Promoters found it cheaper to pay trios or quartets of guitar players and drummers than the seven- and eight-piece bands that played jump blues. Disinvestment in Black communities and destruction of their networks and infrastructures were responsible for the demolition of many of the venues where Black musicians played. Otis remembers realizing he had entered a new era when he showed up at clubs and found that they no longer had in-house pianos because rock bands did not need them. When the Beatles took the music world by storm in the 1960s, they helped destroy the careers of many of the artists they admired most, whose music inspired their own singing and playing. Johnny remembers, "The white boys from England took our music and recycled it, to use a polite term." The damage they did was more than aesthetic. "In a way, it was the end of our lives—our musical lives, at least," Johnny recalls.[51]

The end of those musical lives amounted to more than just fewer jobs and recording dates. It meant more than having to give up the stage and taking nine-to-five jobs outside show business. Popular music itself changed. It pained Johnny to see some musicians become big stars even when they could not so much as keep a steady beat, sing on key, or play their instruments in tune. He regretted that the younger generation did not revere and learn from older musicians the way he had when he first started to play. Otis felt that they missed out not only on important aspects of their musical education but also on the kinds of life lessons about deportment and comportment that he derived from his apprenticeship in the music industry.[52]

This crisis that the 1960s posed for Johnny Otis resembled previous moments of historical change in his life. The rhythm and blues music of the 1940s and 1950s, for which he had developed so much nostalgia by 1965, had actually been forced on him initially because of the demise of the big bands. As a youth in the 1930s, Otis longed to play like Jo Jones and the other great drummers of the swing era. When he formed his own band at his Barrelhouse nightclub in Watts in 1948, he used the Basie band as a model. But then after World War II, Black workers who had been hired in defense industries during the war experienced mass layoffs, ending the prosperity that had sustained jazz during the first part of the 1940s. Consequently, many of the big bands dissolved, and even the Basie and Ellington organizations saw their earnings and opportunities decline. Otis had to break up his band and make the transition to a smaller combo. "We all had big band experience and we longed for that big-band sound," he recalled years later, "but the day came and the money wasn't there. People's tastes changed; the war was over and the economy took a big tumble. We were faced with having to survive in music, so I did what a lot of us did: Instead of seven or eight brass, I cut it down to two brass, and instead of five reeds, I cut it down to two reeds. So right there I chopped off a whole lot of salaries and I made quite a change in the drums, piano, and guitar."[53]

Economic changes altered aesthetics in 1950s music as well. Otis not only changed the size of his band in the late 1940s; he geared the music they played to popular tastes as well. He noticed that while audiences loved and respected jazz, they really came to life when the band played blues, jumps, and boogie-woogies. "That's what really moved them," he recalls, "so when I started recording with the smaller band, I moved in that direction and so did the other guys."[54] Otis replaced the rhythm guitar that he had used in his big band with a lead guitar played by Pete Lewis in the bluesy style of T-Bone Walker. He passed over more talented jazz drummers to hire Leard Bell, who could play a simple backbeat for hours and hours. He selected Lady Dee Williams as his pianist because of her background in gospel music and her skill at playing the blues and boogie-woogie sounds that audiences and dancers alike loved to hear.[55]

The musical changes of the late 1940s came in tandem with dramatic transformations in politics and social relations as well. The postwar period proved to be a big disappointment to Black communities, as postwar economic growth bypassed inner cities. Intellectuals and activists worried that the tools and skills they had developed previously would be inadequate for meeting the challenges of the postwar era. Otis was not the only person challenged by the changes in the postwar period. He shared that difficulty with an entire generation. Harold Cruse remembers, "World War II shattered a world irrevocably. But people who thought as I did were called upon in 1945 to treat the postwar era with intellectual and critical tools more applicable to the vanished world of the thirties—a world we never had time to understand as we lived it."[56]

Thus, the sense that Otis had in the 1960s of the ground eroding beneath his feet came not only from the disruptions of that decade but also from the rapid and dramatic changes that had taken place between the early years of the war and the postwar era and between the early postwar era and the 1950s. Yet the story is still not complete. World War II initiated dramatic changes from the Depression years of the 1930s in more than just the music scene. It produced full employment and full production for the first time in decades. The war disrupted parochial worlds by pulling millions of men and women into military service and jobs in defense industries. In Black communities, successful struggles to desegregate employment and housing set the stage for future activism with the dramatic expansion of membership in the NAACP and other civil rights groups during the war years. Otis left behind his family and the world in which he grew up in Berkeley when he hit the road in 1941 to play music in Denver, Omaha, and Los Angeles amid the economic, demographic, and social changes of the wartime era. The economic scarcity of the 1930s became only a memory in the 1940s with the prosperity fueled by governmental spending on the war.

Yet the 1930s had not been stable either. That decade too was one of extraordinary transformation and change. The Great Depression devastated the economy and undermined the legitimacy of the business-minded Anglo-Protestant elite with its anti-immigrant prejudices. Hard times produced crises that overwhelmed the resources of ethnic fraternal orders and mutual aid societies, leading ethnic working-class families like the one in which Johnny Otis grew up to lessen their involvement in the affairs of their own group and branch out to others through pan-ethnic alliances in trade unions and political mobilizations. Franklin Roosevelt's New Deal forged a new social compact through reforms such as Social Security, the Wagner Act, and the Federal Housing Act. For Johnny Otis's immediate family, the 1930s brought hardship and struggles that played a part in Johnny's move toward Black culture and away from white ethnic identity.

Therefore, Otis's mourning for a lost world in the face of the Watts rebellion may have been as powerful as it was in part because so many of the worlds he had previously inhabited underwent similar transformations. His parents had left Greece because of the chaotic changes they witnessed at the turn of the century that produced a Greek diaspora to all parts of the world. As a child of working-class immigrant parents during the Great Depression, Otis witnessed the decline of the family business and the fraying of social ties in the Greek community. He left his home town and family far behind when he went on the road in the early 1940s as a member of "territory" jazz bands, but then he looked like an immigrant from the Midwest to local residents of Los Angeles when he left Omaha to play in Harlan Leonard's band at the Club Alabam on Central Avenue in 1943. During the postwar period, rhythm and blues combos displaced the big bands, and in the 1960s rock 'n' roll trios and quartets displaced the rhythm and blues ensembles.

Mourning the disappearance of lost worlds played a recurrent role in Johnny Otis's life. Yet his response to the Watts rebellion, like his responses to previous catalysts of transformation and change, reveals a unique ability to turn sad memories about the past into constructive action in the present. Otis intended his 1960 confession about longing for a time machine to be playful and humorous, but he was also serious about not wanting to lose the wisdom of the past in the present. He kept alive memories of people he had known in his past as a way of expanding the present, as a means of summoning into his presence talkative ancestors (whether related to him by blood or not) who could help him see where society had been and where it was going. Otis's sad feelings often proved to be resources rather than liabilities. In remembering and honoring the past, he acted to change the present. His impassioned book about the 1965 riots, *Listen to the Lambs,* deftly blends Otis's personal memories with an astute analysis of race relations in the nation to provide readers with a unique perspective on the present and a provocation for change in the future. For the rest of his life, he would use his writing, speaking, and music playing and producing to build "time machines" through the deployment of stories and arguments that move back and forth across the years, that turn the past into a resource for the present. He wrote books, hosted radio and television programs, produced recordings, and presented shows that viewed the world from the perspective of someone at a crossroads between the past and the present. Although these rhetorical displays might have seemed like innocent nostalgia or self-pitying melancholy to uninitiated listeners and readers, they actually manifested the unique artistry of an acrobat able to leap back and forth across time.

At times, it even seemed to him that he could actually go back in time. In his 1993 book, *Upside Your Head! Rhythm and Blues on Central Avenue,* Otis explains that on nights when his band is playing well and everyone gets into the spirit of their music, a kind of collective trance takes over the room. The band plays brilliantly, and the audiences display the special kind of "finger popping" that he first experienced in Black clubs and dance halls in the 1930s and 1940s. At these times "the music takes on a heightened character. . . . Much as in the Black church, a call and response often develops, and Black magic fills the air."[57] Back in the 1940s, that kind of connection between the band and the audience seemed to happen nearly every night. In those years, Johnny performed regularly at the Barrelhouse nightclub, which he co-owned with Bardu and Tila Ali. Their club was the first nightclub anywhere devoted exclusively to rhythm and blues. It had sawdust on the floor, Johnny's drawings on the walls, and great music on the bandstand every night. Johnny wrote and recorded a song about those times, titled "Midnight at the Barrelhouse," even before the club actually opened. Recorded and released on the Excelsior label, the song was only a regional hit. But it captures a certain mood that Johnny recognized time and time again throughout his career. That recognition enabled him to negotiate the persistence of the past inside the present with consummate grace and skill. As he explains, "That kind of special finger-popping doesn't happen often nowadays for our band. Nor, I suspect, for other traditional black groups. In the rare instances when it does, we are transplanted back in time to the Barrelhouse in Watts, where finger-popping was the order of the day, and everyone understood 'It don't mean a thing if it ain't got that swing.'"[58]

The journey that led Johnny Otis from his white working-class immigrant upbringing in northern California to those glorious nights at the Barrelhouse in the 1940s and those terrible days during the Watts Riots of 1965 required him to adjust and adapt to new circumstances constantly, to reinvent himself many times. During the Depression his parents lost their little grocery business, and only after long stretches of unemployment did his father finally find work in the Kaiser shipyards in Vallejo. Bouts of asthma and deep alienation slowed Johnny's progress in school, leading him to drop out after the ninth grade. Otis's mother refused to give her consent to the marriage between Johnny and Phyllis Walker because she did not want her son marrying a Black woman. When the two married anyway, Irene did not speak to Phyllis for eighteen years, creating a deep chasm between mother and son. Phyllis remained friendly and open to her mother-in-law, however, and welcomed her warmly when Irene reconciled with her in the late 1950s. Johnny and Phyllis eloped to Nevada, because California law at the time did not allow interracial marriages. The couple struggled with the travails that faced mixed-race couples in those days. They endured the consequences of a working musician's life on the road—long separations, low pay, and unpredictable and intermittent employment. Otis found himself forced to face the harsh realities of white racism time and time again, as a member of Black bands touring the country, as a partner in an interracial marriage, as a father of Black children, and as an outspoken activist who felt obligated to challenge injustice whenever he encountered it.

Yet for all of his troubles and struggles, Otis's talent, intelligence, ambition, and hard work enabled him to reach heights that few people in any field ever achieve. Although he was a high school dropout, he went on to write and publish four books. He taught extension courses on the history of Black music for Vista Community College and the University of California, Berkeley. He reveled in his life in show business, yet he also became a preacher who founded and guided a successful Holiness "sanctified" church. His entrepreneurial vision and skills enabled him to make plenty of money in various ventures in show business, but he also proved to be a successful businessman as an organic farmer and apple juice manufacturer. Yet he condemned "predatory capitalism" and donated his services gratis for nearly thirty years to public radio, hosting a weekly music program broadcast on stations in Los Angeles, San Francisco, Fresno, New Orleans, and Fairbanks, Alaska. He left home while still a teenager to travel on the road as a jazz musician, yet he became well known and respected in fields outside jazz. Sometimes hailed as the godfather of rhythm and blues, Otis secured election to the Rock 'n' Roll Hall of Fame, the Rhythm and Blues Hall of Fame, and the Blues Hall of Fame. He resented deeply what the rise of rock 'n' roll as the dominant form in popular music meant for the careers of jazz and blues musicians, but he felt great pride when the Rolling Stones asked his son Shuggie to join them as the replacement for Mick Taylor. He felt even prouder, however, when Shuggie turned them down.

The fame, prestige, and monetary reward Otis derived from his music, however, often left him feeling dissatisfied. His efforts on Capitol Records in the late 1950s made him more money than any of his other recordings, but he considered the music on them generally inferior artistically. He did not mind being one of the key conduits that brought Black music to the Beach Boys, Phil Spector, the Kingston Trio, Frank Zappa, Roy Buchanan, the Blasters, Bob Dylan, and Eric Clapton, but it disturbed him tremendously that the white imitators always secured vastly disproportionate rewards for their work compared with those of the Blacks who had created the music in the first place. The music business executives and journalists who crowned Paul Whiteman as King of Jazz, who named Benny Goodman the King of Swing, and who dubbed Elvis Presley the King of Rock 'n' Roll did so, Otis felt, because they refused to acknowledge, recognize, and reward the real royalty that existed among the ranks of Black musicians.

Throughout his life, Otis believed that music that received mainstream recognition and reward often had an inferior quality to the sounds that he heard nightly played by Black musicians in nightclubs and theaters that whites rarely frequented. He appreciated the acknowledgments he received from white artists, especially when they recorded cover versions of his songs that entitled him to composer's royalties, but he could not forget the struggles of Black musicians who never received their due. Otis considered Big Mama Thornton one of the best people and one of the most impressive musicians he ever encountered. He saw her cheated out of royalties by unscrupulous record company executives, exploited by nightclub owners, and unacknowledged by artists who copied features of her act. While a great, true, and loyal friend to Otis, Thornton could hardly contain her bitterness about her life, frequently bursting out in anger.

Even as a youth, Otis found himself personally offended by anti-Black racism. "As a kid I decided that if our society dictated that one had to be Black or white, I would be Black," he explains.[59] Yet it would be inaccurate to see Otis as simply reacting against white supremacy. He loved Black culture because of the things that he learned from it, for the ways of knowing and ways of being it opened up to him. He thinks of himself as Black not only because of his commitments to racial justice but also because his understandings of individual achievement and collective destiny come directly from the things that Black people and Black communities taught him. To make music in his world was to connect with a whole way of life. As he once recalled,

> I never had to instruct my horn players how to phrase a passage. I never found it necessary to suggest to one of my singers how a song should be handled. I just equipped them with the words or notes, and they supplied the all important elements.... The music grew out of the African American way of life. The way mama cooked, the Black English grandmother and grandfather spoke, the way daddy disciplined the kids—the emphasis in spiritual values, the way Reverend Jones preached, the way Sister Williams sang in the choir, the way the old brother down the street played the slide guitar, and crooned the blues, the very special way the people danced, walked, laughed, cried, joked, got happy, shouted in church.[60]

His biggest hit record testified to those links between music and the community. The core riff that forms the basis for "Willie and the Hand Jive" (played by Otis on piano, along with drummer Earl Palmer and guitarist Jimmy Nolen) is often known as the Bo Diddley Beat because it appeared in many of Diddley's hit songs. Yet Diddley did not compose the riff himself. It comes from a clapping game played by children on playgrounds and street corners. One day while Otis was touring with his band in the South, the bus driver stopped for gas, and Otis took a short stroll. He heard that beat a little ways off in the distance. It sounded like the "hambone" or "shave and a haircut, two bits" pattern that kids chanted in school yards and on playgrounds. He remembered hearing that same rhythmic pattern in San Pablo Park, in Berkeley, when he was growing up. When he played with Count Otis Matthews and the West Oakland House Stompers, he used to play it on tom-toms while Matthews shook a coffee can filled with sand and pebbles and sang, "Mama cooked a chicken, thought it was a duck, put it on the table with its legs stuck up, yes, yes."[61] Otis soon saw, however, that the beat was coming not from children clapping their hands but rather from the rhythms of a chain gang of Black men working on the road. Over the beat, they chanted verses such as "If I'd have known the captain was blind, I never would have come to work on time." The beat stayed in Otis's mind when he got back on the bus. Later he turned that somber scene into the joyous and rollicking "Willie and the Hand Jive." Similarly, when he composed the lyrics for "Double Crossing Blues," a huge hit for Little Esther (backed by the Robins), Otis drew on the comic punch line of a vaudeville routine performed by the team of Apus and Estrelita. His songs drew on Black life, with their lyrics, rhythms, melodies, and harmonies usually coming from the community's practices and traditions.

The skill, intelligence, discipline, and determination that Johnny Otis displayed in many different kinds of work have distinguished him as a uniquely gifted individual in touch with the concerns of others. He attempted to use each of his accomplishments to branch out and create new communities everywhere he has been. Rather than turning his first hit into a solo career, he used his fame to advance the artistry of others. His first recording session produced the hit "Harlem Nocturne." He followed that success with a variety and blues- and jazz-flavored songs featuring vocals by his discoveries, including Little Esther, the Robins, and Mel Walker. In 1951, Johnny sang on the hit "All Night Long." As his song climbed the charts, a promoter in San Diego invited Otis and his band to play a date at a local skating rink. Rather than take center stage himself, Otis proposed a show with many artists, like a carnival coming to town. The show was a success, and from then on, booking Johnny Otis meant booking the Johnny Otis Show or the Johnny Otis Caravan, featuring not only Otis himself but also a talented array of singers and musicians.

Otis did not follow the usual pattern that guided relations between stars and featured acts. Instead of just paying wages to Little Esther and Jackie Kelso to be part of his operation, he made them partners in the business. He did not think of his own talents as a singer and musician as all that special. He viewed himself as a good listener, mentor, arranger, and promoter in a community brimming with talent. He followed the pattern of generosity he established as a musician in his other endeavors as well. When he wrote his column "Johnny Otis Says Let's Talk" in the weekly *Los Angeles Sentinel* in the early 1960s, he often turned it over to others, using long quotes from people whose views he wished to spotlight and devoting many column inches to questions and comments from readers. The book he wrote in the wake of the Watts Riots, *Listen to the Lambs,* devotes several chapters to unedited testimony about the riots by community residents. The introduction to his second book, *Upside Your Head! Rhythm and Blues on Central Avenue,* proclaims that the purpose of the book is "to present the personal memories and photographs of people who were in and of the Black community and to afford the reader a firsthand, insider's view of what it was like during that fascinating time when Los Angeles was giving birth to its rhythm and blues music style."[62] His cookbook, *Red Beans and Rice and Other Rock 'n' Roll Recipes,* features recipes for some of the extraordinary savory dishes that Otis devised over the years while trying to eat well on the road as a working musician, but the book also presents the favorite recipes of a broad range of family members, friends, fellows musicians, and business associates.

For almost three decades, the Johnny Otis radio show provided an extended seminar on the history of Black music to listeners of public radio stations. These shows featured personal testimonies by a long succession of guests eager to speak to Johnny and his listeners about the music they made. Even when Otis decided to move to northern California and retire in 1991, he could not resist using his art to build a community. He established a music school for children on the grounds of his farm in Sebastopol, recruiting parents, teachers, doctors, nurses, and pharmacists to set in motion plans for a nonprofit center to teach children painting, sculpture, dance, drama, music, and poetry, but also to educate them about good health.

In the traditional cultures of West Africa, the purpose of making music is not to display individual virtuosity but rather to create new relations among people through performance. Otis's personal virtuosity manifested itself over and over again through his mastery of three musical instruments, his successes as a singer, composer, bandleader, and arranger, his unique achievements as a television and radio personality, and his visionary political and theological work. His most important work, however, has always revolved around creating new communities and new forms of consciousness. We can say of him what Beat poet Bob Kaufman said about Charlie Parker. He was an electrician because he went around wiring people.[63]

On that hot August afternoon in 1965, however, Johnny Otis thought it might be all over. He worried that he had reached a turning point from which there could be no turning back. The man who composed "Midnight at the Barrelhouse" feared that he had now confronted a very different kind of midnight, that the clock had struck twelve and that a new dawn might never come. Yet he would discover that the trajectory that brought him from his childhood in Berkeley to his adult life in Los Angeles had armed him with everything that he needed to find his way and to move on.

One CENTRAL AVENUE BREAKDOWN

 The period in which Johnny Otis grew up in his Greek immigrant family, the 1920s, was one of the most anti-immigrant decades in U.S. history. In the wake of vigilante attacks on the businesses and homes of German Americans by "patriotic" citizens during World War I, a wave of nativist hysteria spread over the nation, terrorizing immigrants and their families. Throughout the country, local school boards banned foreign-language instruction in high schools. City officials removed foreign-language books from libraries. Some state legislatures tried to make it illegal to speak on the telephone in languages other than English. U.S. Attorney General A. Mitchell Palmer ordered the mass roundup and deportation of some ten thousand immigrants suspected (without due process of law) of holding anarchist or communist beliefs. The Justice Department subsequently deported thousands of immigrants active in the labor movement every year for the next decade. The Ku Klux Klan experienced a dramatic increase in membership during the 1920s, more in the Midwest and West than the South, fueled largely by anti-immigrant and especially anti-Catholic and anti-Jewish sentiment. Even the passage of the Eighteenth Amendment, prohibiting the manufacture, transportation, sale, and consumption of alcohol, was seen by most nativists as a measure necessary to correct the alleged bad behavior of immigrants, whom they believed drank too much.[1]

Immigrants and their children faced repression from the smallest local municipalities to the entire federal government, from armed vigilantes to respectable opinion molders. In the culture and politics of the 1920s, the foreign born and their offspring found themselves defined as unwanted aliens whose entry into the country had been deemed in retrospect to have been a mistake. Congress passed the Johnson–Reed Act in 1924, the most drastic and restrictive immigration law in the nation's history. The new law allocated quotas for future immigration based on preferences for immigrants from northern and western Europe. It permitted only miniscule numbers of people from southern and eastern Europe to enter the United States. Of all the despised immigrant groups from Europe, Greeks received the smallest quota: only one hundred immigrants per year—a sign indicating that they were the least desirable group of all in the eyes of some of the defenders of Anglo-Protestant "100 per cent Americanism." Immigration officials frequently refused to classify Greeks as Europeans at all, designating them as "Orientals." In some states, local application of Jim Crow segregation laws required Greeks to use facilities designated for Blacks. A 1933 real estate appraisal of land values in Chicago advised property owners that the least desirable European immigrant neighbors were Greeks, Russian Jews, and southern Italians.[2]

Even before World War I, Greek Americans had suffered from especially vicious nativist prejudice and violence. In Omaha, Nebraska, in 1909 a mob of one thousand men stormed into Greek neighborhoods, vandalized stores, burned homes, and brutally assaulted people they believed to be Greek. Newspaper articles in Utah referred to Greeks as "ignorant, depraved and brutal foreigners," "a vicious element unfit for citizenship," and "the scum of Europe."[3] The Ku Klux Klan threatened Greeks with violence in Utah, Michigan, and Florida. In the aftermath of World War I, the American Legion in Utah condemned Greeks for reading Greek-language newspapers, speaking their language in public, and sending their children to Greek schools for language instruction.[4] A 1920 candidate for office in Alabama proposed the disenfranchisement of Greeks and Syrians.[5] Restrictive covenants written into deeds to homes in many cities required home buyers to pledge never to sell their property to Greeks. In western mining communities, Greek workers found themselves forbidden to live in housing designated for "whites" and required to share housing with Black, Mexican, Japanese, and in some cases Italian workers, all of whom were deemed nonwhite. Public opinion polls found that more than 40 percent of "Americans" opposed granting citizenship to Greeks.[6]

Yet Greek immigrants became citizens in droves during the 1920s, not because they felt welcomed, but precisely because they believed they family arranged his marriage to Irene, a young woman born on the Greek island of Hydra. Her birth family had been too poor to support her, so they had given her away to a childless aunt and uncle, who immigrated to the United States when Irene was seven years old.[12]

Alexander had gray eyes and a fair complexion. He spoke English with an accent but fluently. He sang featured parts in Greek Orthodox church services that the family attended, and he became a leader in a politically conservative working-class fraternal order, the Greek American Protective Association. After church on Sundays, Alexander usually went to a Greek coffee shop to socialize with his lodge brothers. Irene had dark eyes and dark hair. She was quite introverted when she got married. As she became more assimilated, however, she became more assertive. She taught herself to speak fluent English without an accent and learned how to play the mandolin on her own, without any professional instruction.[13]

Johnny spoke Greek before he learned English. Throughout his childhood, he traveled by bus to attend Greek school. The boy who loved to play outside felt trapped during the two hours of instruction that he received each week from Greek Orthodox clerics in the dingy basement of the church school. The formal Greek language that they taught in Greek school differed greatly from the folk Greek that his parents spoke at home. Having to attend these lessons made Johnny envy his non-Greek friends, who spent their after-school hours fishing in San Francisco Bay or playing sports in San Pablo Park. One day the priest in charge of instruction caught Johnny not paying attention. He walked over to the youth and smacked his hands with a switch the cleric kept for just such an occasion. Johnny ran out of the room with the priest close on his heels. He escaped and hurried back to his home, where he told his father sheepishly what had happened. Alexander sided with his son, saying that he probably should kick the priest's ass, but worried that doing so might be considered sacrilegious. His parents never sent him back to Greek school after that.[14]

On the basketball courts at San Pablo Park, Johnny's friends formed teams by "choosing up sides," with the captains taking alternating turns in picking teammates. The best players were selected first; the last players picked were the ones considered to be the worst athletes. In this circle of friends, the two players always chosen last were Johnny and Don Barksdale. Johnny never got much better at basketball, but Barksdale improved considerably. He went on to play major college basketball at UCLA, played for the U.S. Olympic team in 1948, and later became one of the first

Blacks to play basketball professionally. Barksdale's family background prepared him well for this trailblazer role. Several of his relatives played active roles in the Brotherhood of Sleeping Car Porters, the first Black trade union admitted to the American Federation of Labor. Prejudice on the part of coaches kept Barksdale from making the basketball team at Berkeley High School, but he played so well at the community college level for the College of Marin that he received an athletic scholarship to attend UCLA, where he made the All America team in 1947. In the early years after college, Barksdale could not play professional basketball because of the color line, so he returned to the Bay Area to play for an amateur club team in Oakland. He also launched a career in show business, hosting a popular jazz radio program in the Bay Area and starring on *Sepia Review,* his local television program. When the National Basketball Association desegregated its rosters in 1951, Barksdale became the third Black player in the league, joining the Baltimore Bullets and eventually making the NBA all-star team.[15]

Walter Gordon also grew up in the neighborhood surrounding Dohr and Ward. He went on to become the first Black football player to win All American honors at the University of California before becoming a prominent lawyer, governor of the Virgin Islands, and a federal judge. Another neighbor, Wiley Manuel, became the first Black justice to serve on the California Supreme Court. Johnny's younger brother, Nick, became a distinguished career diplomat, specializing in policy regarding the Middle East and holding many high positions in the Foreign Service and State Department. After retirement from his diplomatic career, Nick Veliotes served as president of the Association of American Publishers.[16]

Although the Greek Orthodox Church and its school held little allure for Johnny as a child, the sanctified churches in his neighborhood that his Black friends attended were a different story. Johnny loved the free chocolate milk and graham crackers these congregations dispensed to children after services. These were rare treats for him during the hard years of the Depression. He also noticed that the cutest little girls in the neighborhood seemed to frequent these particular churches. Initially Johnny believed that it was the refreshments and the girls that drew him to services at these churches, but soon he realized that it was more than that. He loved the fervor of the gospel choirs, the eloquence and intellectual brilliance of the preachers, and the conviviality and moral passion of the congregations. He recalls, "It wasn't the girls or the graham crackers or the chocolate milk that really made the impression; it was the cultural impact of the preaching of the Black preachers and the gospel choirs and the singers and that whole marvelous thing. Black culture captured me," he relates. "I loved it, and it was richer and more fulfilling and more natural. I thought it was mine."[17] The Black culture he encountered was actually no more "natural" than his own Greek heritage, of course, but it seemed remarkable to him because it appeared to be less repressed, more demonstrative, and not quite as hierarchical as the Greek American culture that he experienced.

Alexander and Irene prospered during the 1920s, assisted by their ability to pool resources with an extended family network that revolved around the children's uncle Nick. Irene tended the store counter while Alexander peddled fruits and vegetables from a truck that he drove through the neighborhoods in the Berkeley Hills, where wealthy people lived. The extended family eventually purchased several real estate properties and automobiles as their businesses thrived. When Uncle Nick died in 1928 and the stock market crashed in 1929, however, the family's fortunes reversed. Alexander and Irene lost nearly everything they owned and struggled economically for nearly ten years. They held on to ownership of their home only because of a generous government program that refinanced mortgages for veterans. Plagued by financial problems, Irene and Alexander rented out their grocery store to a Chinese family to run, yet they continued to live in the upstairs rooms of the building. Alexander faced long periods of unemployment that did not truly end until he found work in the Mare Island Naval Shipyard, near Vallejo, just before the start of World War II. Nick Veliotes remembers that the arranged marriage between his mother and his father was "never a love match," but economic pressures contributed to the two of them drifting even further apart. The family spent several years on public assistance, ashamed that they had to stand in line to receive canned goods and secondhand clothing.[18]

Irene and Alexander had two miscarriages before Johnny was born. Perhaps for that reason, they doted on him. He suffered from childhood asthma, however, and his teachers at school initially diagnosed him as a slow learner. Perhaps they did not know about his health problems or realize that, because his native tongue was Greek, he was doing his school work in his second language. He succeeded so well in art classes, however, that he was offered a scholarship to attend the California School of Fine Arts, but he turned it down. Frustrated by both ill health and the puzzling hostility of some of his teachers, Johnny became alienated from school but increasingly interested in activities outside it. Concerned about his absences and vexed by his performance and attitude when he was present, school administrators transferred him from Berkeley High School to the McKinley Continuation School. Years later, Johnny would joke about the contrasts between his struggles in school and the academic and social successes of his younger brother, Nick. "My brother was student body president at Berkeley High School," he would say mischievously, "and I got kicked out!"

Nick Veliotes built on his academic and athletic triumphs at Berkeley High School to enjoy great success in college at the University of California at Berkeley. His career as a diplomat had him serving at different times as the U.S. ambassador both to Egypt and to Jordan. During his days in the Foreign Service, Nick handled delicate negotiations for the State Department throughout the Middle East. He remembers his older brother, Johnny, as a most loving and caring brother, as an extremely compassionate and sensitive person in general. He recalls one especially emblematic incident when Johnny was twelve. The family placed him in charge of raising a lamb in the backyard. Their plan was to kill and eat the animal for the family's Easter feast. When Easter came and his relatives arrived at the house, however, Johnny stood in front of the lamb with his .22 rifle, protecting his pet and refusing to let it be killed.[19] He knew that the family had raised the lamb in order to eat it, but he had grown attached to the creature and felt that it was not fair for it to lose its life.

The young man who loved animals so much that would not let his lamb be killed for Easter dinner also became engrossed in raising pigeons. A neighbor on his paper route, Mr. Williams, raised birds in his backyard. Johnny asked him about them every time he came to the door to collect for the paper deliveries. When Mr. Williams had to move to Arizona for health reasons, he offered the flock to the paper boy on the condition that Johnny's parents would give him their permission to take on the responsibility of caring for them. Alexander refused at first, explaining that the family could hardly afford to feed themselves, much less a flock of birds. Seeing his son's enthusiasm, however, he relented. Johnny promised to pay for the bird feed out of his paper route money, but his kind-hearted father eventually gave him feed from the stock at the grocery store. With only one coop, Johnny could not keep the breeds apart and soon found himself enjoying and taking care of mixtures that purists would never have let develop in the first place.[20]

Music played an important role in the Veliotes household. The family listened to phonograph records by Greek singers Rosa Eskenazi, Rita Abtasi, and Marika Papagika, among others. Important research by Steven Frangos reveals the complexity of Greek music in that era. A significant part of the Greek population lived in Asia Minor before 1923, and the population inside Greece included Turkish Muslims and members of other religious and national minorities. The first commercial recordings of Greek music were made in the diaspora, especially in Germany, England, and the United States. In these countries, Greek immigrants found themselves living and working alongside Armenians, Albanians, Bulgarians, Syrians, and Arabs, who shared with their Greek associates similar (but not identical) histories of displacement, exile, loss, and longing for home. Recorded Greek music in the 1920s contained lyrics sung in Turkish, Armenian, Ladino, and Arabic, as well as Greek. The songs themselves encompassed a wide variety of styles and themes, from nationalist patriotic songs and evocations of village life in Greece to romantic ballads, from semiclassical compositions to *rebetika* songs that merged themes, song forms, and styles from music by the lower classes in urban centers from the Balkans to Asia Minor.[21]

The Veliotes family loved recordings, but they made their own music as well. Alexander sang, Johnny played the drums, Nick played the clarinet, Dorothy played the cello, and Irene played the mandolin. In later years, Irene also became a fan of swing bands, attending dances when the famous orchestras came to town and encouraging her family's interests in all kinds of music. Johnny loved the Greek music that resounded in the rooms inside his house, but he found himself drawn more to the blues music that he heard in his neighborhood. His first brush with the blues came courtesy of Sandy Moore, a Black man who worked as a Pullman porter and lived across the street. Moore often came home from his railroad trips well stocked with blues recordings that he had purchased in the South. A sharp dresser who drove a flashy front-wheel-drive Cord automobile, the porter was a much admired figure by boys in the neighborhood, especially because he always seemed to be accompanied by beautiful women. When Moore hosted parties at his home, the neighborhood youths would gather outside, peek in the windows, and listen to the wonderful music emanating from inside. Johnny remembers that on one of those nights he first heard Robert Johnson's recording of "Terraplane Blues."[22]

Johnson's artistry and the song's suggestive double entendres made a big impression on Johnny. He started taking trips to Seventh Street in Oakland to stand outside nightclubs just so he could hear more blues. He later recalled, "I remember trying to slip into Slim Jenkins' club when I was a kid. We *really* wanted to go where the blues was happening but we were too young. But we'd put on some dark glasses and pull up our overcoats trying to act older and get in there and listen."[23] He tracked down phonograph records by his new heroes. Like the young B. B. King in Mississippi during the same years, Johnny developed a special fondness for vocal recordings made by the artist who called himself Doctor Clayton.

Johnny's deep identification with Black culture and Black people sometimes put him at odds with the people and institutions around him. To please his mother, he joined Boy Scout Troop 25 in Berkeley, graduating quickly from the rank of Tenderfoot to Scout Second Class, with a merit badge in cycling. The adult Scout leaders encouraged him to recruit other boys to the troop, so Johnny submitted the name of his close friend Rudy Jordan. When the scoutmaster found out that Jordan was Black, he explained to Johnny that the troop was for whites only. Johnny quit immediately, disgusted with the chasm between the noble ideals that the Scouts preached and the bigoted behavior they actually practiced.[24]

Like many young men during the Depression, Johnny and Rudy Jordan enjoyed working on cars. They sought out spare parts in junkyards and used their knowledge to repair vehicles for their friends and family. They dreamed of finding an abandoned car and restoring it completely with their customizing and mechanical talents. One day police officers stopped the pair, accused them of stealing parts, and roughed them up. "To that day we had never thought of stealing anything," Johnny later recalled, but "after that we began stealing tires and siphoning gas." We thought "if we're going to be treated like dogs when we're innocent . . . we might as well be guilty."[25]

As he became more immersed in blues and jazz, Johnny started associating mostly with people who played music. A mutual love of swing music launched a lifelong friendship with fellow drummer Hal Kronick, a Berkeley resident who was the grandson of Jewish immigrants. Johnny and Hal built a special bond around their shared love of the artistry of Count Basie's great drummer, Jo Jones. They remained in close contact even after Kronick gave up playing music professionally to become a successful salesman and marketing manager while Otis went on the road for a career in music. One night when they were teenagers, Hal, Johnny, and Bernard Peters (a Black youth who later played drums in guitarist Saunders King's small ensemble) went to hear and see the Count Basie Band play in Oakland. The hall was segregated. For this dance, Blacks danced on the main floor, and whites were supposed to watch from the balcony. Hal and

Johnny, however, crossed the color line and went downstairs to meet up with Peters. The three aspiring drummers stood right in front of the bandstand all night so that they could focus on their personal hero, Jo Jones. At the end of the show, Jones asked the boys if they knew of any good Chinese restaurants close by. They were happy to take him to one of their favorite spots, where they showered Jones with questions about playing the drums. Their hero conducted a clinic for them right in the restaurant. Jones closed the curtains to their booth and demonstrated his incredible paradiddle prowess on the enamel tabletop for the boys with drumsticks provided by Bernard Peters, as Jones's manifestly bored female companion looked on in exasperation.[26]

This scene in which three young men—one Greek, one Jewish, and one Black—found themselves engrossed in a music lesson given by a Black musician in a Chinese restaurant typified one of the main currents of the 1930s, what historian Lizabeth Cohen terms the "culture of unity" that emerged as a response to the vicious nativism of the 1920s.[27] The Depression damaged the credibility of the Anglo Protestant elite and provoked challenges to their exclusionary prejudices. The economic crisis also shattered the viability of ethnic mutual aid and self-help organizations inside ethnic communities by creating demands for relief too great for these organizations to handle. Working people from different national origins began to emphasize their similarities to one another. They may have had different religions, languages, and customs and memories of different ancestral nations, but they also shared common economic problems, similar experiences with prejudice and exclusion. Increasingly, they attended the same motion picture theaters and sports events, shopped at the same stores, and listened to the same radio programs. Mass organizing drives by industrial trade unions reached across ethnic and racial lines out of necessity. Organizers could not gain representation rights by signing up only white workers doing skilled jobs; they also needed to represent the Black and Latino workers in the foundries and on the custodial staffs. In the wake of these changes, young people in the 1930s began to celebrate the multiethnic character of the U.S. nation. Rather than uniting around their own particular ethnicities, they came together around the shared experiences of ethnic formation itself, around the ostracisms, struggles, and solidarities that their individual groups had experienced separately. They lauded the very diversity that 1920s nativists despised, and they worked to transform the image of immigrants from unwanted aliens to redemptive insiders, from people who could never be truly American to the quintessentially true Americans, because they came to the country by choice rather than merely through the accident of birth.[28]

The exuberant pan-ethnic Americanism of the culture of unity emerged out of the unraveling of ties within ethnic communities. Scholars have correctly emphasized the celebration of ethnic difference by the cultural front of the 1930s, but they may have underestimated the degree to which shame and self-doubt fueled the exuberant embrace of that new America. Immigrant children (then and now) have found themselves cut off from the history of their grandparents yet still saddled with the humiliating subordinations that flow from the "foreignness" of their parents. Robert Warshow has written eloquently about the impossible dilemma facing immigrant children. Immigrant parents discover to their great dismay that the values and standards of their nations of origin count for very little in their nation of arrival. They feel demeaned in the eyes of their children, to whom they often must turn for help in translating English words and negotiating American social situations. The parents defend their honor by holding their homelands and traditional cultures as morally superior to what they see in the United States. Yet their children seem to see only that their parents are poor, powerless, and culturally despised. The parents push their children to assimilate but then feel betrayed if they succeed.[29] Robert Cantwell explains that the sons and daughters of immigrant parents crave a sense of yesteryear that might put them on equal cultural footing with their native-born rivals who deploy their families' long histories in the nation as a kind of primordial privilege and entitlement. Immersion in neglected and marginalized cultures can serve a dual role for children from immigrant and ethnic households. In Cantwell's words it can enable them "to gain psychic possession of their adoptive culture," to become "Americans" for the first time.[30] It also eases any guilt they might have about leaving ancestral cultures behind by affirming the importance of ethnic differences in the very process of transcending them. Michael Denning's research enables us to see that this process has served economic and ideological purposes as well, claiming a key role in America for the working class and giving ethnic identity in the nation a profoundly working-class dimension. He argues, "The invention of ethnicity was a central form of class consciousness in the United States."[31]

Johnny and his friends embraced the culture of unity and the opportunities it offered to them. His friend Hal Kronick remembers the 1930s as a time when you could go across town and find more in common with a stranger than with a blood relative. He recalls, "Johnny and I had a mutual good friend, Ike Porter, a portly, Black, good-natured fellow. He'd come by the house, and my dad and mom were delighted. Ike was fluent in Yiddish. He was the drummer in the Saunders King big band that played at Sweets Ballroom and other big dance Bay Area ballrooms for segregated Black dances."[32] Having a Black friend who spoke Yiddish nicely paralleled Kronick's experiences with Johnny Otis, a Greek friend who would go on to a life immersed in Black culture and politics.

During the decade when Otis, Peters, and Kronick came of age and an interethnic culture of unity emerged, Louis Adamic mobilized a grassroots campaign that transformed the meaning of the Statue of Liberty from a tribute to republicanism into the symbol of welcome for immigrants. The Andrews Sisters, daughters of a Greek immigrant father and a Norwegian American mother, had hit records in the 1930s, with one song that had a Yiddish title ("Bei Mir Bistu Shein"), another with a Spanish title ("Cuanto La Gusta"), one that had a Czech melody ("Beer Barrel Polka"), a cover version of a calypso song from Trinidad ("Rum and Coca Cola"), and two songs grounded in the style of African American boogie-woogie piano and guitar playing ("Boogie Woogie Bugle Boy" and "Beat Me Daddy, Eight to the Bar"). The poetry of Langston Hughes, the musical compositions of Aaron Copland, the paintings of regionalist Thomas Hart Benton, and the novels of a new generation of ethnic writers, including Henry Roth, James T. Farrell, and Pietro di Donato, reflected the exhilaration and exuberance of CIO picket lines in which workers displayed signs in several languages and food from a different ethnic cuisine was featured every day. A tidal wave of popular creativity emerged from this new formula, an explosion of little magazines, photography clubs, theater groups, and musical ensembles. Jitterbug dancing and swing music emerged as key expressions of this new culture, as sites where young people from different backgrounds encountered one another in the context of shared enthusiasm for music that originated among Black people and was continually reinterpreted and re-created within that community.[33]

The fervor among working-class white ethnics for a melting pot America, for a nation made up of many nations, reflected the extreme degree to which they and their families had been made to feel unworthy and unwanted by 1920s nativism. They seized the opportunity to present themselves as people capable of realizing the long promised but not yet realized democratic America that some immigrants had dreamed of back in their countries of origin. Although racial and religious bigotry among the working class continued to plague this coalition, and racial divisions worked eventually to shatter it during the World War II and postwar eras, a new openness became evident in the 1930s. Perhaps most startling, the culture of unity that white ethnics forged frequently coalesced around the moral, aesthetic, and political visions of Black people. The descendants of freed slaves, whose activism after emancipation produced what historian W. E. B. Du Bois termed Abolition Democracy—the first real democracy the nation had ever known—knew things about equality and opportunity in America that the advocates of the 1930s culture of unity needed to know. People whose ancestors had been treated as property drew on advanced knowledge about the dangers of elevating property rights over human rights. Racism did not disappear, of course, and many of the white ethnics who made up the culture of unity would eventually go on to secure entry into white suburban neighborhoods, where they banded together to exclude Blacks. And even at the peak of the culture of unity, color still mattered in negative ways. Hal Kronick remembers his sister's embarrassment when he invited his friend Bernard Peters over to their house. She was afraid that Peters's presence would hurt their family's reputation among their neighbors. He recalls that the first time a Black family moved into a particular Berkeley neighborhood near Shattuck Avenue, hostile whites greeted them by breaking one of the front windows in their new home.[34] Yet, something about the combination of the pain of shared economic deprivation and the pleasures of the culture of unity made Black–white interaction more plausible for youth in the 1930s than it had been for their parents.

The culture of unity of the 1930s ultimately influenced the commercial culture of the 1940s and 1950s. Like Johnny Otis, many of the white people engaged in producing, promoting, and selling rhythm and blues music after World War II had been members of immigrant ethnic households in the 1930s. New Orleans studio owner Cosimo Matassa was Italian American. Record label owners Eddie and Leo Mesner of Aladdin Records came from a Lebanese American family. Atlantic Records founder Ahmet Ertegun was the son of a diplomat from Turkey. Jewish entrepreneurs in the business included Leonard and Phil Chess of Chess Records, Arthur N. Rupe (né Goldberg) of Specialty Records, Lew Chudd of Imperial Records, Syd Nathan of King Records, and Herman Lubinsky of the Savoy label.[35]

Many of these men made a fortune from Black music, but among them, only Johnny Otis became an actual part of the Black community and its political, religious, and cultural life.

The culture of unity was especially strong in the San Francisco Bay area in the 1930s, when Johnny entered his teenage years. The San Francisco General Strike and the West Coast Waterfront strikes of 1934 enacted the cross-cultural unity that much of the poetry, art, music, and fiction of the times merely envisioned. As a teenager in Berkeley, Johnny had frequent exposure to this cultural unity, although his interpretation of it may not always have been what its promoters intended. He remembers going to dances in Oakland sponsored by communist and communist-front organizations, not because he cared about their politics, but because the dancing and food were free and the events provided the opportunity to meet "very democratic and 'charitable' chicks," who interested him a great deal.[36] Similarly, his brother, Nick, remembers that in his years at Berkeley the communists and socialists gave great parties. The efforts by the Socialist Workers Party were particularly memorable to him, not because of their Trotskyist politics, but because their membership included a very pretty girl who played the guitar while wearing very tight and revealing clothing.[37]

At eighteen, Johnny purchased a drum set and a vibraphone by forging his father's signature on a sales contract and set up a practice space in a storage shed behind his family's store.[38] His drumming drove the family to distraction, annoying them with a constant racket hour after hour. Yet practice paid off. With the help of instruction books that he bought and borrowed, Johnny taught himself how to play both instruments. By that time, the federal government's defense spending on arms production in anticipation of World War II had begun to revive the economy. Alexander secured work at the Mare Island Naval Shipyard. He labored there alongside a Black worker from Texas, Pee Wee Crayton, who later went on to a triumphant career as a blues singer and guitar player on the very circuits that would feature Johnny Otis. In the early 1940s, however, Crayton had not yet recorded, and Johnny's father took him under his wing to teach him the art of welding. "I'll make a ship worker out of you yet," Alex would say. "I sincerely doubt it," Crayton would quip in response. Years later on the Johnny Otis radio program, the singer remembered how Alex had complained incessantly about Johnny's playing. "My son's got a band, he thinks he can play drums, but he just keeps up a lot of noise in the back of the store," he remembered Alex moaning. Yet when Johnny scored his first hit record, Alex came to a performance and walked up and down the aisles, telling the audience proudly, "That's my son!"[39]

Inspired by the virtuosity of Jo Jones, Johnny pored through books that explained the intricacies of playing the drums. He taught himself to read music and soon started performing with Count Otis Matthews and his West Oakland House Stompers. Matthews's band was a semiprofessional aggregation that played at house parties and for dances in gyms, because most of the members of the group were too young to work in nightclubs. Matthews took the title "Count" in imitation of Count Basie, but his band's music was rooted much more in blues than in jazz. Performing in living rooms while chitlins and red beans and rice cooked on kitchen stoves, the band usually got "paid" in wine and food rather than cash. The interracial band featured Count Otis on piano and doing vocals, a man they called Pops on clarinet, a one-handed trumpeter named Preston, and the younger members: Al Levy on guitar, Bob Johnson on bass, and John Veliotes on drums. The West Oakland House Stompers played the sounds they heard and loved coming through the open windows of joints on Seventh Street and the houses of neighbors who played blues phonograph records.[40]

One summer night when Johnny was seventeen, he and Rudy Jordan went to a party hosted by Curley and Leona, two girls who lived around the block from Johnny's house. When they arrived, Johnny got diverted by the sounds emanating from the trumpet of the girls' uncle as he practiced in an upstairs room. Curley and Leona's uncle played the way that modern swing musicians did on bandstands on the radio, not the down home blues progressions that prevailed in the West Oakland House Stompers. Transfixed, Johnny almost missed the entire party. When he went downstairs, however, he had another profound experience.

He noticed a beautiful Afro-Filipina across the room. He asked Rudy if he knew who she was. "That's Phyllis Walker," his friend related. "You mean little Phyllis Walker from Sixty-first Street?" Johnny asked incredulously. The little neighborhood girl who wore her hair in Indian braids, whom he had hardly noticed before, had now grown up to be a beautiful young woman. Johnny went over to speak with her and to ask her to dance. Two years later, on May 2, 1941, Johnny and Phyllis drove to Nevada (where interracial marriages were legal) and got married. He had discovered both modern swing music and his future bride on the same night.[41]

Johnny introduced Phyllis to his brother, Nick, and confided in him that they were going to get married. Like nearly everyone else who knew her, Nick thought Phyllis was a wonderful person and was happy for his brother. Their mother, however, was shocked by the marriage, attempted to have it annulled, and refused to speak to Phyllis for nearly two decades. Johnny felt that simple racism lay behind his mother's hostility to his wedding, and it made him angry. He had long enjoyed a close relationship with Irene and had great respect for her deeply held moral and religious beliefs. Yet by refusing to accept his marriage to Phyllis, his mother seemed to him to be unable to practice the things she preached. "She was a wonderfully dedicated and loving mother in every way but one—the one that counted most to me."[42] He speculated that perhaps coming to the United States as a child and being immersed in its culture had prepared Irene to have a racist reaction to her son's marriage, in contrast to the stance taken by Alexander, who had come to the country as a young man with attitudes more fully formed from his experiences in Greece.[43]

Nick sees it differently, however. He wonders if his mother was not concerned with her own feelings but rather worried about disapproval from others in the Greek community, especially because their sister, Dorothy, had not yet married. Irene might not have been opposed to Johnny and Phyllis as a couple but merely worried that Johnny's marriage might harm her daughter's life prospects. Because neither Johnny nor Phyllis was yet twenty-one, their parents had a legal right to contest their decision to wed. Irene sent Alexander to Reno to seek to annul the marriage.[44]

Alexander made the journey to Reno, but when he arrived he could not carry out Irene's instructions. An open-minded and tender-hearted man who had worked happily alongside Blacks in the railroad yards and shipyards, who had warm relations with the Black customers who shopped in his store, Alexander viewed anti-Black racism as immoral and foolish. Like most of his neighbors, he had cheered and danced in the streets when Joe Louis, a working-class Black boxer, won back the heavyweight championship of the world by knocking out Max Schmeling, of Germany, in their 1938 rematch.[45] When Alexander located Johnny and Phyllis in Reno, he took his daughter-in-law in his arms and kissed her. "Your mother sent me to annul the marriage," he told Johnny in Greek, "but I came to meet my new daughter." With tears streaming down his cheeks he added, "Besides, I don't want God to get on my case."[46]

It would be years, however, before Irene would accept the marriage fully. Eighteen years went by before Irene reconciled with her daughter-in-law. Phyllis proved to be a hard person not to like. Her personal warmth, love of her family, and gracious acceptance of Irene won her mother-in-law over. Johnny lacked some of his partner's forgiving nature, however. His mother's rejection of his wife had been more than a personal affront; it represented to him a general disapproval of Black people, whom he thought of as his adopted people.

Johnny found work in Reno with a band that reunited him with Bob Johnson, the bass player in the West Oakland House Stompers. When their jobs in Reno ended, they traveled to Denver. They had almost no money and very few prospects for employment. Johnny and Phyllis roomed with a family in the Five Points neighborhood. Phyllis took jobs as a domestic by day and in the evenings cooked large pots of spaghetti that they ate slowly to make the food last as long as they could. Just when he was about to give up and follow the lead of Bob Johnson's uncle and become a Pullman porter, Johnny found work playing drums in one of the Black territory bands operating out of Denver, the George Morrison Band. His last name tended to raise questions and curiosity. So, married to a Black woman, living in a Black neighborhood, and playing drums in a Black band, Johnny Veliotes changed his name to Johnny Otis.[47]

Otis's new band played mostly for white audiences and adopted aspects of minstrelsy in order to do so. George Morrison wore a bellhop's uniform as he played the violin. He got down on one knee to sing Al Jolson's "Sonny Boy" and made his band members wear funny hats and "clown" for the audience. Otis understood the commercial appeal and maybe even the necessity of these antics, but they bothered him deeply. He did not blame Morrison, who had learned to survive in a competitive business by giving the customers what they wanted (and who had given Otis a job he badly needed). The desire for minstrelsy, however, seemed to him to encapsulate so much of the sickness of white identity in the United States. He wondered why it had to be that way.[48]

While playing with the George Morrison Band, Otis sometimes "sat in" playing drums and vibes with the house band at Bennie Hooper's Bar across from the Rossonian Hotel. The Lloyd Hunter Band generally stayed at the Rossonian when they performed at the College Inn in Boulder. One night, Preston Love, who played lead alto saxophone in Lloyd Hunter's band, noticed the skilled musicianship of the tall slender white kid in the band. He found out from his band's drummer, Bobby Parker, that the "kid" was Johnny Otis and that he loved the music of Jo Jones and Count Basie. Love had been enraptured by Basie's sound from the day his older brother Dude brought home a radio and the first music they heard coming out of it contained the sounds of Earle Warren's alto saxophone in the Basie band. Love approached Otis about their mutual admiration of the Basie band, and the two talked long into the night. As Love later related in his extraordinary autobiography, *A Thousand Honey Creeks Later: My Life in Music from Basie to Motown,* "no two men ever agreed more completely and spontaneously than Johnny Otis and Preston Love."[49]

When Bobby Parker was drafted, Love persuaded Lloyd Hunter to audition Johnny Otis. Once he heard Otis play, Hunter was delighted to invite him into the band. They toured the same areas where the Morrison band played, but Lloyd Hunter's stage act dispensed with the overtones of minstrelsy. In Preston Love, Otis found a kindred soul, a great musician who shared his artistic tastes, a thoughtful and creative intellectual, and a person with a deep passion for social justice. For his part, Love found Otis's devotion to Black freedom remarkable. He often told friends that even though Johnny was white, he was the first Black nationalist Love had ever met. In fact, he found it impossible to think of Johnny as anything other than Black, phenotype aside.[50]

The Lloyd Hunter Band offered Otis an advanced education in Black music and Black culture. On the group's first to trip to Kansas City, Johnny wandered into a jam session in progress at Scott's Theatre Restaurant. Accompanied by Preston Love and bass player Curtis Counce, he got up to join the jam session. The three members of the Hunter band felt good about their playing, which Otis remembers as mostly "loud and happy." Then a little guy with an alto saxophone stepped up and joined in. Within a few choruses, he had them all petrified by the complexity of his playing. They later discovered that the name of the saxophonist was Charlie Parker.[51]

As the Lloyd Hunter Band rode from job to job in an old Ford school bus (inexplicably named the Blue Hornet, even though it was painted red), the musicians bantered back and forth.[52] During Otis's first days with the band, he started hearing about Darby Hicks. He had never heard the name before, but Darby Hicks seemed to know him well. Musicians in the band would relate gossip they purportedly heard from Darby Hicks himself, stories about his disparagement of Otis's playing, his nasty comments about Otis's family, and even suggestive comments about the drummer's wife and mother.

By this time, Otis was determined to track down Darby Hicks and shut him up for good. When he demanded to know where Hicks could be found, the other members of the band broke out laughing. There was no Darby Hicks. There never was. The routine about him was just the way to "welcome" new members into the band, a kind of hazing that stung less when the newcomer became a veteran and got to help play the trick on the next unsuspecting initiate.[53]

Yet there was a serious side to the band members as well. In those days, Johnny and Preston Love focused on their playing and their personal lives, but older musicians advised them to pay attention to world affairs, to read the paper and "see what Hitler's doing." Whenever their driver, Brother West, stopped to fill up the bus with gas, the older musicians would purchase newspapers and discuss the day's events. The progress of the war in Europe and the prospects of the Allies defeating Hitler provided a constant focal point of conversation, but the musicians also thought of "Hitler" in a broader sense. When someone asked a fellow band member with a newspaper, "What's Hitler doing?" the response often entailed an account from that day's news about racist incidents, assaults, and lynchings in the United States.[54]

In June 1943, Preston Love and Johnny Otis gave notice to Lloyd Hunter that they were leaving his band. They planned to form their own combo and seek work in Love's hometown of Omaha, Nebraska. Otis and Love respected Hunter and appreciated all they had learned in his band. Yet life on the road was difficult for two recently married men. They put together a group that became the house band in the Barrel House nightclub, the first club in the white sections of Omaha to welcome both Black and white customers. White cattlemen and cowboys mingled with Black hustlers in zoot suits as the band struggled to find a repertoire that would please all the customers. Preston Love's brothers and his mother, Mexie Love, provided an instant and warm support system for Johnny and Phyllis. Jimmy Witherspoon, then working as a cook for the Union Pacific Railroad, sat in with the band as a guest singer whenever he was in town. Otis intended to stay in Omaha, but then an opportunity emerged that changed his life forever.[55]

Soon after Johnny's arrival in Omaha, the Nat King Cole Trio played at a dance in the Dreamland Hall, on Twenty-fourth Street. Otis and Love had encountered Cole on the road while playing with the Lloyd Hunter

Band, and they attended the dance to renew their acquaintance and to enjoy the unique musical stylings of his trio. As they socialized after the dance, Cole informed Otis that a spot had opened up in the Harlan Leonard orchestra back in Los Angeles, because its drummer Jesse Price had just been drafted. Cole explained that he had informed Leonard of Otis's talents and that the bandleader had said Otis could have the job if he came out to Los Angeles. Otis caught the first train west.[56]

Harlan Leonard had been a member of the Bennie Moten band when Count Basie was also in the group.[57] Leonard's Kansas City Rockets held an extended gig at the Club Alabam, one of the most glamorous entertainment venues on Los Angeles's legendary Central Avenue. In the Rockets, Johnny could play in the style of Jo Jones for appreciative audiences who would know what he was doing. He could live in a city with a large and growing Black population, with its own dynamic commercial, cultural, educational, and social institutions. The Club Alabam held special appeal for Johnny also because of its elaborate stage shows by dance troupes such as the High Hatters, who performed in flamboyant costumes made by a woman who called herself Madame Hoodah. When Otis watched the High Hatters perform at the World's Fair on Treasure Island in San Francisco in 1939, he prayed that he might one day be part of their world. Now his prayers had been answered; he played for shows at the Club Alabam produced and choreographed by Patsy Hunter, featuring Frenchy Landry and the High Hatters.[58]

As Black workers left the South to find work in war industries on the West Coast, Central Avenue in Los Angeles became an important crucible for a new kind of Black culture. The Black population of L.A. quadrupled during the war, and full employment and wartime wages fueled discretionary spending on leisure and recreation. "I got here in '43, and at that time the Avenue [Central] was just swinging," Otis later recalled. "It was like a transplanted Harlem Renaissance."[59] Even the streets provided free entertainment that few commercial venues could match. People paraded up and down on weekend nights, hopping from club to club and showing off their stylish clothes. Joyful musical sounds poured out of nightclubs and even some churches, most notably Sweet Daddy Grace's Grace Memorial House of Prayer for All People, on Vernon Avenue near Central. Brightly colored placards placed high up on electric utility poles advertised forthcoming dances and concerts. Most of these had been posted by a man known as Tack-em-up, a six-foot-seven-inch-tall Black man who used his height to place the signs too high up on poles for police officers to tear down. In an era when no radio stations served the Black community, Tack-em-up's placards provided a key source of information for music lovers.[60]

A man who called himself Uncle Blue took a different "tack." Blue sported rundown shoes and made his shirts and pants out of used gunny sacks. He performed on the street as a one-man band. Uncle Blue would not start playing until several coins had been tossed into the chamber pot he used to collect money from passersby. When he felt he had collected enough coins to make it worthwhile for him to start his act, Uncle Blue would make a telephone ring and pick up the receiver. Feigning a conversation as a diversion, he then caused an explosion of flour that simulated a smoke bomb to introduce his performance. Then Uncle Blue would start drumming, strumming, and tooting his instruments while he sang along.[61]

Otis wanted to join in the fun. As soon as he was paid the first time at the Club Alabam, he purchased a brown chalk-stripe zoot suit. With a long coat and pants that ballooned out thirty inches at the knees but tapered down to fourteen inches at the ankles, he thought he looked sharp. Otis proudly wore his new outfit while grabbing a bite to eat at the Brownskin Café between the matinee and evening shows at the club. Instead of admiring glances, however, he found his new "drapes" provoked only raised eyebrows, incredulous stares, and questions like, "What is up with that?" It took dancer and choreographer Patsy Hunter to explain to Otis that his idea of fashion was behind the times, that a zoot suit that might look sharp in Omaha appeared too "country" in Los Angeles, where the musicians emulated the conservative and dignified styles of dress that their heroes in the Count Basie Orchestra and the Duke Ellington Orchestra preferred.[62]

Otis told this story again and again throughout his life. He believed that it demonstrated the importance of intergenerational guidance and mentoring, in life as well as in music. He also felt, however, that it showed desire had to be tempered by knowledge. Otis's youthful self wanted to emulate the flamboyance and flash that appealed to him in the dress and demeanor of the zoot-suiters, without realizing that this choice could compromise the difficult struggle for dignity and respect waged by the older generation. Self-expression could slip into selfishness if one lost a sense of audience or neglected to face up to the fact that one's own actions have consequences for others.

When the job with Harlan Leonard's Kansas City Rockets at the Club

Alabam ended, Otis stayed in Los Angeles. He joined Bardu Ali's band for dates at the Lincoln Theatre. Ali had been a vocalist with the rhythmically sophisticated Chick Webb band and had an advanced appreciation for the kind of drumming that Johnny Otis liked. Soon, Ali and Otis would be partners in the nightclub business as co-owners of the Barrelhouse on Wilmington and 107th Street, named in honor of the club in Omaha where Johnny and Preston Love had formed their first combo.[63] Otis did session work at different recording studios, playing drums behind Lester Young, Illinois Jacquet, and Johnny Moore's Three Blazers, featuring Charles Brown. One night the Basie band came to town to play at the Plantation Club, at 108th and Central. Jo Jones became ill, and Basie asked Johnny to substitute for him.

Johnny almost missed out on the opportunity to play with Basie, because he could not believe his good fortune. His old friend and fellow drummer Ellis Bartee had a habit of making "fake" phone calls to young musicians, pretending to be a famous bandleader such as Earl Hines offering them employment. When his victims enthusiastically accepted these "invitations," Bartee would laugh uproariously and confess his true identity. He had burned Otis once with this particular trick. When Basie called him, Otis believed it had to be Bartee playing a joke. He treated the caller to a torrent of abuse and profanity, vowing that he would not be fooled by the same stunt twice. This time, however, the caller actually was Count Basie. He politely repeated his offer and graciously accepted Otis's embarrassed, awkward apology and then his acceptance of the offer.[64]

Otis was not yet twenty-five. Playing with Basie made him feel that he had reached a peak in music that went beyond his wildest youthful dreams. He knew that he was not "ready" to play drums at that level, but he greatly appreciated the kindness and friendliness shown him by all the members of the Basie aggregation, especially guitarist Freddie Green.[65] Otis remained faithful to the Basie sound for the rest of his life. When he started his own band he secured Basie's permission to copy the bandleader's arrangements so that the Otis aggregation could sound more like the Basie band. Saxophonist René Bloch viewed this link to Basie as one of the great pleasures of playing in the Johnny Otis Orchestra. He remembers proudly the day he heard that Basie had told his own band, "Hey, you guys, Johnny Otis's band is out Basie-ing us."[66] In 1990, Otis recorded and released the album *Spirit of the Black Territory Bands,* which paid tribute to the Basie sound.

Club manager and unofficial "mayor" of Central Avenue, Curtis Mosby contacted Otis shortly after the Harlan Leonard job ended, asking him to return to the Club Alabam as the leader of the house band. Otis assembled an extraordinary aggregation from the rich pool of musical talent available in Los Angeles to form the Johnny Otis Orchestra. Visiting musicians eagerly volunteered to sit in with this band. On different nights, Charlie Parker, Miles Davis, Buddy Collette, and Bill Doggett joined the regular lineup that included tenor saxophonists James Von Streeter (who put the Von in between his first and last names as a tribute to the motion picture actor and director Erich Von Stroheim) and Paul Quinchette, trumpeters Teddy Buckner and Art Farmer, and vocalist Ernestine Anderson.[67] For a time, Hideo Kawano, a Japanese American teenager fresh from a wartime internment camp played with the band, helping out on drums when Johnny played vibes or piano. Kawano carved out a unique career for himself, playing in the Johnny Otis Orchestra and Don Tosti's otherwise all-Chicano Pachuco Boogie Boys under his real name, before heading to Chicago, where he played drums professionally using the name Joe Young.[68] The Johnny Otis Orchestra also exerted influence on musicians who did not actually play with them. As a youth, trumpeter Don Cherry heard Otis's band play on Central Avenue and later credited them for helping form his musical consciousness and artistry.[69]

Johnny used his earnings from the Club Alabam to rent an old apartment building on Washington Boulevard near Hoover so that he and other members of the band could find lodging. Routine racial discrimination by landlords and the city's acute housing shortage made it hard for Black musicians to find suitable lodging. Band members residing in the building on Washington Boulevard saved money on groceries by helping themselves to part of the hearty, tasty, but inexpensive meals that Phyllis cooked for them, meals featuring spaghetti and meatballs, red beans and rice, and tamale pie with red Kool-Aid and thick slices of white bread. Johnny contributed to the communal food supply by cooking the buttermouth perch, opal eye and pile perch, herring, cod, halibut, and barracuda that he caught fishing on barges off the breakwater in San Pedro Harbor. One year some salmon drifted into the waters where he fished, providing the band with a feast that lasted three days.[70]

Johnny and Phyllis eventually moved into a house surrounded by two acres of property in the not-yet-fully-developed area just south of Watts on

118th Street. They needed room for a growing family, as their first daughter, Janice, was born in 1947 and was soon followed by another daughter, Laura (known in the family as La La), and then sons John and Nick. Their property was well stocked with ducks, geese, and rabbits, and Johnny enjoyed raising pigeons and chickens in coops outside the house.[71] The improvement in his personal financial situation seemed to be in step with the rise of the entire Black community. "I saw the whole community lifting," he remembers. "I thought we were going to realize the American dream. We'd say, 'It's a bitch. There's still a lot of racism, but it's going to be OK, because our kids will realize a fresh new democratic America.'"[72]

Yet some things had not changed very much at all. One night a drunken white customer at the Club Alabam started heckling the Black master of ceremonies with racist epithets. Johnny jumped up from his chair behind the drums to go after the heckler, but one of the band members grabbed him and pulled him back as the people at the heckler's table grabbed the man's arms and restrained him. Curtis Mosby called Otis into his office for a scolding from his assistant manager, a man known as Uncle Lou. "Listen, Nat Turner," Lou intoned caustically, "you are hired to play music, not to chastise naughty white folks."[73] It was the first time Otis had ever heard of Nat Turner. When he researched the name and found out that he was being compared to the nation's most famous slave rebel, he wondered why it was an insult and why the club owners could think it was wrong to fight back against racist insults, not yet fully aware of the fine line Black entrepreneurs had to walk in order to stay in business. If Otis had indulged his anger, he might have derived some satisfaction from assaulting the customer. Everyone working at the club, however, might have suffered as a result, because police officers and city inspectors might shut the establishment down if a white customer complained about "uppity" treatment from Blacks.

Otis experienced another lesson in the pervasive presence of white supremacy in the Black community from someone whom he had once idolized. Tap dancer and motion picture star Bill "Bojangles" Robinson approached Johnny one night on the bandstand at the Club Alabam. Pleased to make the acquaintance personally of someone whose talents he had admired, Otis eagerly listened to what Robinson had to say. It shocked him when Robinson proposed to hire Otis and his band for an upcoming tour, on the condition that he dismiss all of the Black musicians and replace them with white ones. Otis quickly and summarily rejected the offer.[74]

In those dynamic times in Black Los Angeles, Otis witnessed people becoming stars overnight. While playing in Sammy Franklin's band at the Elks Hall in Los Angeles, pianist Joe Liggins watched the audience doing a dance called the Texas Hop. His band had no song in their repertoire suited to that beat, so during intermission he fooled around on the piano with a melody to simulate the rhythm of the dance. Couples got up and started to dance to the song while a crowd of admirers surrounded Liggins at the piano. One of the other musicians joked, "Look at this guy; he drips a lot of honey. You're a honeydripper, 'cause all these chicks gather around you, you drip that little tune. You're a honeydripper." Liggins took that phrase as the title of the song, wrote some lyrics, and "The Honeydripper" became a hit on Leon René's Exclusive record label, eventually rising to the top of the rhythm and blues charts in 1945. Five years later, Liggins borrowed the rhythm of the sound of windshield wipers on a rumbling bus to write "Pink Champagne," which became a top-ten record.[75]

Late in 1945, Otis secured an opportunity for his band to make a record. Otis René offered him three hours in the Radio Recorder studio to record four songs for René to release on his Excelsior label. Otis René and his brother Leon were Creoles from Louisiana who had moved to Los Angeles in 1922. They coauthored the classic pop songs "When the Swallows Come Back to Capistrano" and "When It's Sleepy Time Down South." Otis René hoped that the Johnny Otis Orchestra could have the kind of success his label had enjoyed with another Los Angeles–based band, the Nat King Cole Trio. Johnny got Count Basie's great vocalist Jimmy Rushing to front the band on "My Baby's Business," which he thought would be a hit. He filled out the session by recording two instrumentals: "Jimmy's Round the Clock Blues" and "Preston Love's Mansion," a tribute to the dilapidated house in Omaha where Preston Love had been raised, a dwelling that his proud mother, Mexie, had dubbed the "Love Mansion." Everything progressed smoothly, and Johnny triumphantly informed Otis René that he and his group had completed the three record sides without taking the full four hours allotted to them. In fact, Johnny noted, there were ninety minutes left over. He had misunderstood René's instructions, however. René corrected him, telling Johnny that the deal was not for *three* sides in four hours but rather for *four* sides in three hours. That meant that they needed one more recording to release four songs on two two-sided records. Even worse, Johnny had only thirty minutes to create the final recording or René would have to charge him extra for the surplus studio time.

Pressed for time, with no other song prepared, Johnny asked the band to do a number they had played often at the Club Alabam. The band's saxophonist, René Bloch, had brought Johnny the Ray Noble band's arrangement of Earle Hagen's "Harlem Nocturne" for the group to play at the club. Bloch had played the song with a band in Spokane and liked the possibilities it held for solos on his instrument. The saxophonist later went on to a distinguished career in Latin music with Pérez Prado's mambo orchestra as well as an unusual extramusical life as rabbi in the Jewish faith. Johnny slowed down the beat of "Harlem Nocturne," made a few other changes, and put the tune into his band's book. He considered what Bloch had brought him to be a "Mickey Mouse arrangement of a Mickey Mouse song," yet something happened when the band played the song live. The chorus girls at the Club Alabam would stand up and gather 'round the stage when the tune started, swaying sensuously. Soon the musicians followed their lead, slowing the rhythm even more to match the moves of the dancers. Because the band knew the song so well and had fun playing it, Otis filled out the session by recording the song without rehearsal. The recording of "Harlem Nocturne" also featured the piano stylings of Bill Doggett and the trombone artistry of Hambone Robinson.[76] To Otis's great surprise, "Harlem Nocturne" featuring Bloch playing an alto solo in the breathy style of Johnny Hodges became a national hit.

"Harlem Nocturne" launched Johnny Otis on the path toward a successful career as a recording artist, producer, and promoter. Sales of the record created a demand to see the Johnny Otis Orchestra in person. "Harlem Nocturne" took the band right to Harlem itself, to the Apollo Theatre, where their success set the stage for many return engagements. A triumphant tour with the popular Ink Spots vocal group soon followed. The song attracted new fans (and produced additional royalties) when it was selected as the theme song for the *Mike Hammer* television show in the 1950s.[77]

Yet despite this success, Johnny Otis's efforts raised suspicions in some quarters. In 1946, an agent from the Federal Bureau of Investigation came to the Club Alabam and asked Otis, "Do you have a mixed band?" Thinking that a racially integrated band violated no federal law and annoyed by the agent's question, Johnny quipped, "Yeah, I've got men *and* women!"[78] This response angered the agent, who asked whether René Bloch was white or not, evidently puzzled by his looks. With an odd mixture of sophistication and naïveté, Johnny felt deeply offended that an agent of the federal government would try to prevent people of different races from playing together. Yet he noted with some satisfaction that the agent seemed to think what most white promoters, hotel managers, and law enforcement officials in the South thought when Otis brought his band to places where mixed bands were illegal: that the dark-haired man named Johnny Otis, who headed a Black band, must himself be Black. It was an impression he didn't mind conveying. In fact, it brought him a great deal of satisfaction.

Two DOUBLE CROSSING BLUES

The commercial success of "Harlem Nocturne" launched a new era for Johnny Otis. His band was selected to back up the tremendously popular vocal group the Ink Spots on their 1947 national tour. Legendary tap dancers Cholly Atkins and Honi Coles also appeared on the bill. Atkins especially appreciated the Otis band's attentiveness to his particular needs as a dancer. In his autobiography, Atkins remembered that the show was top-notch and that Johnny Otis was "an adorable person."[1] The Ink Spots performed in old movie theaters, and it was a special treat for Otis to hear his band's music resonate against the high ceilings and the width and breadth of those big halls after playing mostly in cramped nightclubs.

Like many couples, Johnny and Phyllis postponed having children during the war. They had been together six years before their first daughter, Janice, was born. The demands of life on the road in the music business interfered with planning a family. Phyllis complained that Johnny often seemed distracted with work concerns and did not really listen to her when she raised the issue of when they would start their family. It had become such a sore subject between them that they ceased talking about it. Shortly before the start of the Ink Spots tour, however, the subject came up again in a conversation. They were in New York, staying at the Hotel Theresa, in Harlem, while Johnny and his band performed an engagement at the Apollo Theatre. He sat up late at night, copying music in the dim light provided by a lamp lit with an orange bulb. Johnny wondered if he should go down to the front desk to get a brighter lightbulb when he realized Phyllis had said something about going back to San Francisco to be with her mother for a few months. Noting that Phyllis's mother had not been sick, Johnny asked why they would be spending time with her. Exasperated, Phyllis replied, "I'm talking about having a baby. Do you mean you haven't understood what I've been telling you all these weeks?"[2]

Not too long after that, Johnny's band started its tour with the Ink Spots. Phyllis had already boarded a train for California so that her mother could help her with the pregnancy and impending birth of the baby. By the time her train had reached Omaha, however, Phyllis realized that she was about to give birth. She walked into the station and asked a porter to phone Preston Love's mother, Mexie Love, and ask her for help. Mexie Love drove Phyllis to the hospital. Phyllis remained in labor for nearly two days. By coincidence, however, the Ink Spots tour arrived in Omaha at precisely that time, enabling Johnny to be present when Janice was born.[3]

At the end of the tour, the Johnny Otis Orchestra came back to its base in Los Angeles, where it performed frequently at the annual Cavalcade of Jazz concerts at Wrigley Field. The Cavalcade lineup included the best big bands of the day and attracted large audiences. Otis especially liked the music of Machito and his Afro-Cubans because of their use of different kinds of percussive instruments. He started employing conga players on many of his recordings because of these encounters with Machito. In 1951, the Otis ensemble recorded "Mambo Boogie" on the Savoy label, featuring the percussive talents of Gaucho Vaharandes, an Afro-Jukla Indian from Brazil.

Soon, however, the financial crisis that impacted all of the big bands in the late 1940s compelled Otis to scale down his orchestra to a small rhythm and blues combo. He enjoyed greater success with this format than with his big band, scoring hit after hit on the *Billboard* charts. Following his established pattern of presenting a full show like a carnival coming to town rather than appearing as a solo act, he charted records featuring several different singers, billing his ensemble alternately as the Johnny Otis Caravan, the Johnny Otis Congregation, and the Johnny Otis Show. He supplemented these activities as a performing and recording artist by running the Barrelhouse Club in Watts on Wilmington between 107th and Santa Ana Boulevard in partnership with his old friend (and now manager) Bardu Ali. Because the club had no license for hard liquor, customers had to be content with beer and wine. Yet business boomed at the Barrelhouse.

The regional popularity of the Johnny Otis Orchestra's recording "Midnight at the Barrelhouse" only added to the club's renown.[4]

During the next ten years, Johnny Otis would find himself at the center of a musical and social revolution. His work took him to Black communities all across the country and enabled him to see firsthand how Black people used cultural creativity to affirm their individual and collective worth in the face of systematic oppression and suppression. During an engagement in Houston, Texas, members of Johnny's band interrupted his lunch at the coffee shop in the Club Matinee, in the Fifth Ward, to tell him about an unbelievably talented musician that they thought he had to see. Otis went to the Crystal Tea Room to check out the act and soon stood stunned in amazement. He encountered a flamboyantly dressed piano player who had substantial amounts of lipstick, eye shadow, and mascara on his face and a huge pompadour haircut offset by a thin mustache that appeared to have been drawn on with eyebrow pencil. The singer jumped all over the room, danced on top of the piano, sang beautifully, and screamed out his importance. "I'm Little Richard. And these are the Upsetters. I'm the King of the Blues! And the Queen too!"[5]

In a talent show that he judged at the Paradise Theater, in Detroit, Otis saw and heard Jackie Wilson, Hank Ballard, and Little Willie John for the first time, all on the same night. Incredibly enough, none of them won the competition, because another act (Johnny no longer remembers which one) was even better on that particular night. Otis would go on to work with all three of the new discoveries. He failed to interest Syd Nathan, his employer at King Records, in the great Jackie Wilson, but he did manage to get Hank Ballard and Little Willie John signed to the label. Otis toured extensively with Little Willie John, which often turned out to be a trying experience. Little Willie liked attention and had an enormous propensity for mischief. As a teenage member of his family gospel singing group, the United Five, Willie liked to stand by the doors or windows of the churches and sing loudly, so that people passing by would hear his voice. Etta James remembers Little Willie John as "a spoiled little brat" who would "pour lemonade over your head, pick your dress up over your head [and] stick his finger up your booty."[6] Little Willie would also help himself to everyone else's food, provoking Otis's drummer Kansas City Bell to coin his catch phrase, "Hide the neck bones quick! Here come Little Willie John."[7]

Musicians on the rhythm and blues circuit competed for attention and took great pains to make themselves memorable. Guitar Slim pranced around in fire engine red suits, occasionally with his hair dyed blue.[8] Larry Williams had manicured fingernails and wore big brimmed hats. He drove a pastel green Lincoln Continental Mark IV convertible with vanity license plates that read "Short Fat Fannie" in honor of his first hit record, complemented by a bumper sticker that proclaimed, "I STOP FOR ALL BLONDES." Etta James remembers that this "gangster" persona was not completely an act. She claims that Williams actually made more money as a burglar than he did as a singer, that he always regretted not putting more time and effort into his music, but simply found illicit forms of work more profitable.[9]

At the Blue Room on Central Avenue in Tampa, Florida, a performer who called himself Iron Jaw Harris presented a particularly unusual act. He danced barefoot on beer bottle caps strewn about the floor until they stuck to his feet and simulated the sound of taps. After executing a few tap steps, he would pick up a table with his mouth and return it to the floor before finishing his performance by eating thumbtacks, broken lightbulbs, glass bottles, and double-edged razor blades, followed by swallowing fire.[10] This was a man determined to be in show business.

Many musicians routinely carried guns with them. They played in some rough joints where violence might break out at any time. When Big Joe Turner performed in after-hours clubs in Watts, he witnessed many fights start because one man approached another's date and asked her to dance. Turner tried to prevent fisticuffs by routinely reminding patrons to "drink hearty, but stay in your party."[11] Bob Koester remembers producing a recording for Big Joe Williams in St. Louis in 1957 during which the singer recognized the piano they planned to use at the session; it had been the house piano in one particularly tough tavern on Olive Street near Vandeventer Boulevard. Koester thought Williams might have recognized the distinctive sound of the instrument, but it turned out that the configuration of the blood stains on the piano was what gave away its previous home.[12]

Sometimes entertainers needed to be armed to protect themselves from robbers. They generally got paid in cash from the evening's gate receipts, and potential thieves were well aware that performers carried cash. At other times, however, they found they needed a gun simply to get paid, to "persuade" club owners to pay them the money they had been promised. Yet carrying guns entailed unexpected risks as well. When Sam Lay played drums in James Cotton's blues band, he once carried a pistol onstage to protect Cotton from a jealous rival who had threatened him with bodily harm. Lay drummed so enthusiastically that he forgot about the pistol in his pants, accidentally discharging it and blowing off one of his testicles.[13] Albert King kept a pistol in his pocket during nightclub performances. Sometimes when a member of his band made a mistake, the guitarist would walk over to the offender and slap him with one hand and fire the pistol with the other. King's victims did not know if they had been merely slapped or shot, a practice that led to high turnover in King's band but also, understandably enough, some incredibly precise playing.

Rhythm and blues singer Wynonie Harris proved to be a flamboyant performer onstage and off. When Harris would encounter a member of Otis's band out on the town with a date, he would sidle up to the woman and intone solemnly that the man she was with was actually married to Harris's sister, adding that he did not approve of him stepping out on her. That usually provoked a fight between the musician and his date while Harris ran off "at top speed laughing like a maniac."[14] Touring with Pete Lewis also presented unusual challenges. A great blues guitarist who once performed with his twin brother in an act aptly named "Pete and Repeat," Lewis could be a strange companion on the road. At one point, Pete stopped speaking to Otis for some reason as they went on tour after tour. His silence lasted nearly an entire year. Then one day, for no apparent reason, Lewis resumed conversation with Otis as if they had been speaking all along.[15]

At one memorable performance in New York's famed Apollo Theatre, Otis picked Big Mama Thornton to open the show. Although she had been on the road as a musician and singer for nearly fifteen years, Thornton had no history of hit songs to present to the crowd. She sang her own version of "Have Mercy Baby," which had been a hit for Billy Ward and the Dominoes. The audience applauded so much they had to pull the curtain down to move on with the show. The manager came backstage and ordered Otis to place Thornton last on the bill from then on, because he thought they would never get on to the rest of the show if she opened. The next night, Thornton came to the theater and saw her name in lights as the star of a show for the first time.

The Johnny Otis aggregation entertained itself by playing baseball games in between shows. Little Arthur Matthews and Big Mama Thornton proved especially enthusiastic about the game, but Arthur Maye and the Crowns generally provided the margin of victory against other teams. Arthur

Maye made passable rock 'n' roll records on Otis's Dig label in 1957, but he distinguished himself in the public as Lee Maye, a star in the Major Leagues for the Milwaukee Braves, the Cleveland Indians, and the Washington Senators, who batted over .300 in three seasons. Before Maye made it to the Major Leagues, Otis hosted a local Los Angeles television program and fielded a baseball team that competed regularly with teams made up of musicians from other bands. The team, sponsored by drummer and singer Roy Milton, proved to be a particularly worthy opponent, as was the aggregation assembled from the popular local Chicano band the Armenta Brothers. Games were held on Wednesday nights at South Park in Los Angeles. As many as one thousand spectators showed up to watch the fun every week. After one game at which Arthur Lee Maye's batting destroyed the Armenta Brothers' pitching staff, his opponents asked Johnny where he got that player. "He's just a singer in my band," Otis answered, telling the truth, if not the whole truth. The next week, the Armenta Brothers' team featured some new players, a couple of dark-skinned Spanish speakers whose play led them to an easy victory. Otis discovered later that the new "musicians" in the Armenta Brothers' band were really professional athletes from the Mexican baseball league, imported solely to even the score in retaliation for the previous week's defeat and to offset Arthur Lee Maye's hitting.[16]

The Otis band also enjoyed following Major League Baseball as fans. Most rooted for the Brooklyn Dodgers because they had been the first team in the modern era to break the color barrier by playing Jackie Robinson. The goodwill that the Dodgers generated among Blacks extended to the whole National League, which desegregated more quickly and more thoroughly than did the American League. When the World Series came around every year in the early 1950s, Johnny and most of his fellow musicians would bet on the National League team in the contest, especially between 1952 and 1956, when the Dodgers played the Yankees four out of five years. Trumpeter Don Johnson, however, thinking like a businessman, did not allow racial allegiances to get in the way of making money. He bet on the Yankees every year and was happy to win his bandmates' money in every one of those years except 1955.[17]

Some artists in those days would create their own show within the show. Big Jay McNeely proved to be an especially memorable performer. At shows where Otis featured the saxophonist, Big Jay often played his instrument while lying on his back onstage and kicking his legs up in the air. In some nightclubs, he belted out a wild solo as he crossed the room atop the customers' tables, leaping from one to the next without a break in his playing. Sometimes McNeely dressed in a Roman toga, painted his saxophone bright colors, and devised a special lighting system that made his horn seem to glow in the dark. Bobby Day remembers that when his group, the Hollywood Flames, sang with Big Jay McNeely backing them up, they would goad him into wilder and wilder playing by chanting the chorus "Blow, Jay, Blow" four times and then turning the stage back to him for more playing.[18]

One night in San Diego, McNeely played with the Johnny Otis Show in a club near the ocean. On an impulse, the saxophonist led the entire audience out onto the beach like a Pied Piper. Johnny stayed on the bandstand pounding the drums, with the sounds of McNeely's horn growing fainter and fainter as he walked toward the sea. When McNeely reached the water, he turned around and led the crowd back into the club, messing up the dance floor horribly with all the wet sand the patrons tracked in on their shoes. McNeely followed up this triumph at another San Diego club a few weeks later. This time, he led the crowd out of the club and into the street. Otis continued to play, pounding the beat until he thought his arms would fall off, not realizing that Big Jay had been arrested by police officers, that he was tooting his horn inside a paddy wagon as it wheeled him away toward the city jail![19]

Johnny Guitar Watson could play guitar while standing on his hands, picking the strings with his teeth. He distinguished himself as a masterful blues player on both guitar and piano, but also anticipated future psychedelic and funk styles with his visionary, innovative, and generative artistry. Former tap dancer T-Bone Walker moved smoothly and skillfully as he played his guitar. He held the instrument behind his head while playing brilliantly, punctuating his solos by dropping to the floor in the splits and then bouncing up again in one fluid motion.

Some performers made their mark in quieter ways, by displaying consummate professionalism. Otis learned that he could always count on Clora Bryant to show up on time and be ready to play. Other artists could be more unpredictable. One night in Pasadena, the Rivingtons started out with six musicians, but by the end of the show only three remained sober enough to stay on the bandstand.[20] Otis, however, did not generally work with musicians who found it a challenge simply to get up onstage, like Jimmy Reed and Chris Kenner. During performances at the 5-4 Ballroom in Los Angeles,

Reed was often so inebriated that stagehands had to tie him to the microphone so he could be heard. "You'd be surprised," observed promoter Billy Diamond, "once we got him tied so he could stand up, he'd give you a real good show."[21] Chris Kenner, on the other hand, almost never gave a good performance live. He charted hit after hit as a recording artist, but his own booking agent, Percy Stovall, confessed that Kenner "couldn't sing. He couldn't dance, he dressed raggedy—he just stood there. He didn't have any showmanship and he was drunk all the time."[22] Yet somehow, audiences came back for more.

Joe August recorded as Mr. "Google Eyes" with the Johnny Otis Orchestra on Duke Records. Excited by his success, August used to drive to gigs in a purple Buick convertible that featured leopard-skin upholstery, leopard-skin floor rugs, leopard-skin lining inside the trunk, and leopard-skin padding covering the dashboard.[23] August came out of the rich performance culture of Black music in New Orleans, where at one show Ernie K-Doe found himself on the bill with the great James Brown. Determined not to be eclipsed by Brown's energetic antics onstage, K-Doe changed suits nine times during his performance of the song "A Certain Girl." He positioned a clothes rack and a valet behind stage, and every time K-Doe reached a certain instrumental break in the song, he ran backstage and came back out the other side wearing a different-colored suit.[24]

During these years, Otis taught himself to become a remarkable musician: a multi-instrumentalist who did fine work on drums, piano, and vibes, who enjoyed commercial and critical success playing jazz, rhythm and blues, and rock 'n' roll. His innovative arrangement held the key to the success of "Harlem Nocturne" (1945), but he also proved himself adept at singing lead vocals on "All Night Long" (1951), "Willie and the Hand Jive" (1958), "Crazy Country Hop" (1958), "Castin' My Spell" (1959), and "Mumblin' Mosie" (1960). Otis also sang on "Country Girl" (1969), in which the lead vocal was sung by Delmar Evans. Yet many of his most important contributions to Black music came from his efforts at promoting other musicians. He had developed his appreciation of great Black music to such a degree that he recognized what he believed to be his own limitations. "I'm not a good singer," he maintained. "I get by, I sing, and I've had hit records—and that's ridiculous—but know thyself. I had the talent, I don't have the voice. I don't have the big masculine baritone bottom, or the nice high bright tenor. I don't have that. So if I'm going to try and sing a song, I've gotta be doggone sure the range is right. So what am I going to do? Jump out in front of a band and sing? Sometime I do, but there's too much marvelous talent out there, people who deserve a break, a chance at it."[25]

Otis "blames" T-Bone Walker and Joe Adams for convincing him to do a vocal on "All Night Long." They said, "You sound as bad as the rest of them cats that's making hit records singing, go ahead and make one yourself."[26] When the song became a hit, Otis felt "almost for a moment" that he actually could sing. He came face to face with his limits once again, however, when he asked Phyllis what she thought of his singing. Diplomatically, she replied slowly, "Well, it's nice." Otis felt she was right. "Not only was it just nice," he chuckles, "in reality, it wasn't nothing."[27]

Dave Marsh and other discerning critics disagree with Otis's self-assessment. They believe that he had all he needed to become a star as an individual.[28] Johnny certainly knew that many pop singers have been commercially successful with vocal talents greatly inferior to his. Voice coaches can train singers to increase their range. Coaching helped Frank Sinatra expand his range considerably.[29] Studio equipment and production techniques can hide vocalists' flaws and foreground their strengths. Limited vocal range did not keep Rod Stewart, Olivia Newton John, Madonna, or Tony Bennett from successful careers as singers. John Lee Hooker made a virtue out of his limited range by finding new and innovative ways to sing the things within his grasp. In addition, Johnny did some fine "singing" through the Lester Young–inspired melodic lines he played on the vibes on many of his recordings.

Otis's primary point, however, was less an expression of personal modesty or an assessment of his own skills than it was an indication of his commitment to promoting an advanced appreciation of Black music when played and sung well. He wondered why anyone would want to listen to Johnny Otis sing when they could be listening to Little Esther Phillips, Charles Brown, or Etta James. He took pride in his success in putting talented singers before the public in settings where they could show off their artistry, and he felt deeply gratified by his role in discovering, nurturing, and producing previously unknown talents. "I can hear the raw talent before it develops," he noted as an explanation for his roles as session producer and career mentor for Etta James, Sugar Pie DeSanto, Linda Hopkins, Margie Evans, and Barbara Morrison, among others.[30]

Otis's deep respect for the collective riches embedded within Black culture guided his efforts as a composer as well. Working in the dialogic tradition of the blues, in which artists talk to one another across generations by reworking a common repertoire, Otis's compositions almost always reference something that came before. Otis's 1953 song "Rock Me Baby," on Don Robey's Peacock label, presented a thinly veiled remake of the gospel song "Thank You Jesus." "Willie and the Hand Jive" reworked the "hambone" beat of "shave and a haircut," as well as Count Otis Matthews's version of "Mama Had a Chicken." Otis's composition "So Fine," a hit for the Fiestas and many years later for the Oak Ridge Boys, turned Willie Dixon's "My Babe" inside out. Hank Ballard's "Work with Me Annie" provided the basis for "Roll with Me Henry," the answer record written by Etta James and Johnny Otis and recorded by James with the approval of Ballard, who received songwriter's credit and royalties as well.[31]

At times Otis believed that artistry in one area proved to be a hindrance in another. When drummer Ellis Bartee left his band, Otis had an opportunity to hire the great Art Blakey. Members of the orchestra were excited by the prospect of playing with a musician whom all of them admired, but Otis knew that the sophisticated bebop drumming that Blakey had mastered would be wasted in a band that played the comparatively simple tempos of rhythm and blues. Even the most skilled bebop drummer found it confining to lay down the steady pulse needed by Otis's band. Instead, Johnny hired Leard "Kansas City" Bell, not because he was a better drummer than Blakey (as if that were possible), but because he was virtually a human rhythm machine who was perfect for the rhythm and blues music of the late 1940s and early 1950s—a big, strong, consistent musician who could play all night. When rhythms got more complex by the late 1950s, however, Kansas City Bell could no longer keep up, and Johnny had to fire him. Bell was hurt and never spoke to Johnny again. It was probably the most painful decision Otis had to make in his career.[32]

Just as the virtuosity of Art Blakey did not necessarily translate into the type of artistry required for rhythm and blues and Kansas City Bell's more limited skills did work better for that purpose, the limitations of some singers could make them ill suited for solo work but fine for membership inside groups. Tom Reed, known as "the Master Blaster" when he was the most popular disc jockey in Los Angeles in the mid-1960s, notes how Johnny Otis's shows and caravans made use of the same principles that nurtured gospel harmony groups in Black communities. "Not everybody is Sam Cooke or Herb Jeffries," Reed observes, but carefully delineated roles and skilled arrangements can make five average singers sound great together. From the Robins to the Royals, from the Click Clacks to the Nic Nacs, from the Penguins to the Premiers, from the Sheiks to the Sultans, from the Tears to the Twilighters, Johnny worked his magic in arranging and producing on behalf of many vocal groups who might otherwise not have been able to succeed in the business.[33]

While Johnny Otis ran the Barrelhouse nightclub, toured the nation with his band, and scouted and produced new artists for a variety of labels, he transformed part of his property off Wilmington Avenue into a chicken farm, incorporated as the Progressive Poultry Company. He worked in partnership with bass player Mario Delagarde, an independent thinker who later composed "Motor Head Baby" with Johnny Guitar Watson (and is rumored to have died in Cuba fighting alongside Fidel Castro in overthrowing the dictatorship of Fulgencio Batista). The company raised and sold chickens. It owned an old ice cream truck that Delagarde drove throughout Watts during the day, peddling chickens and eggs from the vehicle, just as Johnny's father had sold fruits and vegetables in the Berkeley Hills in the 1920s and 1930s. Otis fed, watered, slaughtered, and dressed the fowls so that they could be sold. Transplanted southerners in Watts especially appreciated the opportunity to select their own birds for supper.[34]

Professional entertainers today may invest in other enterprises, but very few spend time actually running their own businesses. In the post–World War II period, however, the wages and royalties paid to rhythm and blues artists were so low that several artists conducted other business on the side. As R. J. Smith notes in his fine book about African American Los Angeles in the 1940s, Roy Milton slept in the back room of the twenty-four-hour grocery store that he owned and managed in downtown Los Angeles while he was recording and performing with his band. Joe Liggins had a huge hit record with "The Honeydripper," but that success did not divert him from his other job—selling sewing machines to Black women, many of whom worked as seamstresses for white customers.[35]

Johnny Otis liked the work of raising birds. He enjoyed doing business with his neighbors, and he appreciated opportunities to busy himself with carpentry work in building coops for the chickens. Yet while sawing some wood one day, his hand slipped. The saw cut the second and third fingers of his right hand down to the bone, severing the tendons in his fingers. For a time, it looked like the attending physicians might have to amputate three fingers, although that later proved unnecessary. One doctor who treated him, however, mistakenly left the hand in the flexed position, leaving Johnny permanently unable to grip a drumstick in the proper manner with his right hand.[36]

The accident made it impossible for him to continue playing as a swing drummer, although he could get by on most rhythm and blues and rock songs with what he was still able to play. This serious injury and subsequent disability presented him with new challenges. He faced these with a confidence rooted in his experience. Otis's entire life had entailed rapid changes and adaptations to new circumstances. He forged ahead in the face of obstacles. He had made himself into a professional musician largely through will and hard work, learning drums and vibes from instruction manuals. He went from being an appreciative member of the audience at a concert by the Count Basie Band to playing with that aggregation less than a decade later. He had even made himself Black.

Otis found that he could still perform on the vibes despite his injury. He began playing the piano in a more percussive style because of the change in his right hand. Otis's disability constrained his piano playing in some respects, but like Tiny Parham, another piano player with a crippled hand, he found he could work within his limitations and actually use them to accentuate the rhythmic possibilities of the instrument.

One night when he was recovering from his injuries, Johnny's hand hurt so badly he could not sleep. Fearing addiction to painkillers, he took a walk to get his mind off the pain, so that he would not take another pill. Strolling up Wilmington Avenue to 103rd Street, he found himself in front of the Largo Theatre. Big Jay McNeely was playing, so he went inside. Before the main act came on, the theater hosted a talent contest. A thirteen-year-old contestant named Esther Mae Jones competed but did not win the contest. She sat sobbing in the back of the theater when she discovered she had lost. Impressed by her talent, Johnny consoled her by inviting her to sing with his band.

Under contract with Savoy Records as a performer and producer, Otis brought Esther Mae Jones into the studio to record. Intimidated by the studio, by the backup group the Robins, and by the pressure of the situation, Esther could not stop giggling as precious studio time ticked away on the clock. Just as he had done with "Harlem Nocturne," however, Johnny produced a hit with a song put together in a hurry at the end of a session. Esther later recalled, "At the end of the [recording] date they had 20 minutes left, so he [Otis] wrote out this song about lady bears in the forest. We only had time to make one take. It sold a million."[37]

The song that Otis cobbled together at the last minute was "Double Crossing Blues." Its lyrics did contain a joke about lady bears in a forest taken from a Black vaudeville routine by Apus and Estrellita, just as Esther remembered. The song, however, really revolved around some good-natured teasing between two lovers, "performed" by Esther and Mel Walker. Evoking a young Dinah Washington, Esther sounded much older than she was. Not knowing if the record would be released, Otis sent it off to Savoy's president, Herman Lubinsky, at the label's headquarters in Newark, New Jersey. In the midst of transacting some other business, Lubinsky told Otis, "You'd better come up with a stage name for that girl." Initially, Otis did not know to whom Lubinsky was referring. "What girl?" he asked. Then it dawned on him, "Oh, you mean little Esther?" "That's perfect!" Lubinsky replied, and from that moment on, Esther Mae Jones became known as Little Esther. When she grew up she performed as Esther Phillips.[38]

"Double Crossing Blues" surged to the top of the rhythm and blues charts and stayed there for five months. *Time* magazine compared Little Esther to other "coffee colored coloraturas such as Lena Horne and Dinah Washington" and saluted her "big warm billowing voice adrift on the blues."[39] She recorded five top-ten rhythm and blues hits in 1950 and went on to place seven single records and seven albums on *Billboard's* best-seller charts in the 1960s and 1970s. Otis made sure that Little Esther received not only royalties but also half of the profits garnered from the public appearances and record sales of the Johnny Otis Show. On tours, he brought along Esther's mother, her manager, and a tutor to supervise two hours of school work each day.

In addition to his work with Savoy, Otis also produced recordings for Don Robey's Duke and Peacock labels in Houston, as well as for Syd Nathan's King and Federal labels in Cincinnati. Robey was a light-skinned Black man who reportedly had used his winnings as a professional gambler to start a taxi cab business and the Bronze Peacock nightclub along Lyons Avenue in Houston's Fifth Ward. Robey had a reputation as a rough character, as a man not reluctant to push his artists around to keep them in line. But Johnny Otis had only good experiences with him. Working for Robey opened the door for Otis to work with Big Mama Thornton, Marie Adams, and Johnny Ace. Otis produced eight of Ace's twenty-one recorded songs, including his biggest hit "Pledging My Love." Ace's brilliant career ended on Christmas night in 1954, when he blew his brains out playing Russian roulette backstage before a concert at Houston's Civic Auditorium. The tragic death did not surprise Otis. He remembered Ace's road manager complaining about the singer's fascination with guns and his propensity for courting danger. During a tour in Florida, the manager told Otis, "He's got that goddamn gun and he spins the barrel and points it at me and it just scares the shit out of me. He does it while we're riding along the highway."[40]

Johnny greatly appreciated his relationship with Don Robey's organization, especially the exposure it gave him to the extraordinary pool of talent that existed in the Houston–New Orleans Gulf Coast area. In 1952, Otis rented studio time in Los Angeles to produce recordings of Big Mama Thornton for Robey's Peacock label. He selected the song "Hound Dog," written by two local nineteen-year-old song writers, Jerry Leiber and Mike Stoller. Otis changed the chorus and removed the horn parts, enabling Thornton to take center stage. The record was a smash hit in 1953, reaching the top of the rhythm and blues charts. It remained a hit for fourteen weeks. In 1956, Elvis Presley recorded his version of the song, which reached number one on the pop charts and stayed a hit for twenty-seven weeks.

"Hound Dog" became a classic in the rock 'n' roll pantheon, but it also generated one of the biggest controversies of Otis's career. Before "Hound Dog" had been written, he invited Leiber and Stoller to attend a rehearsal with Big Mama. Inspired by Thornton's singing and stage presence, they went home and quickly composed the basic contours of "Hound Dog" in fifteen minutes. They returned to the rehearsal and ran through the song with her. At the actual recording session at Johnny's home studio on August 13, 1952, however, things did not start off well. Leiber and Stoller suggested that Otis replace Kansas City Bell on drums, because Otis had played something they liked when they first rehearsed the song. The first take worked, and the second one went even better. Don Robey released the record, and it became a hit. The composing credit on the label gave one-third authorship to Leiber, one-third to Stoller, and one-third to Johnny Otis. Leiber and Stoller protested, claiming that they had written the entire song. They admitted they had assigned Otis one-third of the "mechanical rights" on record sales (not on radio or television airplay), but they claimed they owned all of the composers' rights.

Otis explained his side of the story to journalist Norbert Hess. "Leiber and Stoller wrote 'Hound Dog' and I helped rewrite it and we had an arrangement where I became co-writer for my contribution to the song, as we did many other songs. I wrote 'You made me feel so bad. You make me weep and moan. You ain't looking for a woman. You're just looking for a home.' They [Leiber and Stoller] had some derogatory crap, I constantly had to edit their songs."[41] Otis remembers that initially Leiber and Stoller gave him a one-third share of the writers' credits on the song, but when Presley's record became such a big hit, they claimed that when they signed the contract with Otis they were minors, and thus the contract was not valid. He recalls that Leiber and Stoller insisted on a new agreement that gave them 46.25 percent of the song while allocating Don Robey 28.75 percent and giving Elvis Presley the remaining 25 percent. The courts supported their claim, awarding them the rights to "Hound Dog" on that basis. The decision cost Otis millions of dollars in royalties, but he accepted the legal decision, always expressing sincere admiration for Leiber's and Stoller's extraordinary talents as song writers.[42]

Working for Syd Nathan's King and Federal labels proved less pleasant to Otis than working for Don Robey had been. Nathan was a short, balding, gravel-voiced man who chomped a big cigar and looked out at the world through Coke-bottle glasses. He directly supervised most of the recording done for his labels. He thought of himself as a perceptive judge of musical talent, but many of his decisions indicated otherwise. When Johnny brought Jackie Wilson to audition for the label, he knew that Nathan would not understand the greatness of Wilson's amazing melisma-filled rendition of "Danny Boy," so he wrote the song "Every Beat of My Heart" especially for the occasion. Yet Nathan did not want Jackie Wilson at all. He grudgingly gave "Every Beat of My Heart" to Hank Ballard and the Midnighters but then did not promote the recording. Later, it became a hit for Gladys Knight and the Pips on the Fury label. Ballard wrote and recorded the original version of "The Twist" (based on Clyde McPhatter's "What You Gonna Do?"), but Nathan dismissed the song as a mediocre record with limited appeal. Dick Clark disagreed with Nathan's assessment and produced "The Twist" for Chubby Checker. The song became a number-one seller on the *Billboard* charts twice, becoming the first record since Bing Crosby's "White Christmas" to reach number one, fall off the charts, and then reach number one again on its subsequent release. Hank Ballard enjoyed proving Syd Nathan wrong, especially when he discovered that Clark's Parkway label was actually going to pay him songwriter's royalties on the song, a payment he could not count on when his records were released on the King label.[43]

While doing some work at the King and Federal studios, Johnny went to hear his old friend Lowell Fulson at a club in Columbus, Ohio. Because pianist Lloyd Glenn did not like to travel, Fulson hired a replacement to accompany him and open the show, a then virtually unknown musician who called himself Ray Charles. Fulson got through only a few bars of his first song that night before a fight broke out that eventually led to the cancellation of the entire show. Johnny had heard enough in those first few bars, however, to bring Charles to Nathan. He explained that the blind pianist and singer was one of the greatest talents he had ever encountered. Nathan listened to the demo that Otis made and sneered that Ray Charles sounded like a "poor man's Charles Brown," adding, "I don't need any poor man's Charles Brown. I've already got Charles Brown."[44]

Nathan was equally unimpressed by the music of James Brown. His company profited tremendously from the success of James Brown's sixty-five best-selling recordings on the King label, but Nathan never liked the way Brown's music sounded. "Nobody wants to hear that noise," he growled after hearing the Godfather of Soul's first demo.[45] Disc jockey Magnificent Montague remembers receiving a dub of James Brown singing "Please Please Please" from Nathan while producing a daily radio show in Chicago. The mogul wanted Montague's opinion of the recording, because Nathan felt that no one would buy a song in which the singer stuttered one word over and over. The disc jockey informed King's president that he had a hit on his hands, and when Montague played the song on the radio, his phone lines lit up like never before with eager requests to hear the song again.[46]

A failure to appreciate talent was hardly the least of the sins committed by the executives who controlled the labels that recorded Black music in the 1950s and 1960s. Syd Nathan seemed to take pride in not paying his artists. When Gladys Knight and the Pips scored a top-ten hit with Otis's song "Every Beat of My Heart" on the Vee-Jay label, Otis never realized a dime of the royalties until Nathan's publishing and record companies were sold after Nathan's death in 1968.[47]

Nathan was not alone in his attitudes toward musicians. New Orleans artists felt cheated so routinely by Johnny Vincent that Huey Smith and Mac Rebennack (Dr. John) organized a posse of artists to "stick him up." They made Vincent hold his hands in the air as one of them pointed a gun at him and the others went through his trousers, shoes, and drawers looking for the money he owed them. Vincent took the holdups in good humor but almost immediately withheld their royalties again. The artists had to track him down and stick him up once more to get their money.[48] Other label owners were even more callous. When musicians asked Morris Levy of Roulette Records when they would receive their royalties, he reportedly snarled, "Royalty? You want royalty, go to England."[49]

Herman Lubinsky of Savoy Records was the worst of them all in Johnny's experience. Known to musicians as "Herman the Vermin," Lubinsky profited greatly from jazz and rhythm and blues but consistently withheld royalty payments to musicians and composers. Otis produced hit after hit for Savoy but received almost nothing in return. For eight hit records in 1950 alone, Lubinsky gave Otis the seriously deflated payment of fourteen hundred dollars. Then the label owner deducted six hundred dollars from the total for a television set that he had sent to Otis, which Otis thought had been a gift. When Lubinsky died, a reporter called Johnny Otis and asked him to comment on his dealings with the impresario from Savoy Records. "You shouldn't say anything about the dead unless you can say something good," Otis replied. "So all I'll say is, he's dead. Good!"[50]

Working as a producer enabled Johnny Otis to see the inner workings of capitalism in the record industry. He was often shocked and offended by what he observed. Life on the road as a touring musician, however, offered Otis and his band members an opportunity to interact with other artists they admired. Backstage, in hotels, and at cafés where their tour buses stopped, they socialized with gospel, jazz, and blues artists who had been only names on phonograph records to them previously. Don "Sugarcane" Harris and Dewey Terry were popular because they threw the wildest parties. Solomon Burke cooked wonderful barbecued chicken sandwiches backstage. Johnny especially enjoyed encounters with the singing group the Five Royales. They featured the fine singing of brothers Johnny and Eugene Tanner and the distinctive guitar playing of Lowman Pauling, and they wrote great songs like "Think" (later covered by James Brown) and "Dedicated to the One I Love" (later covered by the Shirelles). Aside from enjoying their musical talents, Johnny looked forward to running into them on the road because, as he explains with a twinkle in his eye, "they *thought* they knew how to play poker."[51]

Life on the road also offered opportunities to connect with old and cherished friends. Playing an engagement at the Dreamland Ballroom in Omaha enabled Johnny to spend time with Preston Love, who had returned to his home in Omaha after a stint in the Basie band. Performing with Basie had been a dream come true for Love. He first took up the saxophone because he loved the rich tone and consummate artistry of Basie's lead alto player, Earle Warren. In the later 1940s, Warren had to quit performing because ulcers and other stomach ailments made him too ill to play well. Warren became Johnny Otis's professional manager, while Preston Love replaced his hero in the Basie band for a brief spell. During the 1952 date at the Dreamland, Johnny had the tour bus let him off in front of the housing project where Preston and Betty Love lived. He stayed with his old friends in their apartment while the rest of the band stayed at a local rooming house.[52]

On one tour through the South, Johnny's driver stopped the bus to fill up with gasoline. Johnny recognized country music singer Hank Williams standing outside a limousine beside a gas pump. Otis loved Williams's sincerity and artistry. He felt that pure country singers like Williams came close to capturing the feel and intent of the blues, and he admired their work greatly. Accompanied by Little Esther Phillips, Otis struck up a conversation with Williams, who immediately recognized Otis and warmly praised his music. After saying good-bye, Otis and Little Esther got back on their bus. As it pulled away, Esther's mother, Lucille, asked what kept them so long. Esther said, "Johnny and I were off talking to some cowboy." Amazed that Esther did not know to whom they had been speaking, Johnny replied, "Esther, that was not just some cowboy. Don't you know that cowboy was the great Hank Williams?" Lucille's jaw dropped. She stood up on the bus and screamed, "Johnny Otis, you turn this bus around. I have to meet that man!" Apparently, Mrs. Jones shared Johnny's admiration for the "drifting cowboy."

Traveling on the road as working musicians, however, also compelled the Johnny Otis Caravan to confront the harsh realities of race hatred everywhere they went. In 1947 at a dance in Boise, Idaho, a white hoodlum in the crowd insulted one of the women in Otis's show. Her husband demanded an apology, and a minor fight erupted. As a result, a lynch mob of approximately one hundred people gathered outside the ballroom, threatening the band. Otis and his entourage had to slip away quietly. "We were lucky to get out of town in one piece," Otis remembers. In South Carolina in 1950, a police officer arrested one member of the band for using a restroom intended for use by whites only. A judge fined the offender fifty dollars, even though no signs had been posted indicating that the bathroom was restricted. A year later, in Augusta, Georgia, one of the musicians in Otis's group failed to say "sir" in response to a question by a white man and was beaten brutally as a result. That same year, a white road manager traveling with the show in Fort Lauderdale, Florida, was arrested and fined for being in a Black neighborhood after dark. Police officers interrupted a performance of the Johnny Otis Show in Memphis in 1952 and made the entire audience line up against the walls to be searched. When the police found some weapons, the officer in charge took the microphone and shouted racial epithets at the crowd.[53]

Johnny found himself in another no-win situation later that same year in the same city. Police officers ordered the manager of a hotel that accommodated Blacks to deny Otis a room because the policemen thought the entertainer looked white. A few minutes later, the manager of a hotel for whites turned Otis away because the manager thought he looked Black. On the road in southern Illinois in 1953, the band went all night without eating because no restaurant or café would serve food to them. The next year, police in Alabama jailed one of the performers traveling with the Otis show because he was driving a Cadillac with New York license plates, which they claimed must have been stolen. Once they had the musician locked in jail, they beat him for good measure.[54] "If they'd known I was white in the South we'd have gotten killed," Otis observes calmly. Yet he felt that he had no choice but to cast his lot with Black people. "I feel black, I can't explain it; it's a mystery. Ethnically I'm a Middle Easterner, but psychologically and culturally, I'm black. I chose to be."[55]

Life on the road proved so vexing for Black performers that Big Jay McNeely turned down offers to tour when his first recording, "Deacon's Hop," reached the top of the best-seller charts in 1949. He had learned from Bardu Ali (then Johnny Otis's manager and co-owner of the Barrelhouse nightclub) that gangsters often signed performers to contracts that robbed them of all their tour earnings. He chose to stay in Los Angeles and perform for local crowds at venues where he could be paid immediately in cash. Yet the large crowds he attracted also drew the attention and intervention of the police department. "At the time, people were so prejudiced," he recalls, "they couldn't understand why the white kids responded the way they did, and there'd be Mexican kids by the thousands watching us jam. People thought the kids must all be on drugs, and it got to the point where I was blocked out of Los Angeles—either the cops would come and shut us down or they wouldn't give me a permit."[56]

Dramatic incidents of racial harassment took a toll on Otis and his musicians, but even the ordinary circumstances they faced bothered them.

Johnny remembers that when the bus crossed the Mason–Dixon Line everybody got quiet, as if a blanket had been thrown over them. Black musicians could not count on finding a place to eat, a gas station that would serve them, or a room to rent no matter how much money they had. "You could have a pocket full of money," Johnny relates, "and have no place to stay. Joe Turner used to say, 'I got a pocket full of pencils and can't even write my name.'"[57]

Many of the things that happened to Otis and his musicians in the South differed little from the treatment they received back home in Los Angeles. The western metropolis had a good reputation as a hospitable place for African Americans in the 1920s, but by the 1940s the area had become a center of anti-Black racism. When Nat King Cole purchased an English Tudor–style home on South Muirfield Road in the previously all-white Hancock Park neighborhood in 1948, his new neighbors protested by burning crosses on his lawn and circulating petitions demanding that the Cole family move out. One member of the newly formed Hancock Park Property Owners Association, who had evidently never laid eyes on Nat King Cole, telephoned the singer's road manager, Mort Ruby, and asked, "How would you like it if you had to come out of your home and see a Negro walking down the street wearing a big wide hat, a zoot suit, long chain, and yellow shoes."[58] Angry neighbors made threatening phone calls to the Cole family's real estate agent. The Los Angeles Realty Board organized a campaign to amend the U.S. Constitution so that restrictive covenants (ruled unenforceable by states in a 1948 Supreme Court decision) could be reinstated so that neighborhoods could remain all white.[59]

White residents of Leimert Park burned a four-foot cross on the lawn of John Caldwell's house on Sixth Avenue in 1951 when the family moved in and desegregated the neighborhood. A year later, a dynamite bomb wrecked the new home of a Black junior high school science teacher and his wife when they tried to occupy a dwelling at 2130 Dunsmuir in a predominately white neighborhood. A ritual cross burning on the lawn of a Black family that had recently bought a home in Eagle Rock attracted the participation of the president of the Kiwanis Club, members of the Chamber of Commerce, a local realtor, and a police officer in uniform as part of the mob.[60]

In Los Angeles, Black bands could play dances at the YMCA on Twenty-eighth and Naomi, but only if they were sponsored by "reputable citizens." Black people were not allowed to swim in the YMCA pool. They could not enter the pool in Centinella Park in Inglewood either. On public beaches, like those adjoining the popular Santa Monica Pier, Blacks were restricted to a small area far from where whites entered the ocean. Whites could stay on the beach at night for campfires and barbecues, but police officers escorted Blacks away from the beach at dusk. Activist attorney and publisher Loren Miller Jr. remembers what those days were like for African Americans like himself growing up near Jefferson Boulevard. They knew that segregation barred them from entering private pools, such as the Bimini Baths on Vermont, and they understood they would be stopped and harassed by police officers if they drove too far south on Western or out into Compton, Glendale, or Inglewood.[61] It was not until 1947 that Blacks could secure admission to the 5-4 Ballroom, located on the second floor above retail stores at Fifty-fourth and Broadway.[62] The city of Inglewood posted a sign that warned, "No Jew and No Coloreds Are Welcome in This Town."[63]

When Johnny Moore and the Three Blazers played in a nightclub in Riverside (some seventy miles from Los Angeles), they discovered that the owner had segregated the audience. Black service personnel from nearby March Air Field were allowed to listen to Moore's band, but the owner guided white customers to another room on another floor of the club to be entertained by white musicians. The band resented this treatment, so they quit. As they left the stage, pianist and singer Charles Brown explained that the band was quitting because the owner "doesn't like colored people." From the parking lot, Brown and his bandmates could hear turmoil behind them. The Black patrons were turning over tables and breaking bottles in protest. In subsequent weeks, the African American service personnel stationed at the base boycotted the establishment. Eventually, the owner telephoned Moore contritely, asking the band to return and letting them know he would no longer segregate the audience.[64]

Other musicians found segregation in Los Angeles less susceptible to challenges. The local branch of the American Federation of Musicians union admitted only whites, giving them sole access to choice jobs at motion picture and recording studios. Blacks formed their own union, Local 767, but despite the plethora of entertainment venues, jobs and decent wages were hard to come by. Trumpeter Clora Bryant had to work as a maid in Hollywood, while pianist and vocalist Babs Gonzales did a stint as a chauffeur for actor Errol Flynn. Musicians bitterly referred to Los Angeles as "Mississippi with palm trees." After starring in a show at the Club Alabam in

1952, Jimmy Witherspoon was followed by police and arrested on charges of driving while under the influence of alcohol. Police officers beat Witherspoon in the stomach and knees and then kept him locked in the station all night, refusing his requests for a sobriety test to prove his innocence. Lionel Hampton viewed Hollywood as so oppressive that he claimed it was like the South. "You had to sit on the back of the bus, go into the white nightclub by the back door. Taxis wouldn't stop for you. Also, black musicians didn't get paid as much as white musicians—in fact, blacks got about 20 percent of what whites made," Hampton complained.[65]

Black musicians in Los Angeles found that they had to accept "escorts" by police officers back to Black neighborhoods after playing music in white clubs.[66] In order to perform in Glendale, Black musicians had to apply for police permits granting them special permission to be within the city limits after 6 P.M. When the nightclubs closed at two in the morning, officers in squad cars lined up to transport the Black musicians across the Los Angeles city line. Inside the city limits, law enforcement personnel patrolled the west side of the city, "accompanying" Black performers back to areas south of Pico Boulevard, the street that marked what the police considered to be the acceptable northern border of the Black community. Vocal coach and pianist Eddie Beal remembers being "asked" by managers at the Cotton Club in Culver City to sit at a separate table from a white colleague when the two went to hear the Count Basie Orchestra there. Discrimination prevented Blacks from entering most clubs on the west side, where Black musicians like Art Tatum played (at the Swanee Inn on Westwood Boulevard), leaving Central Avenue as one of the few areas where whites and Blacks could mix socially.[67] Soon even the avenue came under siege by the police.

In their memoirs, many of the musicians who thrived on Central Avenue in the 1940s pointed to police harassment as the reason for the demise of the neighborhood in the 1950s. Ernie Andrews, Hampton Hawes, Art Farmer, Clora Bryant, and Horace Tapscott have all claimed that the police could not stand to see interracial harmony, so officers harassed citizens at interracial gatherings. Police officers routinely harassed and intimidated any interracial couples walking along Central Avenue. A police officer once arrested African American trumpet player Howard McGhee and his blond wife, Dorothy, for sitting side by side at a showing of a James Cagney motion picture in downtown Los Angeles. The arresting officer claimed that an interracial couple who looked as they did had to be a prostitute and her pimp.[68]

Trumpet player Clora Bryant remembers, "Central Avenue closed up when they found out how much money was being dropped over there and City Hall started sending the cops out there to heckle the white people."[69] She recalls roadblocks, traffic stops, and sidewalk arrests. According to the memories of pianist Hampton Hawes, on any weekend night, mixed-race couples would be "frog-marched" from Central Avenue to the Newton Street police station for "inspection."[70] Art Farmer reflects, "The police really started becoming a problem. I remember, I would walk down the street, and every time they'd see you they would stop and search you." Integrated clubs seemed to pose a particular challenge to the police department. Farmer played regularly at one "black and tan" spot until police officers threatened to close it down, "because they said they didn't want this racial mixing there, and if the club didn't change its policy there was going to be trouble."[71] The L.A. City Council passed an ordinance in 1948 requiring cocktail lounges to maintain minimum lighting standards, evidently believing, as R. J. Smith phrases it, that low wattage led to low morals. Enforcement of laws like this depended on the discretion of building inspectors and police officers, who could be influenced by their own racial prejudices, as well as by their desires to extort kickbacks from vulnerable merchants and musicians.[72]

Horace Tapscott argued that it was not just police repression that "shut down" Central Avenue, that city officials made zoning decisions that destroyed the quality of life in the neighborhood. "They started rezoning the areas in the district," he explained, "which would call for this and not call for that, certain beverages, and this type of establishment in the block or in the neighborhood . . . you know, anything to become a nuisance."[73] The Los Angeles Police Department cracked down on nearly every establishment where whites and blacks might mingle. Black businessman John Dolphin complained about a "campaign of intimidation and terror" waged by the Los Angeles Police Department against Dolphin's of Hollywood, the rhythm and blues record store that he owned and operated near the corner of Vernon and Central. Because his business attracted clientele of all races, the police blockaded the store and warned all its white customers that they were in danger simply by being present in a Black neighborhood. Dolphin called his business "Dolphin's of Hollywood" in the first place as a sarcastic statement about the policing of racial boundaries in the city. With the store located far from Hollywood, Dolphin reckoned that if Blacks could not travel freely to Hollywood, then he would bring Hollywood to them.

Aggressive policing, changes in zoning, and disinvestment by mortgage lenders combined with urban renewal and suburbanization to destroy the urban spaces that had produced the interracial culture and commerce that gave rise to rhythm and blues in Los Angeles and other cities. Federal highway projects combined with government housing and home loan policies that favored development in suburban areas over urban locations. New shopping malls in outlying areas lured customers away from downtowns by offering shoppers branch stores with free parking. Suburbanization also helped undermine public mass transit, exacerbating traffic jams and creating a chronic shortage of parking spaces in inner cities. Migration to the suburbs pulled customers away from traditional sites of public entertainment, encouraging the growth of home-based entertainments like the television set and the high-fidelity phonograph. The demise of streetcar lines, the introduction of diesel buses, and automobile-based suburban sprawl left inner-city areas like Central Avenue and Watts as spaces of last resort for people unable to escape to the suburbs.[74]

All public entertainment venues felt the impact of suburbanization. In 1951 alone, 126 Los Angeles motion picture theaters went out of business while the number of television sets in use climbed to nearly 900,000.[75] In her visionary work on the introduction of commercial television in America, Lynn Spigel chronicles an extraordinary drop in spectatorship at motion pictures, sporting events, concerts, and other public events between 1947 and 1955, accompanied by a 2 percent decline in total recreational spending despite an unprecedented rise in disposable income for middle-class Americans. Between 1947 and 1953, nine million people moved to suburbs, a 43 percent growth that brought the suburban population to around thirty million. Three-quarters of suburban dwelling units were owner-occupied, and business commentators noticed a clear correlation between consumer spending and suburban life.[76] Expressly discriminatory federal home loan policies subsidized Euro-American consumers in many ways, freeing them from having to save for large down payments on homes, giving them tax breaks and increased disposable income through the homeowner's mortgage interest deduction, and supplying them with better housing at less cost compared with the housing market available to members of aggrieved racial groups.

People of color found themselves confined to an artificially small housing market that compelled them to pay high prices for inferior dwellings. Quality of home maintenance made no difference to appraisers from the

Federal Housing Agency and the Home Owners' Loan Corporation. One appraiser described the neighborhood near Jefferson and Arlington populated by Blacks, Japanese, Russians, Poles, and Jews as "the best Negro residential district in the city," but the mixed population of the area precluded it from receiving home loans despite "stability of values and evident pride of ownership."[77] A neighborhood bounded by Silver Lake, Sunset, and Alvarado received a "blighted" rating because the presence of "Japanese, Negroes, Russians, and Mexicans" convinced the appraiser that "adverse racial influences are noticeably increasing inevitably."[78] A section of Hollywood would have received a higher grade "were it not for a scattering of Japanese and Filipino residents," and a section of San Gabriel received a low rating because its "American-born" population "are still 'peon Mexicans' and constitute a distinctly subversive racial influence." The appraiser noted favorably that "pressure is being exerted to confine the population and keep it from infiltrating into other districts."[79]

As urban space became increasingly segregated and the nightclubs where Johnny Otis played started to close down, he turned to one place where Black music could still reach a broad and diverse audience: on the radio and, to a lesser degree, on television. At the conclusion of the 1953 national tour of the Johnny Otis Show, Frank Schiffman, the owner and manager of New York's Apollo Theatre, suggested that Johnny think about becoming a radio disc jockey. Back home in Los Angeles, Otis opened the telephone book to the page that listed radio stations. He selected station KFOX on a whim and dialed the number. At the other end of the line, station program manager Hal Scheidler said hello. Johnny blurted out, "My name is Johnny Otis. I'd like to become a disc jockey." Scheidler paused and replied, "Johnny Otis, the Duke Ellington of Watts? Are you serious?"[80] Soon Johnny was hosting a one-hour evening program. When Otis went down to the station to sign his contract, the first thing the station owner told him was, "I don't wanna hear none of that goddam nigger music." Yet if Johnny got his way, he would hear plenty of it—and soon.

Three WILLIE AND THE HAND JIVE

 During the 1950s, Johnny Otis became one of the best-known personalities in popular music. Through recordings, live performances, and broadcasts on radio and television, he became Southern California's most recognizable representative of Black music. That visibility gave him special responsibilities. At a time when Black communities across the country were mobilizing for freedom, racial issues took center stage in national life. Chaotic, contentious, and often violent struggles challenged the status quo with a vexing mixture of progress and retreat. The Supreme Court declared segregated schools to be unconstitutional, yet the men who murdered fourteen-year-old Emmett Till in Mississippi went unpunished. The Montgomery Bus Boycott desegregated public transportation in that Alabama city, propelling Martin Luther King Jr. into prominence as a civil rights leader. Yet massive resistance blocked implementation of the Supreme Court's school desegregation orders in both the North and the South. The governor of Arkansas even closed the high schools in Little Rock for a year to prevent them from being integrated. Grassroots groups in Black communities all across the nation demanded an end to discrimination in education, employment, and housing, yet new and old forms of mortgage redlining, private discrimination, and urban renewal subsidized the accumulation of wealth in the white suburbs at the expense of the inner cities. As one of the most prominent public faces of Black music in a largely white supremacist society, Johnny Otis found himself in an unusual role as a mediator between increasingly antagonistic social groups.

Radio turned out to be a perfect medium for Johnny Otis. He ran his disc jockey programs the way he had served as master of ceremonies at his live shows: as a performer himself but also as a presenter of great entertainment by others. He hired comedian Redd Foxx as his on-air assistant and comic foil. Foxx had toured with some of Otis's shows (including the 1947 Ink Spots tour) and was always funny onstage. Offstage, however, he was frequently sullen, grumpy, and morose. Yet Foxx's irascible and audacious humor worked wonderfully on the radio. The comedian told listeners that Los Angeles had nothing to fear from an invasion by the Russian army, because in their city the invaders would never be able to find a place to park.[1] It was not always pleasant, however, for Otis to witness the comedian's mean-spirited, and sometimes even cruel, behavior off the microphone. Johnny once watched Foxx ridicule a member of his own entourage so cruelly before a group of celebrities that the man broke down in tears. Once Foxx informed Johnny that he had no room in his house to lodge his mother and stepfather, who were coming to Los Angeles for a visit. He requested that Johnny host the couple for a few days. Johnny welcomed them into his home. They stayed for five years. When Johnny asked Redd if he would take his parents into his own dwelling, Foxx explained that he did not really like them, that his stepfather was all right, but as far as his mother was concerned, he said, "I can't stand that bitch."[2]

Each program began with Otis's drummer Kansas City Bell announcing, "And now it's time for *The Johnny Otis Show.*" Then a female duet sung by singer Marie Adams and Johnny's wife, Phyllis, chanted rhythmically, "John-ny O-tis, John-ny O-tis." With up-tempo music playing in the background, Johnny would then come on the air and say, "Hi, everyone, this is Johnny Otis, and that means it's time to rock . . . and it's time to roll . . . and we're gonna get way back in the alley with the blues." A recording of Pete Lewis playing a bluesy riff on guitar introduced a short selection from the entire band, featuring Johnny on vibes, and the show would begin to the sounds of the Bo Diddley Beat from "Willie and the Hand Jive." In the early years, Otis broadcast the show live from Scribner's Red Hut Broiler on S. Western Avenue. In subsequent years, the program originated from the window of Dolphin's of Hollywood record store at Vernon and Central or from Conley's Record Rack (a business in which Johnny was part owner) on Wilmington next door to Smith's Bar-be-cue.[3] Listeners generally loved the liveliness of Otis's program, but sometimes it got too lively. On one occasion, Johnny interviewed an artist who had the nickname "Sweet Cakes." When he asked the musician how he had acquired his unusual alias, the man answered in detail, resulting in Johnny receiving a four-day suspension from the air for violating the FCC's obscenity prohibitions.

Johnny Otis's passion for the music, his dramatic and eloquent language drawn from the everyday vernacular of the Black community, and, most of all, his voice made him a natural for radio. "Now no one talks like Johnny Otis," singer Etta James asserts. "He's got this deep molasses honey-dripping deejay voice. It's a jivetime jazzman's voice, but it's also sincere and filled with wisdom."[4] Otis used that voice to generate enthusiasm for Black music and Black culture, to help build an inclusive festive culture for young people in Southern California, and to deliver public service announcements with wit and conviction. He deployed his personality to sell his sponsors' products effectively. He made it sound like a rare treat to eat at Scribner's Red Hut Broiler, to get a new hairdo or a process at Le Coiffure Hair Salon, or to savor the fabrics and fashions at Mister Charles Limited, an establishment where all measuring took place with the aid of the fabulous Charles-Scope—"an invention so new it defies description."[5]

At a time when Black people and their concerns were virtually invisible in the mainstream newspapers, in Hollywood films, and on network television, disc jockeys programming Black music held a strategically important position in society as cocurators of a wonderful but devalued culture. The "Master Blaster" Tom Reed remembers how his years as a rhythm and blues and rock 'n' roll disc jockey led to friendships with John Coltrane and Miles Davis. He valued their consummate artistry and complex thinking on a wide range of issues, but most of all he recognized Coltrane and Davis as artists who were aware of their own people, as musicians and citizens who drew upon the politics, the geography, and the wisdom that comes from experiencing life as a Black person in America. "That's my thing and I held true to that," Reed relates. "I took up Black causes."[6]

Reed viewed Otis as a kindred soul. He noticed big differences between him and other white disc jockeys. "Johnny was a Black disc jockey in the context of 'This is where I want to go with my life. I do not want to be a white man,'" Reed explains. Otis did not separate the music from the lives of the people who gave birth to it. "I saw him involved in the community. He stayed within the context of the soul and the source of the music and the importance and the power of that music," Reed recalls. This was the choice Reed made in his own life, but it was significant that Otis could make the same decisions even though he was not Black by birth. "As a white man he chose to do this," Reed explains, referring to Otis's public political activism and promotion of Black culture. "He could have gone the other way, but he chose to get involved in Black causes. The respect that I give him is that he chose to be Black. It wasn't a gift to him; it wasn't a birthright."[7]

For a while, Otis's combination of social commitment and show business flair worked together beautifully. Amazed by the enthusiastic embrace of *The Johnny Otis Show* by eager listeners, KFOX executives increased the time allotted to the program from one hour to three hours a night. As the show became more popular, it became a constant presence in the lives of millions of young people in Southern California. Strollers and sunbathers listened to the show blaring from battery-powered portable radios all up and down the region's beaches. On many thoroughfares, especially those selected by young drivers for cruising, the show could be heard blasting from car radios. One listener told Johnny that he had driven all the way from Los Angeles to San Diego on the coast highway with no radio in his car, but still heard the entire show by simply leaving his windows open and listening to the sounds of portable and car radios all along the way.

Otis continued to perform and make records while developing his career as a disc jockey. He felt constrained, however, by the reigning practices in the recording industry. Engineers would not adapt their customary techniques to the needs of rhythm and blues performers. They followed their own personal musical tastes in the studio, refusing to let the drums and bass "crack" the rhythm and muting guitar players who produced a "twangy sound" on the strings. Frustrated by recording engineers who distorted the music to suit their own personal tastes, Johnny decided to open his own studio on Washington Boulevard near his new house on Harvard Avenue.[8] Johnny hired saxophone player Jackie Kelso to find artists and put sessions together in exchange for a share of the profits made by the enterprise. Kelso felt sure that the business would succeed because he considered Otis one of the smartest people he had ever met, "a very, very sharp, highly developed intellectual." His recording business had the potential to be a fully integrated monopoly. Otis could record songs in the morning, play them on his show in the afternoon or evening, and then sell them at a record shop in which he owned half interest the next day. Yet the control over national airplay and distribution by the major recording studios proved to be too much to overcome, and while artistically successful, his Dig records label produced only a few minor regional hits. Sometimes a song that did not become a hit immediately secured sales in another incarnation later on. For example, one day while fooling around in his garage studio, Johnny had Jesse Belvin, Mel Williams, and Harold Lewis record a song he had composed titled "So Fine." Otis released the recording under the group name he gave them on the spot, the Sheiks. It did not sell well, so he recorded it again with Mel Williams alone, but that version did not sell either. Five years later, the song became a hit on an East Coast label for the Fiestas, a Newark, New Jersey, quartet.

Otis's popularity on radio led to a weekly show on television that lasted eight years, first on Channel 11 (KTTV) in 1955, and later on Channel 5 (KTLA) and Channel 13 (KCOP). The first telecast on November 15, 1955, featured Marie Adams, Don Julian and the Meadowlarks, the Sheiks, Little Arthur Matthews, and Jeannie Barnes. Between 1954 and 1961, Otis's radio and television shows defined Black music for a generation of young people in the nation's second largest media market. Otis not only presented his own band and other local acts on his television show but welcomed as well guest appearances by nationally known artists, including James Brown, Sam Cooke, Ray Charles, Fats Domino, Little Richard, the Drifters, the Moonglows, and the Everly Brothers.

The locally televised Johnny Otis Show replicated the look of the Club Alabam and other elite spots on Central Avenue in the 1940s. His band wore matching uniforms and sat on raised platforms behind music stands decorated with stylized piano keys and the name of the show's sponsor, Metropolitan Ford. Moving at a fast pace, Johnny served as master of ceremonies, interviewer, and performer, moving from drums, to piano, to vibes on different songs. He mixed musical performances from different genres, turning the stage over to Lionel Hampton on vibes on the same show in which Marie Adams and the Three Tons of Joy sang "Goody Goody."

Tom Reed remembers the impact of Johnny Otis's television show. "In the 1950s and '60s, it was the only Black thing going" in the world of television, he contends. "It was our *Soul Train*. Johnny Otis had a *show*, and it was finger popping. It wasn't no jive ass show. It was some serious Black stuff in television. We're talking blues and jazz. He was able to mix the two." Guests on the television program included Ben Webster and other greats from the world of jazz, as well as contemporary rhythm and blues, rock 'n' roll, and even folk music performers. "This is the greatness about our culture and our music," Reed notes, pointing to "musicians who were good and talented and could play both jazz and blues. They were that talented."[9]

Otis's prominence in Los Angeles equaled the fame that Dick Clark had on the East Coast (and later nationwide), but there were important differences between the way the two television hosts presented the music. Johnny took special pains to call attention to the Black originators rather than the white imitators of rhythm and blues and rock 'n' roll. At his live shows and television dance parties, he welcomed youths of all races. Dick Clark, on the other hand, favored white cover artists on his playlists and had his staff screen out Black youngsters who wanted to dance on his broadcasts. He required written applications that afforded him the opportunity to give preferences to names that sounded Italian, Jewish, or in some way "foreign" to decrease the likelihood of Blacks dancing before the camera. Clark neglected the veteran blues musicians who created the popular music he played, omitting Big Mama Thornton, Chuck Berry, T-Bone Walker, and Pee Wee Crayton from his shows while preferring to showcase teenage white imitators of decidedly lesser talent, like Fabian, Bobby Rydell, and Frankie Avalon. Clark made stars out of previously unknown artists recording on labels that he controlled. He had one of his biggest hits with the Black (but youthful and clean-cut) Chubby Checker covering Hank Ballard's "The Twist." Clark also relentlessly plugged the instrumental music of white guitarist Duane Eddy on his show. Johnny Otis received invitations three different times from Clark to appear on *American Bandstand,* but Otis refused the offers each time as a protest against what he viewed as Clark's racism. "Dick Clark rode to glory on a gravy train that was largely built by black bands," Otis observes, "and when he became one of the 'owners' of the railroad, he would deny them a ride."[10]

Like Clark and many other disc jockeys of that era, Otis augmented his income from his radio and television shows by promoting live shows and starting his own record labels. He also accepted payments from record company promoters to play certain songs on the air, a practice that later became known as payola when it served as the focal point of a congressional investigation into rock 'n' roll music. The amount of money Otis received from song pluggers was small, about seven hundred dollars total, but he realized when the practice was exposed that it was wrong. "I thought it was a perfectly legitimate thing, though, until the payola probes came," he remembers, but admits, "I did not understand then that the airwaves belong to the people and are a trust and that you should not prostitute it in that way."[11]

The entrance of television into American homes after World War II transformed a great deal in U.S. society: its consumer culture, its household dynamics, and its intergroup relations. The new medium had a special significance, however, in a rapidly changing and growing city like Los Angeles. Only three million TV sets were purchased nationwide during the entire decade of the 1940s. By the 1950s, however, five million sets were sold every year. Like radio before it, commercial network television turned the private home into a site for advertising and entertainment. It also divided the family into separate market segments, broadcasting different kinds of programs at different times of the day to reach different age groups: game shows in the morning, soap operas in the early afternoon, news programs at the dinner hour, and variety and action/adventure shows in the evening. Rock 'n' roll shows filled the late afternoon after-school hours between the soap operas and the news with programs suited for selling the attention of young consumers to advertisers, although sometimes the Otis show appeared in the early evening hours before the network prime-time shows started.[12]

Surveys showed that households with only one person were the least likely to own television receivers, and those with from three to five people were most likely to own them. Advertisers viewed young people as a burgeoning consumer market with as yet unfixed tastes, so they proved especially eager to sponsor shows aimed at younger viewers. In Los Angeles, television played a unique additional role for young viewers. Children of migrants from other parts of the country had few attachments to local spaces. The decentralized sprawl of Southern California dispersed its population over a wide area and produced no single downtown area to serve as a focal point for recreation, shopping, or culture. Television became the public square of Los Angeles, the vernacular space accessible to the greatest number of residents. Yet in order to serve that role, television programs in Los Angeles focused on already-existing, albeit marginal, public spaces. Before the completion of the coaxial cable in 1953, which made it possible for people on the West Coast to view television programs produced in New York and Chicago, local programming dominated the air waves. Programmers needed to air shows that would motivate large numbers of people to purchase television sets. Just as the early radio industry had turned to country music and jazz as a means of promoting the sales of receivers, local television programmers in Los Angeles relied on a schedule ranging from wrestling to western swing music, from Roller Derby to rock 'n' roll. When these seemingly marginal public activities appeared in television broadcasts, they helped constitute a new public square, a mass-media-created multicultural space that exposed broad new audiences to what had previously been particularistic cultural practices and traditions.

Television enabled ethnic cultures to transcend physical barriers. Johnny Otis remembers getting bags of mail from exclusively Anglo neighborhoods praising his rhythm and blues television programs featuring Black artists.[13] Poncho Sanchez, now an influential Latin jazz musician, remembers growing up in Los Angeles hearing music he liked in church and at community dances, but he also cites Otis's television show as a profound musical influence in his home.[14] Mexican American jazz musician Eddie Cano remembered being denied entrance to the dance halls on Ocean Park Pier, near Venice, because he was a Chicano, but Cano brought his own music into millions of homes through television when Channel 9 began broadcasting the program *Momentes Allegres* in 1954, featuring the Pachuco Boogie Boys.[15] Chicano rock musician Cesar Rosas, of the group Los Lobos, remembers that his mother listened to Mexican *ranchera* music at home but that she also watched country and western shows like *The Melody Ranch* on the independent local television stations.[16] Jimmy Espinoza, bass player and leader of the Chicano rock band Thee Midnighters, recalls spending afternoons with his "eyes glued" to the television set watching *The Johnny Otis Show.*[17]

In August 1947 (when only three thousand television receivers were in use in Los Angeles), sports events accounted for two-thirds of the programs on the air.[18] Sports promoters feared that television would hurt attendance, but in Los Angeles, wrestling and roller derby audiences actually increased after televised broadcasts.[19] Similarly, live broadcasts of country music performers Spade Cooley and Tex Williams on KTLA initially added to their appeal as live performers. The blues and jazz singer Hadda Brooks attracted new fans with her extremely popular Sunday night program on KLAC.[20] Johnny Otis's television show built on this legacy by broadcasting rhythm and blues music with a local accent to the broad metropolitan audience.

Otis used his television program to advertise live extravaganzas at local venues, which proved to be lucrative ventures in themselves. Shows at the Million Dollar Theater, Angelus Hall, and the Long Beach Civic Auditorium attracted eager and enthusiastic rhythm and blues fans from diverse backgrounds. Young people enjoyed the shows. Musicians made money and won new fans. Johnny Otis exulted in his ability to bring the people and the musicians together. City officials, however, viewed the shows as threats to public order and public decency. Local authorities worked tirelessly to ban rock 'n' roll dances inside the city limits of Los Angeles. Police officers began to make their presence felt at these shows, disrupting perfectly peaceful gatherings. They enforced long-forgotten ordinances that made it illegal for someone under sixteen to dance with someone over sixteen. Otis knew that racism motivated this kind of policing. "They see Black kids and Hispanic kids and Asian kids, and they don't like it," he later recalled. "They just didn't want to see that. If it were all Asian and Hispanic and Black, they wouldn't care, but there were whites there, and they're mixing with the Blacks and what not."[21]

The harassment backfired in some significant ways. Prohibitions within the city of Los Angeles forced Otis and other promoters to move dances farther out into unincorporated areas of Los Angeles County that had large Chicano populations. "We found we could not play in Los Angeles," Otis remembers. "We tried the ballrooms. They hassled us to death successfully."[22] These attempts at censorship by city officials in Los Angeles drove Johnny to stage his weekly dance parties at El Monte Legion Stadium, in the city of El Monte, in Los Angeles County. Coupled with continued television exposure, these shows *increased* rather than *decreased* interracial interactions in Los Angeles, because they attracted so many young Mexican Americans. As early as 1948, Johnny had been playing shows at Angelus Hall that attracted enthusiastic Mexican American rhythm and blues fans. The shows in El Monte further cemented the allegiances of this community to his music.

Musician Ruben Guevara (later with the Armenta Brothers, Ruben and the Jets, and Con Safos) credits Otis with sparking new kinds of music in the eastside barrios. "His swing didn't just swing," Guevara remembers, "it jumped. And the Eastside jumped right along with him."[23] Don Tosti's Pachuco Boogie Boys and other Chicano ensembles blended Johnny Otis's jump blues and boogie-woogie rhythms with Spanish-language caló lyrics that delineated the everyday concerns and cares of people in the barrio.

Chicanos flocked to the shows in El Monte, where they rubbed elbows and danced with Black, white, and Asian youths attracted to the same music. Black saxophonist (and sometimes piano player) Chuck Higgins, born in Texas but dwelling in Aliso Village near a huge Mexican population, composed and performed the song "Pachuko Hop," a tribute to the style, slang, and poses affected by young Chicanos in zoot suits.

El Monte Legion Stadium proved to be an important venue in an unlikely place. In 1857, Anglo mobs had lynched four Mexicans in El Monte. During the Depression the area was inhabited mostly by whites who used restrictive covenants to exclude people of Mexican origin from their neighborhoods. Postwar population growth and the Supreme Court's 1948 decision declaring restrictive covenants unenforceable by the state combined to promote the movement of a new population into the area. Constructed as a potential site for sporting events during the 1932 Olympics, El Monte Legion Stadium generally hosted boxing and wrestling matches, and also served as the home for the Los Angeles Thunderbirds roller derby team. About fifteen miles from downtown Los Angeles and close to the new freeways, which promoted suburbanization while destroying many inner-city neighborhoods inhabited by Chicanos and Blacks, El Monte Legion Stadium helped redefine the experience of race for young people in Los Angeles during the 1950s. Its exuberant diversity stood in sharp contrast to the monochromatic homogeneity of many of the new suburbs. As Herman "Sonny" Chaney, the lead singer of the Jaguars, remembers, "We used to play a lot at the El Monte Legion Stadium, and the audiences were a good cross section of whites, Chicanos, and blacks. . . . I don't think kids today even think in those terms; it's common to see racially mixed groups now. . . . But that was the beginning of rock 'n' roll and they were all into the music, so they didn't care (that the group and audience was mixed)."[24]

Yet many of the old problems persisted in El Monte. When Otis's business manager and partner, Hal Zeiger, went to City Hall to get a license to stage dances at the Legion Stadium, an official told him, "Speaking as one white man to another, we can't have these niggers dancing with these white kids."[25] Zeiger sought help from the musicians union, the National Association for the Advancement of Colored People, and the Jewish organization B'nai B'rith. Representatives from these groups confronted city officials at a public meeting, forcing them to back down and allow Otis's dances at the venue.

Just as he had noticed the enthusiasm that Chicanos displayed for rhythm and blues music earlier in his career in shows at Angelus Hall, Otis noticed and welcomed their attendance at his shows in El Monte. "I would have had less of a career if it were not for the Chicano audience," he told David Reyes and Tom Waldman, authors of *Land of a Thousand Dances,* a book that chronicles the history of Chicano engagement with rock 'n' roll in Southern California. "They were the most loyal and responsive, and they would show up everywhere we went."[26] One day, one of them showed up at Johnny's door.

The young man introduced himself as Julian Herrera. He explained to Otis that he wanted to become a singer. After a brief audition, Johnny started to groom the young man for a spot on the show. Herrera had limited range and lacked the voice control of a talented singer, but he knew how to phrase a song. He was handsome and had good stage presence. When Herrera came onstage at El Monte Legion Stadium, young women, especially the Chicanas, roared their approval. Starved for attention, acknowledgment, and recognition in a media market that virtually ignored them, young Chicanos and Chicanas turned L'il Julian (as he was then known) into a local hero.

L'il Julian joined Otis's band, lived in his house, and made his first recording at Otis's home studio, with Johnny producing. Otis's Dig record label released "Lonely Lonely Nights" by L'il Julian Herrera and the Tigers in 1957. The song became a regional hit. Shortly after the record peaked on the charts, however, a visitor came to Johnny's door. Displaying identification and a badge that showed him to be an officer with the juvenile court, the visitor asked Otis where he could find Ron Gregory. Not knowing anyone with that name, Otis shrugged his shoulders and started to close the door. The officer then held up a photograph. It was a picture of L'il Julian.

To his surprise, Johnny discovered that the bilingual Chicano he knew as Julian Herrera was really Ron Gregory, a Hungarian American Jew from Massachusetts who had run away from home to live with relatives in the ethnically diverse Los Angeles neighborhood of Boyle Heights. Apparently, Ron Gregory had not found his relatives, or else they would not take him in. He did encounter a lady named Mrs. Herrera, however, who took him into her home, raising him as if he were her son. Thus, the first Chicano rock 'n' roll hero in Los Angeles turned out not to be a Chicano at all but rather a Hungarian American Jew who thought of himself as Chicano singing Black music in a band run by an ethnic Greek who thought of himself as Black![27]

Herrera became another in the long line of Johnny Otis's discoveries who stretched back to Little Esther. One of his most important finds was Etta James. During a 1954 engagement of Otis's band at the Primalon Ballroom, in San Francisco, his manager, Bardu Ali, telephoned Johnny in his hotel room from the lobby. Ali said he was with a girl singer who wanted to audition for the band. At first Johnny resisted. He felt tired, and his band did not need another girl singer. Ali persisted, explaining that he thought Johnny would want to hear *this* singer. When she arrived in his room, sixteen-year-old Jamesetta Rogers did not look or act like someone ready to begin a professional career. Too shy to audition for Otis in the room, she walked into the bathroom, where the acoustics were better and where she could not be seen from where Johnny sat. The teenager started to sing. Instantly, Johnny knew she would be a star.

Because the young woman said her age was sixteen, Otis insisted that she get her parents' permission to sing professionally. Never having known her father and aware that her mother, Dorothy Hawkins, was in jail at the moment, Etta walked to the telephone and pretended to call her mother, using one hand to hold the receiver to her ear and the other to discreetly press her index finger down on the button to stay off the line. She conducted one side of an imaginary conversation, convincing Johnny that her mother had given her approval. Later when Johnny asked for written consent, the young singer, now dubbed Etta James in the Johnny Otis Show, forged a letter allegedly from her mother indicating that she was eighteen and that she had Dorothy's permission to go on tour with the band.[28]

Over the Thanksgiving holiday in 1954, Johnny Otis produced a recording session with Etta James that yielded "Roll with Me Henry." James remembers that Johnny drove the lead car in a caravan of six automobiles traveling to the recording studio in Culver City across the street from the RKO studios. It was a foggy night, and Johnny had to lean out the window to see where they were going. Once they finally reached the studio, Kansas City Bell could not quite get the drum part right, so Johnny took over. Richard Berry sang the part of "Henry," Willard McDaniel played piano, and Etta James's neighborhood friends, sisters Jean and Abye Mitchell, sang backup vocals.[29]

Earlier that year, Johnny Otis had produced a recording with Hank Ballard's Midnighters that became a number-one rhythm and blues hit on Syd Nathan's Federal label. Ballard originally titled the song "Sock It to Me Annie," but Otis convinced him to change the title to "Work with Me Annie." The song stayed on the charts for twenty-six weeks. Etta James composed the beginnings of an answer song to Ballard's hit, singing "You've Got to Roll with Me Henry." Johnny wrote verses around that refrain and secured Hank Ballard's permission to record the answer song in exchange for royalties as cocomposer. Etta James and the Peaches did the song at their first recording session, and the record soared up the charts. It was renamed "The Wallfower" when some radio programmers found the phrase "roll with me" too suggestive for their tastes. This success introduced Etta James to a mass audience and was the first of nineteen rhythm and blues best sellers that she would record. The prevailing practice of the day, however, was for the major labels to pick white singers to "cover" hit songs by Black artists. Mercury Records released an artistically inferior but commercially more successful version of the song by Georgia Gibbs. This version lacked the phrasing, range, and rhythmic complexity that Etta James brought to the song, but it outsold the original, topping the pop charts for twenty weeks in 1955.

The business relationship between Etta James and Johnny Otis brought two highly assertive and self-confident people together. They often disagreed with each other, yet somehow remained friends. Touring with the Johnny Otis Show, Etta James disliked having to sit onstage when the other acts performed, waiting for her chance to sing, but Johnny insisted that all the performers remain onstage to give the show the feel of a caravan of stars. James contends that she wrote all the lyrics to "Roll with Me Henry" herself and that Johnny claimed coauthorship to make more money from the record. For his part, Otis recollects asking Hank Ballard for permission to write an answer record to the song they had made together, "Work with Me Annie." Otis insists that he never gave himself songwriting credits unless he participated meaningfully in the creation of a song. Otis and James even disagree about how and when they met. Otis remembers Bardu Ali phoning him from the hotel lobby and urging him to hear James sing. She claims that her friends Jean and Abye Mitchell went to the hotel and told Otis and Ali that she could sing, leading Johnny to call her on the phone, ask her to come to the hotel, and even volunteer to pay her cab fare. Otis, on the other hand, recalls James being brought up to his room by Bardu Ali. Otis remembers James pretending to speak with her mother on the phone, while James recalls forging a note ostensibly from Dorothy, granting permission to tour with the Otis band.[30]

Otis and James experienced many ups and downs in their relationship over the years, but remained friends. He always salutes James's artistry as the apex of achievement in singing. She has returned the compliment many times, most notably when she delivered his official induction speech at the Rock and Roll Hall of Fame. In her autobiography, James describes Otis as "much more than a promoter and a musician," as "a guru, a man with encyclopedic knowledge and appreciation of black music."[31] James has repeatedly expressed appreciation of Otis's many talents and his influence on her career, but she also admires his personal decisions. "I dig how Johnny Otis reinvented himself as a black man," she wrote in her autobiography. "People took his Greek shading as Creole, but Johnny took it even further; he viewed the world—and especially the musical world—through black eyes. His soul was blacker than the blackest black in Compton."[32]

By 1957, poor distribution caused Otis to fold his Dig record label. In that same year, however, a member of his management team, Hal Zeiger, brought musical comedian Mickey Katz to see one of Johnny's live shows. Katz, father of Broadway actor Joel Grey and grandfather of *Dirty Dancing* star Jennifer Grey, knew the ins and outs of show business from his decades as a clarinetist, singer, and Yiddish parody artist. When Jo Stafford had a hit with the song "Shrimp Boats" in 1951, Katz produced a successful parody titled "Herring Boats." He answered Perry Como's 1952 hit "Don't Let the Stars Get in Your Eyes," with an answer song, "Don't Let the Schmaltz Get in Your Eyes, Don't Let the Lox Get in Your Socks." Georgia Gibbs's "Kiss of Fire" became "Kiss of Meyer" in Katz's hands. Although his klezmer-accented pop music differed greatly from Otis's down-home rhythm and blues, Katz recognized in his fellow white ethnic a marvelous ability to touch audiences successfully. He telephoned executives at his record label, Capitol, and urged them to sign Johnny Otis to the label. Except for a brief stint recording jazz-oriented numbers for Mercury in 1951 and 1952, Otis had never before had the opportunity to secure the kinds of promotion and distribution that a major label could provide.[33]

Otis's first release for Capitol featured Marie Adams and the Three Tons of Joy doing the vocals on a remake of a big band classic, "Ma, He's

Making Eyes at Me." Adams initially came to Johnny's attention when he worked for Don Robey's Duke and Peacock recording labels and she was a Houston resident who aspired to a career in music. Adams recorded one of Duke's best-selling records, "I'm Gonna Play the Honky Tonks," which climbed to number seven on the rhythm and blues top-ten best-seller charts in 1952. Otis had produced her on a 1954 session that yielded "I'm Gonna Latch On" and a 1955 tribute song to Johnny Ace, both released on the Peacock label. By 1957, Adams and her sisters, Doris and Francine, called themselves the Three Tons of Joy and appeared regularly in the Johnny Otis Show. Their recording of "Ma, He's Making Eyes at Me" became a sensation in England, reaching the second position on that nation's pop music best-seller charts. It sold few copies in the United States, however.

A year later, Capitol released Johnny's biggest hit ever, the Count Otis Matthews–Hambone–Bo Diddley–influenced "Willie and the Hand Jive," featuring the drumming of Earl Palmer, an unforgettable guitar riff by Jimmy Nolen, and Johnny's vocal performance. When Johnny wrote the music for "Willie and the Hand Jive," he blended the sounds of a chain gang that he had heard singing while he was on one of his tours with his band in the early 1950s with the arrangement that he had worked out with Count Otis Matthews and the West Oakland House Stompers when he was a teenager. The rhythmic beat of the song evoked children's clapping games and rope-jumping rhymes. In 1952, the Hambone Kids from Chicago turned this beat into the hit recording "Hambone." The song's lyrics, however, have another history. While scouting British rock 'n' roll shows in anticipation of a Johnny Otis tour in England, Hal Zeiger noticed that the theaters there did not allow dancing in the aisles. Teenagers at rhythm and blues and rock 'n' roll shows stood at their seats and let their hands do the "dancing," waving them in synchronized motions not too dissimilar from the "eephing" and "hambone" clapping and patting that accompanied the Bo Diddley Beat on street corners throughout the United States. Armed with this information, Johnny wrote a song about a "cat named way-out Willie" who did the "hand jive." At live shows, Marie Adams and the Three Tons of Joy would demonstrate the movements of the hand jive. With fists closed, they would place one hand over the other and "clap" them together to the beat of the song. Then, after reversing hands, they would extend the fingers of their hands and roll their arms like a football official signaling a penalty for illegal motion. The hand jive moved the focal point of rock 'n' roll dancing from the hips to the hands, but it was the infectious beat that made the song a dance floor favorite.

Most musicians aspire to have just one hit record, little knowing that if they succeed, they will probably have to sing that song nearly every night for the rest of their lives. No Johnny Otis performance is complete without a rendition of "Willie and the Hand Jive." He grafted the Jimmy Nolen riff from the song onto the theme song of his radio show, letting listeners know in advance what they might hear from him. The song provided Otis with two of his rare motion picture appearances, one in *Juke Box Rhythm* in 1959 and the other in *Play Misty for Me* in 1971. Whenever Johnny Otis performs, the audience expects to hear "Willie and the Hand Jive." Fortunately for him, the song does not bore Otis but rather is one that he continues to enjoy playing. "People say 'Don't you get tired of playing 'Hand Jive'?" he relates. "I say no. It's a piece of nonsense, it's not deathless art, but it's fun and as long as somebody out there likes it, I'm delighted."[34]

"Willie and the Hand Jive" hit big. During the summer of 1958 it reached number nine on the *Billboard* pop charts and number five on the rhythm and blues charts. It stayed a hit for sixteen weeks. It did more than Bo Diddley himself to popularize the Bo Diddley Beat, sometimes known as "the postman's knock," which subsequently appeared again and again in an amazing range of rock 'n' roll songs, including Elvis Presley's "Marie's the Name," Smokey Robinson and the Miracles' "Mickey's Monkey," and the Strangelove's "I Want Candy," later remade by the group Bow Wow Wow. Capitol's promotion and distribution apparatuses outstripped anything Otis had seen on the small labels for which he had worked previously. He followed up "Willie and the Hand Jive" with three more "top one hundred" hits in the next two years—"Crazy Country Hop," "Castin' My Spell," and "Mumblin' Music." He was at the peak of his career and could have spent the rest of his life at Capitol following the formula that made these records successful.

Commercial success, however, did not necessarily bring happiness. Although he often jokes, "I'm too well raised to turn down large sums of money when they come my way," Otis did not like much of the music he made while under contract to the major label.[35] "My Capitol Records time was very lucrative in dollars and cents, but very negative creatively," he explains. "I tried to chase the almighty dollar and listened to bad advice from profit-motivated sources when I should have been my own Black self, recording my own Black R&B sounds, and not gone into contrived rock 'n' roll shit. With a few exceptions, of which 'Willie and the Hand Jive' is one, I am quite ashamed of some of the directions I took in those days."[36]

Even when he played the music that he respected and loved onstage or on his radio and television programs, Otis became increasingly dissatisfied with the commercial music industry. He did not object to capitalism itself. He had a long history as an entrepreneur, and he profited from nearly every enterprise in which he engaged. He made money from the Barrelhouse nightclub, the Progressive Poultry Company, Dig Records, Conley's Record Rack music store, and from his radio, television, and stage shows. Although working for Herman Lubinsky at Savoy Records provided him with a painful lesson in exploitation, he had held his own and come out ahead in his dealings with Don Robey (whom he liked) and Syd Nathan (whom he did not). His years at Capitol and the general direction of the music industry troubled him deeply, however. He felt that what existed in the United States was not actual capitalism but rather predatory capitalism, a system "based on profit and power with no consideration for artistry and cultural integrity." He deplored the way the entertainment industries catered to the most juvenile tastes, how they grabbed consumers at a young age before they had the opportunity to make decent artistic decisions and used powerful forms of advertising to "make up their minds for them." He wondered if some kind of parallel system should exist in the mass media, some kind of blue ribbon committee that would identify "heritage" music worth preserving even if it had no contemporary commercial presence. He envisioned obligating every media outlet to play at least one of these pieces every hour so that the blues of Bessie Smith or the jazz of Duke Ellington or the concert music of Paul Robeson would be available to young people in their formative years.[37] Above all, Johnny Otis wondered what he was doing as an entertainer onstage when the struggle for racial justice had reached a crucial moment of decision. Sometimes, events on- and offstage seemed closely connected.

In February 1960, Los Angeles singer and composer Jesse Belvin died in an automobile accident. A creative genius who could write great songs on the spot during recording sessions, Belvin formed and sang with several Los Angeles rhythm and blues acts. He secured great popularity from his recordings of "Dream Girl" on the Specialty label, "Goodnight My Love" on the Modern label, and "Funny" and "Guess Who" for RCA. For a time he was the "class act" of Class Records. Belvin had been performing in Little

Rock with Jackie Wilson and Arthur Prysock. In keeping with custom and law in that part of the country, the promoters designated one show for Blacks and one for whites. When whites showed up well past the time appointed for their show, however, Wilson refused to play for them. Each of the performers received death threats when they refused to do another show. Investigators quoted in a story in the *Los Angeles Sentinel* claimed that disgruntled white "fans" had slashed the tires on Wilson's and Prysock's cars in retaliation for not getting to see a show put on especially for them.[38] Belvin died immediately when his car collided head-on with another vehicle just outside future president Bill Clinton's hometown of Hope, Arkansas. An article in *Sepia* magazine reported that Belvin's car had been parked near the ones that had their tires slashed, adding that when Prysock and Wilson drove away from Little Rock they developed tire trouble very close to the spot where Belvin's car crashed.[39] Citing research by Sam Cooke biographer Daniel Wolff, singer Jerry Butler notes that no evidence emerged proving that the tires on Belvin's car had been slashed. Yet Butler considered Belvin's death a sign of the times, another suspicious incident when considered in the context of the subsequent deaths of Sam Cooke, Malcolm X, and Martin Luther King Jr.

As the NAACP, the Congress of Racial Equality (CORE), and other civil rights organizations stepped up their campaigns against discrimination, Johnny threw himself into the struggle. He worked on a campaign to pressure the Helms Bakery Company to hire Black workers but noted that his own entertainment industry was hardly blameless about segregation. He used his column in the *Sentinel* to let his readers know that in all the years he had been doing television programs, he had never seen any Black people employed at the TV stations in anything other than janitorial work.

At about three o'clock in the morning on March 14, 1960, Johnny Otis heard some noise outside his house. He got up and looked out the window. He saw a cross burning on his lawn. Soon the phone rang, and a voice informed him that this was merely a sample of what was in store for him if he continued his agitation for Black rights. He checked to make sure that Phyllis, Laura, Janice, Shuggie, and Nicky had not been harmed; then he came back to the window to view the cross once again. As he told the local chapter of the National Association for the Advancement of Colored People at a meeting later that week at the Tabernacle Baptist Church on 113th and Central, "Looking at that cross, I couldn't help but wonder if the original bearer of the Cross had died in vain."[40] A week later, he joked to his readers in his next *Sentinel* column that he had been trying to "light a fire" under the Negro community in Los Angeles, but he did not expect to see that fire break out on his lawn! He vowed, nonetheless, to continue writing about racial issues in his column and to continue his participation in demonstrations and rallies.

Otis's stance on civil rights frequently jeopardized his career. An anonymous letter complaining about one of his *Sentinel* columns illustrates the kind of reactions his activism provoked. It read:

> Dear Johnny Ignoramus Otis,
> Why don't you stick with stupid rock and roll music and stop trying to solve the "race problem." There is no race problem here and radicals like you keep trying to stir up trouble so you can have something to write about. . . . the government should take you and all your civil rights idiot friends and send you all to Berlin and put you on the front line. Then the Germans can take care of you mongrels the same way they took care of the Jews.[41]

Otis devoted a 1962 column to a contrast between the Cinnamon Cinder nightclub on Sunset Strip, one of the city's most popular rock 'n' roll clubs, and the Peppermint Stick in Sherman Oaks. The Cinnamon Cinder pretended to be a private membership club in order to keep out Blacks. When whites came to the door they were signed up for club membership instantly, but when Blacks appeared they were turned away because they did not have membership cards. The Peppermint Stick, on the other hand, welcomed youths of all races. The police left the Cinnamon Cinder alone but routinely harassed the Peppermint Stick, because it was, in Johnny's words, "too colorful." He proposed that the activist Congress of Racial Equality broaden its repertoire from sit-ins at lunch counters and conduct a "twist-in" at the Cinnamon Cinder.

Otis devoted his April 19, 1962, *Sentinel* column to housing discrimination, noting that Los Angeles was three times as segregated as Atlanta and Houston, five times more segregated than New Orleans, and ten times more segregated than Memphis. Housing discrimination remained on his mind six years later when he wrote his first book. "Integrated housing has never actually existed in recent times in Los Angeles," he observed in *Listen to the Lambs*. "A neighborhood may become integrated briefly, but it stays that way only as long as it takes the white residents to get out; then it becomes part of the main body of the ghetto. The periphery inches out at a snail's pace and the ghetto gradually expands, but integrated housing remains an idealistic theory."[42]

Otis felt that leaders and civil rights organizations could do only so much, that it would require the coordinated efforts of Black people as a group to erase discrimination and injustice. He found himself working closely with Mervyn Dymally, a special education teacher and activist in the Black community, to help build a broad-based movement among Black people. He first met Dymally in New York backstage at the Apollo Theatre in 1946. A reserved young man wearing an elegant suit and speaking with a faint West Indian accent, Dymally wanted to tell the bandleader how much he liked "Harlem Nocturne." A native of Trinidad who moved to Los Angeles in 1949, Dymally drew on a complex racial, ethnic, and religious background. His East Indian ancestors on his father's side and Haitian ancestors on his mother's side had both migrated to Trinidad to work in the island's coconut and sugarcane fields. Pressured to become a Muslim by his father's side of the family and a Catholic by his mother's relatives, he "compromised" and became an Anglican. He declared his race to be Negro when he immigrated to the United States, because racist restrictions in immigration law denied naturalized citizenship to South Asians but allowed for diasporic Africans. Dymally washed dishes and pushed a garment cart as a laborer at ten different jobs during his first year in New York. After moving to Los Angeles, he obtained a degree in education at Los Angeles State College while working on the assembly line at the Cannon Electric Company plant during the Korean War. Schooled in activism by the Oil Workers union in his home country and by subsequent trade union activity in the United Auto Workers union and the American Federation of Teachers in Los Angeles, Dymally helped found Attack, a Black political awareness group.

While driving home from a Democratic Party meeting in 1960, Dymally heard news on the radio about the start of student sit-in demonstrations attempting to desegregate lunch counters in Greensboro, North Carolina. He asked himself what he was doing attending a Democratic Party meeting as the only nonwhite person in the room when his fellow Blacks were mobilizing *by* themselves and *for* themselves about the issues that concerned them most. In 1962, he won election to a seat in the California State Assembly. The next year, Attack helped three Blacks win election to seats on the Los Angeles City Council. Dymally introduced legislation in the Assembly requiring schools to teach Black history, the first successful law of its kind anywhere in the nation.[43] He also introduced the Equal Rights Amendment and a law recognizing women's rights to community property. Dymally felt that abuse by police officers created one of the main problems for his constituents, and he helped organize the activist group Stop Terrorizing Our People to push for more respectful conduct by police officers.[44]

Working with Dymally, Johnny Otis secured election to the Central Committee of the Democratic Party in Los Angeles County. He became chairman of the party's Speakers Bureau and ran for a seat in the Assembly himself, unsuccessfully despite an endorsement from his friend Maury Wills, then starring at shortstop and tearing up the base paths for the Los Angeles Dodgers baseball team. Attack worked to elect Blacks to office as it mounted campaigns against discrimination in employment, housing, and education. The group also organized study and discussion groups. Noted author James Baldwin presided at one of these sessions.

Arriving early at one Attack meeting at a friend's house, Otis pulled a couple of art books down from the living room bookshelf. One featured the cubist art of Pablo Picasso, and the other presented page after page of African wood sculpture. He was stunned by what he saw. "It was like a bombshell exploded in me," Otis later confessed. He remembers perceiving a close connection between the two kinds of art and admiring both. He begged his friend to let him borrow the books. He took them home and read them over and over again. Soon he found books on Henri Matisse and the Mexican muralists: Jose Orozco, Diego Rivera, and Alfaro Siqueiros. Otis started making his own paintings and creating sculptures and mixed-media installations. His art would eventually win prizes, find space in prestigious exhibition venues, and be purchased by serious collectors and prominent celebrities.[45]

One meeting of Attack featured a presentation by someone Johnny had first met on bandstands in the 1940s as a hustler selling drugs to touring musicians: Detroit Red, later known as Malcolm X, a minister of Islam and the leader of the Organization of Afro American Unity. Malcolm told the members of Attack that racism was like a Cadillac: they make a new model every year. Just as a 1963 Cadillac could not be repaired with a 1953 owners' manual, the racism of 1963 required up-to-date methods of struggle. Malcolm did not attempt to recruit Johnny and his associates to his religion but instead emphasized standing together, respecting Black traditions, defending the community, treating women with love and care, acting responsibly as parents, and, above all, not accepting any abuse from racists.[46]

Otis accepted an appointment to serve as deputy chief of staff in Assemblyman Dymally's Los Angeles office. As he increased his involvement in politics, music became less and less important in Otis's life. Changes in popular culture also contributed to this trajectory. "The black audience was no longer interested in us, and the white audience had moved on to the Beatles and things," he remembers.[47]

Changes in society altered the nature of the audience for Black music. African American listeners demanded levels of consciousness and social concern that frightened many whites. Black artists and entrepreneurs chafed at the censorship they experienced as a consequence of white control over the recording and broadcast industries. Station executives at KGFJ fired Tom Reed (aka the Master Blaster) for being "too Black," even though he was the city's most popular disc jockey. The station managers dismissed Reed largely because of his work as regional president of the National Association of Radio and Television Announcers. Reed argued in public that Black broadcasters received less money than they deserved, so the station fired him, even though he had the top-rated show in the market. Reed played James Brown's great song "Say It Loud, I'm Black and I'm Proud" on the air as soon as it came out, before it was on any other station. The program director telephoned him and told him not to play it. Brown's song expressed no anti-white sentiments, but its joyful expression of Black pride proved too much for the owners of KGFJ. They also banned the record on a Charlotte, North Carolina, station they owned, firing the legendary Hatty Leeper in the process. Now a member of the Black Broadcasters Hall of Fame, Leeper had been broadcasting successfully as Chatty Hatty on WGIV in that city for many years, but the company that owned the station dismissed her in retaliation for playing "Say It Loud, I'm Black and I'm Proud" on the air. James Brown took out a full-page advertisement in the *Los Angeles Sentinel* to protest KGFJ's decision, declaring, "It seems to be the policy of KGFJ to despise all Black men unless they are a 'Tom.' Any Black man or any White man who stands up to KGFJ's policies must suffer the consequences of being ostracized and isolated from exposure to the public through the radio medium in so far as KGFJ controls the exposure of rhythm and blues recording."[48] Brown helped Reed financially when he got fired. Soon the Master Blaster had a new job on another station, playing "underground rock."

Reed had grown up in St. Louis, where his mother ran a restaurant and his father served as a police officer. The repressive racial order and residential segregation in St. Louis relegated the Black community mostly to dwellings on the city's north side. Black police officers, including Reed's father, were not allowed to arrest white suspects or charge them with crimes. The city's schools, theaters, stores, and restaurants practiced racial segregation. Yet the Black community in St. Louis offered wonderful educational and cultural resources for the young Tom Reed. He was the nephew of blues singer, composer, pianist, and Blues Hall of Fame member Walter Davis, the nephew of gospel singer Vance "Tiny" Powell, the godson of jazz trumpeter Charlie Creath, and the cousin of Elston Howard, who broke the color line in 1955 as the first Black player ever on the roster of the New York Yankees baseball team. Reed's father worked closely with Jordan Chambers, a prominent Black politician who owned the city's most vibrant jazz and blues nightspot, the Riviera, on Delmar Boulevard. Young people growing up in St. Louis had the privilege of listening to disc jockey Spider Burks on radio station KXLW between 1947 and 1960. Burks selected great songs to play and introduced them in an entertaining way, but he also provided a role model for his listeners as an intelligent, educated man with wide-ranging interests.

Nonetheless, the pervasive and intense racism in St. Louis made Reed feel he was on a collision course with the authorities, and he feared he would wind up in jail for thinking the way he did. He moved to Los Angeles to attend college and to get away from the racial order he had known all his life in the Midwest. By comparison, "Los Angeles was a piece of cake."[49] Reed first broke into radio as a student at City College in Los Angeles, where he attended classes with a young man named Ron Everett, later to become famous as Maulana Karenga, the leader of US, the city's most important Black Nationalist organization. Karenga created and popularized the Kwanzaa holiday. Reed and Karenga shared a common belief that it was good to be Black, that Black pride was a positive force. After leaving Los Angeles for stints on the air in Kansas City, Detroit, and New York, Reed came back in 1966, when he quickly became the most popular disc jockey in the market as the Master Blaster on KGFJ. Back on the air shortly after the 1965 Watts uprising, Reed understood the riot as a collective expression of frustration about the ways Black people had been treated in the city. He became an important force for unity and uplift in the Black community, eventually writing a regular music column for the *Sentinel*, producing his own television shows on Black culture and Black history, and publishing an extraordinarily comprehensive and beautifully illustrated book, *The Black Music History of Los Angeles—Its Roots*. In that book he wrote a warm tribute to his fellow disc jockey Johnny Otis. Reed observed, "Otis was not the kind of White man who came into the Black community, laughing and joking, scratching and itching and all along taking the 'soul' and 'money' out of it. Otis believed he was Black; psychologically, politically, environmentally, artistically, and sexually. He felt the same as his 'brothers' and 'sisters.' He caught some hell and began to question why."[50]

This questioning led Johnny to give up his radio and television shows and start to play engagements with his band only rarely. He continued to produce some rhythm and blues records for the King label. For a while in 1963, he produced gospel recordings by the California Gospel Caravan, featuring Billy Preston (who later went on to become a favorite accompanist for the Beatles and a pop solo artist in his own right), Mel Carter, the Angel Aires, Burma Floyd, the Cavaliers, and Reverend Claude Keller. Yet employment for Otis in the music business became so infrequent that Phyllis had to take a job working for the Los Angeles branch of the United Nations Association to support the family. Johnny stayed at home as caretaker and cook for their four children.[51] Even when he needed money badly, he found it hard to compromise his artistic standards. One time a friend arranged for Johnny to perform on a session with white trumpeter Shorty Rogers, a well-known "cool" jazz artist. Otis showed up and started to play but felt so alienated from the music being played that he politely begged off and went home.

Fortunately for him, the same white flight that kept Los Angeles segregated had enabled Johnny to purchase a large Victorian home. As Blacks started moving into previously white neighborhoods, whites sold their houses in a panic for far less than they were worth. This fear worked to the advantage of the Otis family at this time, enabling them to purchase a home at 2077 Harvard Avenue, which was paneled with imported redwood, its bathroom equipped with slabs of marble, and its dining room decorated with silver and crystal chandeliers. That home became the base of operations for his subsequent work in politics. He rented it out to earn money during hard times and even eventually turned it into a church when he became a sanctified preacher during the 1970s.

The insurrection in Watts took place at a time when Otis had developed deep pessimism about the music business and his place in it. The economic and political isolation of Watts and other ghettos seemed to mirror the marginalization of the originators of Black music and the undue acclaim and reward accruing to their white imitators. The destructive violence that swept Watts and South Los Angeles in August 1965 destroyed what remained of many of the places that Otis loved best. As he drove down Central Avenue on August 13, the rebellion forced him to confront his whiteness in new and disturbing ways.

Yet Otis also felt an uneasy satisfaction and a kind of vindication from the insurgency. It confirmed the arguments he had been making in his columns and his civil rights activism about police brutality, residential and educational segregation, and employment discrimination. He noted that the rioters displayed careful calculation amid their rage and fury. They left a Black-owned bank untouched but burned down every other building on the block. On one street in Watts, a storefront that housed an employment project run by the Urban League remained standing while a next-door furniture store owned by whites was looted and burned to the ground. When looters entered department stores and clothing stores that charged high interest rates on installment purchases of inferior goods, they destroyed the establishments' credit records before helping themselves to the goods on display.[52] Rioters and arsonists demolished many commercial buildings but almost no private homes, churches, or libraries.[53]

Despite the tragic loss of lives and destruction of property, the mass participation in the insurrection by tens of thousands of ghetto residents and the attention their actions attracted all over the world produced a strange sense of collective power and pride. A psychoanalyst who interviewed participants in the insurrection reported that they saw themselves as "freedom fighters liberating themselves with blood and fire" and that they differentiated themselves from their parents, whom they described as helpless and frightened when encountering white police officers.[54] Black journalist Almena Lomax reported "a certain sense of triumph" among Blacks in the wake of the riots, "a strange, hushed, secretive elation in the faces of the 'bloods.'"[55] Poet and spoken-word artist Richard Dedeaux of the Watts Prophets performance group proclaimed that while it takes millions and trillions of watts to light up most big cities, it took only one "Watts" to light up Los Angeles.[56]

In the aftermath of the Watts Riots, Otis briefly became a political candidate again, running for a seat in the Assembly from the 55th District. He vowed that he would try not to tell the lies politicians generally tell in order to get elected. Otis came close to winning and might actually have triumphed if the secretary of state had allowed his name to be listed on the ballot as Johnny Otis rather than as John Veliotes. Yet Otis did not mourn his defeat very much. He did not really believe that electoral politics held the solution to the problems facing Black people. "The whole thing was a lie and I knew it," he wrote later. "One night . . . a young black man asked me, 'Do you really believe that the Negro community can ever make meaningful progress under the white man's Democratic or Republican parties as they function today?' I hemmed and hawed for a moment. My head began to throb painfully. Finally I answered, 'No.' 'Then what are you doing?' he asked. 'That's a good question,' I said."[57] Even with the passage of civil rights legislation in 1964 and 1965, it seemed to Otis that the pace of change was too slow, that the meager concessions made to Blacks by whites were intended more to produce peace and quiet than peace and justice, and that freedom for his people was still a long way off.

Four LISTEN TO THE LAMBS

Almost as soon as the fires had been extinguished in Watts and South Los Angeles in August 1965, Johnny Otis started to write about the riots. He penned a long letter to a friend about the uprising less than a week after he drove down Central Avenue into the heart of the conflagration. During the weeks that followed, he collected oral testimonies from eyewitnesses to the insurrection and began to compose a series of short essays about the uprising and its importance. These writings grew into a book, *Listen to the Lambs,* published in 1968. It is an impassioned and incendiary volume that supports the insurrection and the people who waged it.

Otis argues that the destruction in Watts in August 1965 stemmed from pressures built up over centuries throughout U.S. society. He rejects accounts of the riots as acts by deranged or criminal elements in the community, depicting the uprising instead as a political statement by people deprived of any other effective way of getting their grievances heard. The book delineates the complex constraints that shaped life and death in the ghetto. In one poignant passage, Otis points to the multiple indignities and disappointments that preceded the rebellion, asking, "Do we bury the dead in American flags . . . or canceled welfare checks . . . or Baptist choir robes? . . . or Los Angeles Police Department handcuffs? . . . or eviction notices? . . . or selective service questionnaires?"[1]

As an entertainer whose career relied on public approval, corporate support, and police toleration, Johnny Otis took a huge risk in writing *Listen to the Lambs.* By publishing this book in the wake of the fires that had consumed much of Watts, Otis was seemingly willing to light a match and torch the rest of his career. He surrendered any future viability he might have had as a mainstream commercial entertainer in exchange for the opportunity to speak truth to power. In associating himself with the rage of the urban poor and connecting himself to the principles, commitments, and beliefs of the most ferociously disaffected opponents of white supremacy, he revealed himself as someone willing to surrender money, fame, and prestige for ideas in which he believed. This radicalism had professional and personal consequences. In those years of government programs like COINTELPRO, designed to monitor and harass dissidents, Otis set himself up as someone who could be singled out for repression. The book guaranteed that some doors would be closed to him forever. It marked him as someone who might be dangerous to know. In writing *Listen to the Lambs,* Otis made certain that in the future he would not be the person selected to host *New Year's Rockin' Eve* specials on television, like Dick Clark, that he would not become the subject of mainstream Hollywood films about rock 'n' roll, like Jerry Lee Lewis and Buddy Holly, and that he would not be able to leverage his fame later in life into a successful career in politics, like Sonny Bono.

When he wrote *Listen to the Lambs,* Johnny Otis was a forty-six-year-old high school dropout who had never written a book before. He had no credentials as a sociologist or political scientist. He held no elected office and led no organization. No one had asked him to volunteer his opinions. He was not even Black. Yet Otis believed he had something important to say. *Listen to the Lambs* remains one of the most unusual books ever written. It mixes impassioned polemics about the present with whimsical anecdotes from Otis's past. It blends bold diagnoses of major social issues with loving descriptions of everyday life events in the Black community. It is, in many ways, a work of improvisational art, a book written quickly in the heat of the moment, a virtuoso performance of verbal bravado designed to serve immediate ends: to salve a community's wounds and lift its spirits. It is in every respect a vernacular text, a message from and for a particular place and time, speaking to contemporary issues in the language of the day, replete with the new slang words and the new language patterns being forged in the wake of the turmoil of the 1960s. It resonates with the tones and textures of twentieth-century Black political activism, with what Cedric Johnson aptly describes as the culture of the soapbox, the pamphlet, and the bullhorn.[2]

Listen to the Lambs focuses on the lessons learned by Black people in the United States from centuries of exploitation, oppression, and brutality. In this book, Otis offers a model of how to be pro-Black in a society in which the rewards for being anti-Black are enormous. In the sections that deal directly with the riots, Otis presents a frank interpretation of their causes and consequences. He argues that people who had been completely oppressed in the past and were economically strangled in the present had nothing to lose from the insurgency. If only meaningful concessions had been made to nonviolent protesters in the past, the terrible destruction wrought by the riots might not have happened. Yet recounting the history of anti-racist campaigns dating back to the 1940s and beyond, Otis insists pointedly that Blacks have made gains only when they made the status quo too painful or too costly for whites to endure. He contends, moreover, that whites simply have no idea what Black life is like. "The races have grown so isolated from one another in big urban areas like Los Angeles," he explains, "that it is sheer nonsense to ask the majority what's plaguing the minority."[3]

Throughout the book, Otis relates stories about his encounters with defenders of the white supremacist status quo. One of his opponents at a public debate after the riots accuses him of wanting too much. After all, his opponent argues, the Supreme Court ruled segregation unconstitutional, and Congress passed the 1964 Civil Rights Act. "What do you want now?" he asks in exasperation. "I want the same life expectancy and birth survival rate for Negro children that whites enjoy," Otis retorted.[4] After emphasizing the importance of job opportunities and quality education on an equal basis, he concludes, "Perhaps the best answer to the question is that the average black person in America wants a full, unadulterated position in this society, an equal, uncut share of America."[5] But he sees little hope of these demands being met. "If the plight of the Negro in the big urban areas is not cured, and quick," Otis predicts, "we can expect plenty of the same. This thing is not going to go away."[6] In the years that followed, he would discover, much to his own dismay, that he was absolutely correct.

Listen to the Lambs follows a format as unconventional as its author. Otis turned over nearly thirty pages of his book to direct testimony by Black people about what they had witnessed during the insurrection. These firsthand reports from the front lines contained evidence and arguments that were ignored by the corporate media and political leaders at the time and that remain repressed and suppressed to this day in most accounts of the insurgency, save Gerald Horne's important volume, *Fire This Time*, first published in 1995. The testimonies Otis presents refute the dominant accounts of the rebellion by journalists, social scientists, historians, and politicians who attribute the uprising to the blind rage of uneducated and criminal elements in the community. What Otis presents challenges the prevailing view of the ghetto as a tangle of pathology and traces the origins of the fighting, looting, and arson of the rebellion to the long history of brutal police violence in the community, enacted to protect and preserve white supremacy and its unbearable inequalities and injustices. Perhaps most important, these testimonies reveal that while the riots began as a popular uprising against the police, they soon turned into police riots against the populace.[7]

Explaining that his own direct experiences with the riot were limited, Otis devotes chapter 4 of the book to testimony by Lily Fort, Taft Hazely, Maxy Filer, Stan Saunders, and Roberta Anderson. He provides brief descriptions of their professions and places of residence to establish their authority to speak. Just as the master of ceremonies in a rhythm and blues review introduces featured acts, Otis sets the scene and then retreats to the background, letting his informants speak for themselves in their own words. Lily Fort (lead singer with the famous Roulettes and resident of 6610¼ South Broadway) describes one event she witnessed from her front porch: the execution of a teenage looter by a police officer. She relates how she watched a youth accompanied by two friends enter a store directly across the street from her home. His two friends ran away when a police car drove up, but the youngster seemed unaware of their presence. Fort and her brother-in-law yelled to the young man that he should leave, but he did not seem to hear them. They watched as one officer calmly walked up to the store, peered inside, and aimed his weapon. Fort tried to scream out a warning, but she was so frightened no sound came out of her mouth. The police officer yelled, "Halt!" at the exact moment that he fired his gun. Fort and her brother-in-law saw the youth drop to the ground. The officer turned around and signaled to his partner in the squad car by pressing his index finger and thumb together in a "bull's eye" sign. Fort recalls that it was "just as though he had shot a tin can off a fence, not a human being."[8] For ten or fifteen minutes, the officers stayed outside the building, waiting for the ambulance to arrive, but they made no effort to see if the young man was dead or alive. When the medical technicians arrived they found him dead. Fort watched in horror as they dragged the youth

from the store "like he was a sack of potatoes."[9] A station wagon belong-
ing to one of the news outlets rolled up to get the officers' version of the
shooting. Suspicious that the officers might cover up their act of cold-
blooded murder, Fort and her brother-in-law and her husband (who had
now come out of the house and joined them) tried to tell the reporters
what actually happened. They walked out to the gate in their front yard and
tried to speak with the journalists. The driver of the station wagon, however,
looked directly at them but simply drove away. One of the officers came
across the street and ordered the three of them back into the house. When
Fort's husband hesitated, the officer drew and aimed his gun. Fort thought
he had "that same murderous look in his eyes" that she had seen before.
Fort explains, "I pulled my husband [back into the house] because I was
scared for him, and I had seen what they had just done to the other kid."[10]

Businessman Taft W. Hazely (of 1671 East Eighty-fourth Street, owner
of a cleaning and pressing shop in the riot area) contributes harrowing testimony about police officers and National Guard soldiers brutalizing citizens inside his store. He tells of being unjustly arrested himself.[11] Law
student Maxy Filer (age thirty-five, president of the Compton, California,
branch of the NAACP) reports seeing rioters commit "suicide by cop" during the rebellion. "These were people," he noted, "who had cracked under
the social pressure piled on through the years. Here was the chance to go
out like a man. They knew they were going to die, but with some Negroes
it has come to that: just die and get it over with; nothing to live for really,
anyhow."[12] Stan Saunders (Rhodes Scholar, Yale law student) relates his
shock in reading a story about the riots in *Look* magazine, learning there
about the riot-related death of his childhood friend Charles Fizer, once the
lead singer in the popular rhythm and blues group the Olympics.[13]

It takes a special kind of author to cede nearly thirty pages of his or
her first book to the words of others, but this kind of sharing flowed logi-
cally from the life Otis had led. As a promoter and performer, he credited
the entire Black community for his own artistry and accomplishments.
Unlike most of the white people who have made a living from Black culture, Otis has always been able and willing to connect that culture to the
full history and social life of the Black community. In his musical career,
Otis continually did what he does in *Listen to the Lambs*: deflects the spotlight from himself and turns it back onto the Black community. In doing
so, he reflects not only his own moral choices but also the rich practices of

Black life itself. From the dialect poetry of Paul Laurence Dunbar to the Nobel Prize–winning fiction of Toni Morrison, African American writers have long drawn directly from the oral traditions of their community. Richard Wright frequently established his own authority as a writer about Black life in *Native Son* by paraphrasing the words of ordinary people, introducing stories with phrases like "Sometimes I'd hear a Negro say. . ."[14]

The statements by neighborhood residents that are presented in *Listen to the Lambs* also reveal Otis's deep attachments to Los Angeles's Black neighborhoods and the people living in them. His experiences helped him see the important role of housing segregation in the skewing of opportunities and life chances along racial lines. Unlike slums in eastern and midwestern cities, Watts consisted largely of small bungalows with front lawns on streets lined with palm trees. Yet the physical and social isolation of Black neighborhoods in Los Angeles made their residents vulnerable to exploitation. The city had long been a center of restrictive covenants: deed restrictions that required white homeowners to pledge that they would never sell their property to nonwhites. The U.S. Supreme Court ruled these covenants unenforceable by the state (although still permissible as voluntary agreements among whites) in its *Shelley v. Kraemer* decision in 1948, enabling some Blacks in Los Angeles to move into previously all-white neighborhoods. Yet they faced ferocious opposition in the form of mob violence, cross burnings, and constant harassment. Efforts to end housing discrimination proved unpopular. The California legislature passed the Rumford Act, a bill outlawing housing discrimination in 1963, but a ballot initiative sponsored by the real estate industry the next year promptly overturned that law. White voters in California made it clear that they intended to retain the privileges (and the profits) they derived from discriminating against people of color. As Otis explains in *Listen to the Lambs,* "Integrated housing has never really existed in recent times in Los Angeles. A neighborhood may become integrated briefly, but it stays that way only as long as it takes the white residents to get out; then it becomes a part of the main body of the ghetto. The periphery inches out at a snail's pace and the ghetto gradually expands, but integrated housing remains an idealistic theory."[15]

Yet while he opposed exclusionary segregation, Otis did not necessarily endorse integration as an end in itself. In his view, there was nothing wrong with a Black neighborhood, as long as its composition came from voluntary choices and as long as it did not receive second-class amenities and services because of the complexion of its residents. Black neighborhoods throughout the country served as resources for Black people. Out of necessity they made productive use of the spaces to which their residents were confined. They countered the dehumanization created by white exclusion with a rehumanization grounded in Black solidarity. As historian Earl Lewis argues, Black people have been adept at turning segregation into congregation. Faced with the radical divisiveness that flows from lives in which they find themselves constantly pitted against one another in competition for jobs, housing, romantic partners, and prestige, residents of ghettos like Watts cultivate their commonalities. They create common ground through creative, spiritual, and political imagination and invention. Otis condemned the oppressive conditions that created the ghetto, but he insisted that "in Watts, as in any other spot on earth where the human spirit refuses to yield, there is deep and startling beauty. In the heart of Watts, one can feel the surging glory of the African character. It continues to endure like some indomitable, indefatigable, will-o'-the-wisp that denies the separation of thousands of miles . . . defies the span of hundreds of years, and tenaciously holds fast.[16]

These associations and affiliations help explain the expansive intellectual vision that pervades *Listen to the Lambs*. Otis's bold statements about the depths, dimensions, and duration of white supremacy draw deftly on well-established intellectual and political traditions in the Black community. He takes special pains in the book to connect racism at home with U.S. foreign policy overseas, treating white supremacy as both a national and a global issue. He follows W. E. B. Du Bois in arguing that the capture and exploitation of African labor provided the necessary precondition for the creation of wealth in North America. He points to the hypocrisy of a government that seems eager to police the world overseas, yet remains unwilling to defend the lives, labor, and property of its own Black citizens. Otis condemns the war in Vietnam as unjust and immoral, as a drain on resources needed to fight poverty and racism at home, and as symptomatic of the unrestrained arrogance and imperial ambitions of a white supremacist nation. He advocates a global rather than a purely national solution to racial oppression, suggesting, "It might be an idea now to examine the entire world in terms of white and non-white."[17]

This global vision demonstrates Otis's immersion in important social and intellectual currents in the Black community. Otis's friend, mentor, and employer Mervyn Dymally grew up in Trinidad before migrating to the United States. He became the first African American born outside the United States to be elected to Congress when he won a seat in the House of Representatives in 1980. One of his first initiatives in Congress entailed support for reparations for Japanese Americans placed in internment camps during World War II.[18] Widespread awareness of anti-colonial struggles by nonwhite people informed the global vision of Malcolm X as he argued that African Americans should take their grievances to the United Nations rather than to the U.S. Congress. Martin Luther King Jr.'s opposition to the Vietnam War reflected his commitment to rejecting narrow nationalisms in favor of world-transcending citizenship. During the Harlem Renaissance, Alain Locke had proclaimed, "As with the Jew, persecution is making the Negro international," a claim that may have had special resonance for Johnny Otis as a child of the Greek diaspora.[19] Theophus Smith notes that for centuries sacred practices in the Black community promoted collective commitment to transcending "the oppressive conditioning of their host cultures in order to acknowledge, support, and advance the humanity of peoples elsewhere and everywhere."[20]

Otis also spoke for and from the collective vision of the Black community in his impassioned defense of Black women in *Listen to the Lambs,* devoting a memorable section of his book to a tribute to their strength. In response to the Moynihan Report and other social science studies that promoted the idea that the disadvantages that Black men encountered in U.S. society did not stem from white racism but from the deficiencies in Black families that left Black women in too prominent positions, Otis responds by pointing to Rosa Parks and other freedom fighters as evidence of how the strengths of Black women work to the benefit, rather than the detriment, of the Black community. While granting that one dimension of white supremacy includes systematic efforts to demean and infantilize Black men, he refutes the accusation that Blacks suffer from having too many households headed by women and argues for the importance of viewing gender as a political identity as well as a personal one. He asserts, "Because the American black man has been preempted, the Negro woman has been forced to assume the impossible role of both mother and father, breadwinner and homemaker. The entire world of womanhood stands taller and prouder as a result of the American Negro woman's historically supreme job of holding her race together with her bare hands. In the finest tradition of womanhood, Rosa Parks struck the spark that lighted fires in twenty million hearts, and started an emotional surge that transcended mere survival."[21]

For a book with deadly serious purposes, *Listen to the Lambs* proceeds in a peculiarly playful fashion. Interrupting his serious sustained attacks on white supremacy, Otis intersperses autobiographical stories from his past throughout the book, presenting seemingly casual personal reminiscences about joining the Boy Scouts, learning about sex as a teenager, his first days on the road as a working musician, his early experiences at Central Avenue's famed Club Alabam, his memories of the Barrelhouse, his encounters with Jim Crow segregation in the South, his fondness for fishing, hunting, and raising pigeons, and his nervousness about being a new parent. It is almost as if the political points he wants to make are too harsh to make in undiluted form, so he chooses to lighten up the mood with personal reminiscences. Yet all of his stories serve serious purposes. They do not merely foreground Johnny Otis's personal biography, but instead present incidents in his life as illustrative anecdotes fashioned to teach lessons about racism. They connect the macrosocial structures and conditions that Otis condemns throughout the book to the actual lived experiences of ordinary people like himself. Rather than celebrating himself, he tries to share what he has learned from life. Otis provides evidence and arguments drawn directly from his efforts to become and remain an anti-racist white person in a white supremacist society. He expresses his conclusions simply and directly. Racism kills, literally as well as figuratively. Otis reminds readers that Blacks have higher levels of infant mortality and shorter life spans than whites. "This is not some biological phenomenon linked to skin color, like sickle cell anemia," he points out; instead, "this is a national crime, linked to a white-supremacist way of life and compounded by indifference."[22]

Perhaps most important, at a time when people purporting to be experts responded to the upheavals of the era with diagnoses about the defects of Black people and Black culture, Otis correctly understood that the real problem lay elsewhere. "The real danger for the future . . . ," he explains, "grows not out of the Negro community's struggle for justice, but out of the white community's historical and continuing rejection of these demands."[23] If the United States is ever to solve its "black problem," he maintains, it must first deal with the problem of whiteness.

The problem of whiteness was something Johnny Otis knew well at the time. Yet the riot forced him to deal with his identity in a new way. He had lived much of his life as an anti-racist white who felt completely comfortable inside the Black community. But was there a place for him in an increasingly polarized society in which even the best of personal intentions meant little in the face of systemic structural racism and enduring injustice and inequality? Was it possible for any white person to be actually anti-racist as long as the privileges and advantages of whiteness persisted? The Watts Riots forced Johnny Otis to face this reality in stark and unmistakable ways, to confront the limitations and contradictions of the choices he had made. He came to believe that he could not be genuinely anti-racist unless he became an advocate for Black Power.

The concept of Black Power emerged from the grass roots of the Black freedom movement of the 1950s and 1960s. It emanated from a recognition by the Black working class that newly passed civil rights laws, which were weak to begin with, were not even being enforced, and from a collective realization that desegregating access to public accommodations or the ballot box did too little to address deeply entrenched economic inequalities. Black Power adherents defined the racial problem as more a matter of power than a matter of prejudice. Systematized as a theory in a groundbreaking book by Charles Hamilton and Stokely Carmichael (later Kwame Ture), Black Power proceeded from the premise that racism amounts to more than irrational prejudice and aberrant acts of hatred by isolated individuals, that primarily it entails systematic subordination of an entire people for economic and political gain. Racial subordination renders Black workers powerless to bargain freely over wages and working conditions. It prevents Black families from accumulating assets that could appreciate in value and be passed down to subsequent generations. Racial control precludes Black communities from running their own institutions and solving their own problems.[24]

Advocates of Black Power viewed white supremacy as a matter of interests as well as attitudes, as a question of property as well as pigment. They believed that no one would care more about the freedom of Black people than Black people themselves, that the road to freedom required the creation of new democratic practices and institutions that would act in the interests of Blacks. Black Power did not rule out alliances and affiliations with other races; indeed, it argued that the critiques of society emerging from the Black Power movement could benefit everyone. Yet the concept of Black Power presumed that Blacks had a unique need to come together because outsiders owned the stores, ran the schools, and even dominated the institutions in the Black community. Hamilton and Carmichael maintained that "before a group can enter the open society, it must first close ranks."[25]

White sympathy, empathy, or pity did not translate into justice. Even friendly whites did not seem willing to give up the privileges, preferences, unfair gains, and unjust enrichments they secured as a result of discrimination against Blacks. Of course not all whites profited equally from white supremacy. Yet even in the days of slavery, whites who did not own slaves received preferential treatment because of their group position. Before and after emancipation, the subordination of Black workers meant that white workers had the security of knowing there was a floor through which they could not fall. They knew that they had immunity from the worst indignities, because those were reserved for Blacks. The Black Power critique charged that these realities hurt people other than Blacks. It contended that racism works to protect and preserve a fundamentally unjust social order that oppresses even many of those who benefit from its racial rewards. Racism functions as a crucible in which other cruelties are created. Racism makes inequality seem natural, necessary, and inevitable. Hamilton and Carmichael assert that Black Power demanded a fundamental revolution in values that included an emphasis on the dignity of man rather than the sanctity of property, that it required a society based on free people rather than free enterprise.[26] They warn that nonviolence had been tried and found wanting by the masses of Black people, that "a nonviolent approach to civil rights is an approach black people cannot afford and a luxury white people do not deserve."[27]

Martin Luther King Jr. remained committed to nonviolence in the wake of the riots, but he too recognized the logic that made ghetto residents attack the symbols of their subordination. As he explained in his important, but often overlooked, last book, *Where Do We Go from Here: Chaos or Community?*, "When there is rocklike intransigence or sophisticated manipulation that mocks the empty-handed petitioner, rage replaces reason."[28] In arguments similar to those Otis makes at the end of *Listen to the Lambs*, King warns, "The cohesive potentially explosive Negro community in the north has a short fuse and a long train of abuses. Those who argue that it is hazardous to give warnings, lest the expression of apprehension lead to violence, are in error. Violence has already been practiced too often, and always because remedies were postponed."[29]

Johnny Otis was one of the people who gave that kind of warning. At the end of *Listen to the Lambs,* he observes, "White America stands at a critical crossroad. She can meet ghetto disorders with increased police power in the belief that oppressive punitive actions will make the problem go away, or she can start getting at the economic and social causes of the riots. Unfortunately, but typically, the trend is toward punitive police power."[30]

Four decades later we know that what emerged from the cry for justice that erupted in Watts in 1965 was not an honest reckoning with the tragic legacy of racism but rather a counterrevolution that promoted incarceration instead of education, that funneled resources away from the masses and toward the upper classes. Our problems today are so severe because warnings like Otis's went unheeded when they first appeared in print. He would spend the rest of his life immersed in the struggle against white supremacy, not merely as an anti-racist white person, but as a tireless advocate and promoter of the unique vision of racial justice that emerged from centuries of struggle, suffering, and sacrifice. He rooted himself in Black culture: its music, religion, and visual art. He kept the past alive in the present by referring again and again to the rich aesthetic, political, and moral traditions of the Black community. Without ever denying or disavowing his own biological bloodlines, he drew on common histories of bloodshed to remember, praise, and honor his adopted ancestors, such as Count Basie, Bessie Smith, and Duke Ellington. His writing, broadcasting, speaking, and recording endeavors coalesced around producing understandings of the past that could serve as tools for solving problems in the present. In the process, Otis connected himself with the lives of people who came before him, with well-known preachers, teachers, artists, and activists to be sure, but also with the previous generations of Black people fighting for freedom, whose bodies now "lie in graves as unmarked as their place in history."[31]

Five ALL NIGHT LONG

Like other musicians during the 1950s, Johnny Otis often had to defend himself against charges that he was "polluting" the youth of America by performing and promoting sensual, provocative, and even "obscene" Black music, music that purportedly poisoned the minds and morals of young whites. Crusaders opposed to rock 'n' roll and rhythm and blues music alleged that these genres promoted illicit sexual behavior. Executives at major record labels, radio and television programmers, and watchdogs of public morality in and out of government sought incessantly to censor lyrics and smooth the rough edges off rhythmically complex songs. When Mercury Records selected white singer Georgia Gibbs to record the cover version of the Etta James and Johnny Otis song "The Wallflower" (originally "Roll with Me Henry"), the label's executives renamed the song "Dance with Me Henry." The record company's officials knew that when stations had played the Etta James song, broadcasters received warnings from the FCC complaining that the word *roll* in the lyrics (as in "rock with me Henry, roll with me Henry") could be construed as obscene. The FCC censors believed that *roll* was a slang term for having intercourse. An incredulous and annoyed Johnny Otis telephoned Etta James to inform her that the FCC had virtually banned their record because of the word *roll,* even though that word appeared in hundreds of other songs.

Gibbs's record became a big hit, however, and Otis, James, and Hank Ballard profited from the writers' royalty payments they received. Nevertheless, Otis felt that the FCC and Mercury Records had deprived Etta James of her just recognition and reward, that a combination of racism and an excessive fear of sexuality was responsible for the inferior cover version of this song outselling the artistically superior original. Puritanical policing of sexuality was detrimental enough in itself, he believed, because it portrayed beautiful things like sensuality and pleasure as dirty, but in so many cases in the United States it also had a racial agenda. White supremacists channeled popular anxieties about sexuality in general against Blacks. They turned a threat to their racial privileges into a threat to sexual purity in an attempt to make desegregation appear unnatural and obscene. They drew on a long history of sexual racism that portrayed Black men and women as hypersexual, licentious, and likely carriers of sexually transmitted diseases. Like people in power all over the world, they tried to preserve their privileges by treating what they viewed as a social transgression as if it were a biological threat.

Censoring popular songs sometimes backfired. Telling young people in a sexually repressed society that an innocent song like "Roll with Me Henry" had obscene connotations probably made the song *more* attractive to them. Yet these efforts to police the racial border with sex-negative censorship inevitably distorted relations between Blacks and whites, subjected Black artists to higher levels of scrutiny than white musicians faced, and systematically channeled unfair gains and unearned rewards to mediocre white performers. In the case of "The Wallflower," the decision to censor struck Johnny Otis as especially ridiculous. "If ever a song was about dancing with no sexual connotations, this was it," Otis argues. Yet he adds in disgust, "Not that there's anything wrong with honest sexuality—it's a dance record. Try to tell that to the establishment of 1954."[1]

The same scenario repeated itself with "Willie and the Hand Jive." Even though the song's lyrics expressly compare the Hand Jive to other dances (the Walk, the Stroll, and the Suzie Q) and even though the Three Tons of Joy demonstrated the Hand Jive on stage countless times while Johnny sang the song, would-be censors complained that its lyrics presented a coded tribute to masturbation, an interpretation that has persisted for years. An interviewer for National Public Radio in 1992 asked Johnny if the song was really about masturbation. He thought, "Damn! Can't you understand the lyrics? It's about dancing . . . DANCING!"[2] Fears of teenage sexuality in general, and of interracial sex in particular, permeated the moral panics about popular music in the 1950s, as they have propelled many other attacks on Black music before and since. On several occasions, however, complaints about the alleged immorality of rock 'n' roll hid other motives. In certain cities where the authorities informed Otis that some had objected to the possible indecency of his show, he found that "under the table" payments of cash to police officers and fire inspectors solved the problem, enabling the show to proceed as scheduled. The guardians of public morals simply wanted a little kickback. Other times, Otis just got lucky. Before one engagement at the Long Beach Civic Auditorium, Johnny was informed that a group purportedly representing that city's church congregations and parents' associations would be present at the show to make sure that all the performances were in good taste. Knowing that the lyrics of the songs to be played that day were harmless, Johnny assumed that he had nothing to worry about. Headliner Chuck Berry, however, concluded his act with a verse of one of his songs that he often used to close his shows in adult nightclubs: "We boogied in the kitchen, we boogied in the hall, she boogied on my finger, and I wiped it on the wall!" Otis expected the police to shut down the show immediately. Fortunately for him, however, the noise of screaming fans in the arena was so deafening that the observers evidently did not hear the offending lyrics.[3]

Captivated at an early age by the beauty of Black music and Black culture, Otis felt that the charges of obscenity lodged against blues music were simply wrong. "I don't understand the word *dirty* as it relates to the blues," he contended. "I've never understood that, because I never saw Black music as dirty. I saw it as beautiful, sexy sometimes and earthy, but beautiful."[4] To Otis's relief, popular culture in the United States during the 1960s changed dramatically in respect to what might be considered obscene. Although he objected to many of the other changes that transformed popular music during that decade, he believed that the trend toward more open expression of sexual desire demonstrated some progress. Songs that had provoked censorship during the 1950s seemed tame and innocent by comparison with the frank lyrics and affirmative sexual imagery prevalent in music and society during the next decade.

Otis made his own contribution to that frankness with an unusual album in 1969. One of the leading lights of the new hippie counterculture made that recording possible. Frank Zappa, founder and leader of the innovative group the Mothers of Invention, had grown up in Los Angeles listening to Johnny Otis's music and attending his live shows. He delved deeply into the musical archive Otis played such a large role in creating. As a young songwriter in 1963, Zappa composed "Memories of El Monte" for the Penguins, a tribute to the rock 'n' roll shows that Otis and others had hosted at that venue. When he began to record his own music, Zappa frequently consulted Otis in order to get in touch with musicians who were known for their work with Johnny and whom he wanted to hire to play on his recordings, including Don "Sugarcane" Harris, Preston Love, and Shuggie Otis. Johnny himself sometimes played in rehearsals and on recordings with Zappa. Although the free-form compositions on albums with titles such as *Hot Rats* and *Weasels Ripped My Flesh* seemed a long way from "Willie and the Hand Jive," Otis and Zappa respected each other and enjoyed their collaborations. At one recording session, however, Zappa's devotion to the avant-garde seemed over the top to Johnny. "This part is in B natural, and you take it," Zappa said. This key rarely appears in rhythm and blues songs, and its five sharps make it extremely difficult to execute. Johnny replied, "Well, if it's in B natural, *you* take it!"[5]

Zappa urged the owners of Kent Records in Los Angeles to bring Otis and his musicians back into the studio to cut an album in 1968. The session produced *Cold Shot,* a marvelous collection of soulful and funky numbers. Executives at Kent released the song "Country Girl" as a single, and it reached the best-selling rhythm and blues charts in 1969, remaining a hit for six weeks. The success of *Cold Shot* led to a contract for an album on the Epic label, owned by Columbia Records.[6]

Buoyed by the success of *Cold Shot* and emboldened by the changing culture of the times, Otis decided to produce an album of music that he would not have been able to record previously, a collection of the songs based on the things he had heard over the years in taverns, jails, and pool halls. Along with singer Delmar "Mighty Mouth" Evans and Johnny's son Shuggie (only fifteen years old, but already an extremely talented musician), Johnny selected songs that spoke about sexuality in frank, explicit, and sometimes obscene language. Built on African American folk tales, street corner rhymes, comedy routines, and the teasing and bragging styles of "the dozens," the new album presented sex as something to be laughed at, marveled about, and celebrated. Its liberal use of profanity and racy subject matter no doubt fulfilled the worst fears of the moral crusaders against "Roll with Me Henry" and "Willie and the Hand Jive." Otis titled the album after the deliberately vulgar moniker he chose for the group playing it, *Snatch and the Poontangs,* a name made up of vernacular slang words for a woman's vulva and for sexual intercourse.

For all of its frankness, however, *Snatch and the Poontangs* was not intended as an exercise in transgression. The album attempted to capture, preserve, and disseminate a rich ghetto culture that Otis felt had been too glibly dismissed by the dominant society as simply a tangle of pathology. He wanted the songs to speak in the idioms of the streets, to use the words spoken every day by Black working-class people on Elm Street in Dallas and Hastings Street in Detroit, on Beale Street in Memphis and 125th Street in Harlem. "The Signifying Monkey" and "The Great Stack A-Lee" adapt Black folk tales about tricksters and bad men to the rhythm and blues idiom.[7] "Hey Shine" archives a half century's worth of stories and songs about actual events, including the treatment of Black workers on the *Titanic* as it was sinking. "That's Life" presents a series of salacious limericks, and "The Pissed Off Cowboy" delivers a wide range of insults in narrative form. "Big Time Slim" and "Big John Jeeter" anticipate many of the forms of bragging and aggressive teasing later popularized in hip-hop. Otis acknowledged the grounding of these songs in the long history in Black culture of "playing the dozens" by recording a version of Speckled Red's "The Dirty Dozens" during Snatch and the Poontangs' session. This cut was not released with the other songs, however, until a British label reissued the album in 2002.

The celebration of sexual desire in these songs did not sound obscene to Otis. To him, they manifested what he thought of as a healthy sexuality in the face of a puritanical, repressive, and sex-negative social climate. The liveliness of the toasts, boasts, rhymes, and raps in these songs chronicles the survival mechanisms of an often broke but never broken people. The profane teasing and bragging that pepper the album's lyrics have a tone not too different from the revelry of carnival celebrations dating back to the medieval era in Europe. Yet like many cultural expressions of sexual awakening in the 1960s, the album's lyrics remained rooted in normative masculinist and heterosexist understandings of sex. The name "Snatch and the Poontangs" certainly did not affirm the desires of women, but rather objectified and demeaned them. The song "Two Girls in Love (with Each Other)" foregrounds two women's voices making sounds of arousal and climax over a bluesy musical background, displaying the very lascivious and prurient approach to sexuality that Otis often criticized as well as both sexism and homophobia. Yet the best songs on the album display an open, frank, guiltless, and pleasure-affirmative approach to sex. They also offer Black working-class cultural traditions as healthier alternatives to the snickering and shame-filled stance toward sexuality that still predominated in the larger society at that time.

The lyrics on the *Snatch and the Poontangs* album leveled social distinctions by emphasizing bodily desires that cut across social groups. These sentiments are evident not only in the album's songs about cuckolded husbands, same-sex love, and the pleasures of certain body types, but even more in an intensely pointed political song that was recorded when the album was made but not released until thirty years later. "It's Good to Be Free" was cowritten by Johnny Otis and vocalist Mighty Mouth Evans shortly after Johnny published *Listen to the Lambs*. "It's Good to Be Free" revolves around the chasm between white America's idealized promises and its actual ignoble practices in regard to race. The song's narrator describes reading newspaper stories that salute all the progress purportedly made by Blacks. He sees that the newspaper claims that opportunity has really arrived, that Blacks can succeed if they take advantage of the educational opportunities offered them, as long as they "don't socialize with those crazy militant fools." A preacher says that practicing the golden rule is especially important now that freedom is here. As the narrator gives thanks in prayer for all these signs of progress, a policeman arrests him for a crime he did not commit. A list of lofty promises follows, pledging factories to be owned by Blacks, peace in the streets, and freedom for all. Before these can be realized, however, the narrator is offered a gun and told to go to Vietnam, to join the "free Americans" saving that land from the communist Viet Cong. After every verse, the narrator sings sarcastically, "Oh it sure is good to be free, but who do they think they're fooling with that bulls––? Not me."

Otis wrote the lyrics to "It's Good to Be Free" to give musical expression to the sentiments he heard every day in the ghetto. At first the record company executives approved his lyrics. As the recording worked its way up the corporate chain of command, however, a minor executive became frightened by the song and ordered the deletion of all expletives. The song remains a favorite of many of Johnny's closest associates and friends, but when he listens to it, all that he hears is the censorship that prevented him from doing what rap artists would do so successfully twenty years later: chronicle their community's political ideas and feelings with a documentary honesty that spoke the language of the streets.

Even in 1969, no record company executive had the temerity to release even the cleaned-up version of "It's Good to Be Free" as a single. The song remained virtually unheard in the United States until a British company re-released *Snatch and the Poontangs* and *Cold Shot* as a double album in

2004. The mixture of politics and sex on Otis's *Snatch and the Poontangs* album, however, offers important evidence about the complicated currents running through Black music and Black culture at the time Otis recorded it. During the years when Johnny Otis attained his greatest professional success, all music, but especially blues and gospel music, served important needs for Black people. As they struggled every day against racism, exploitation, and ostracism, music provided significant psychic, moral, spiritual, and even political resources. At a time when the enemies of Black people controlled every major communications outlet in the society, popular music reached out to them with what Horace Tapscott called the "songs of the unsung." The rhythms, melodies, harmonies, and lyrics of popular songs served as archives of everyday experiences, repositories of collective memory, and sources of moral instruction. Dancing to popular songs created a fully embodied experience of coordinated movement with other people. Dancing transformed the body that labored five days a week into a vehicle for play, expression, and display.

Richard Wright, one of the best-known Black authors of the post–World War II era, believed that the most important function popular music served in Black communities was to affirm desire. He meant desire for a better life, of course, but something else as well. Wright believed that erotic desire serves important social purposes. It embodies the deepest form of connection to other people. Its intimacy, affection, and reciprocity produce utopian models for human interaction. It channels somatic frustration, nervous energy, and selfish needs into selfless love. Wright argued that fulfillment of sensual desires can serve important social ends, that erotic love plays a part in moving people toward the love of humanity and even the love of God. Aware that his analysis could be misused to reinforce degrading stereotypes about Blacks as being lascivious, undisciplined, and immoral, Wright nonetheless insisted on acknowledging the sexual dimensions of the music of African Americans. "This aspect of black music has been denied for too long," he maintained, insisting, "the faith of mystics and of most blacks has a sexual ingredient which well meaning people are too timid to dare to admit, but which must be proclaimed." Wright believed that Baptist and Holiness ministers use gospel music successfully to co-opt these sexual energies for apolitical but valid purposes, channeling erotic desire into love of God through what he described as "aphrodisiac music." Wright argued that it is a short step from church music to the music of Ray Charles, that Charles could say things directly that the preachers have to couch in more respectable language.[8]

The suspicion that music might encode secret sexual messages has often been a source of fear, anxiety, and censorship. From the times of antiquity to the present, musicians have been accused of possessing powers capable of subverting sexual propriety, of appealing so directly to the body that the mind becomes powerless. In the United States, where human sexuality has so often been viewed as obscene, where sex-negative messages far outnumber sex-positive ones, and where vicious forms of sexual racism have fabricated images of Black people as sexually licentious, indiscriminate, and even rapacious, the erotic dimensions of popular music have provoked repeated moral panics castigating the music as a threat to the dominant white population. Yet for working musicians, sensuality and sexuality are omnipresent and inescapable. People dancing and listening to music in public are often looking for love, pursuing pleasure, and aiming for erotic connection and fulfillment.

For musicians not to notice this or to participate in it would be to misunderstand the nature of their jobs. Yet this reality has sometimes made them uneasy. Jazz musician Ornette Coleman often complained about the social forces that connect music and sexuality. The saxophonist felt that his work made him into a kind of a pimp who got paid for setting up the circumstances that enabled other people to have sex. Knowing full well that jazz music got its start in brothels, Coleman was upset by the realization that his playing often served as an excuse for nightclub audiences to get drunk and pursue one another into bed. From Thomas A. Dorsey to Little Richard to Al Green, musicians raised in Holiness churches have sometimes experienced crises caused by the tension between the sacred and the sensual elements of their music, giving up secular music altogether at times to play church music exclusively. For many musicians, however, erotic pleasure played a positive role. It affirmed life and people's right to be happy and often offered musicians the reward they wanted most. It had a lot to do with why they became musicians in the first place. Johnny Otis is one of those people.

"It's funny how some people can't stand flesh," Otis observes. "I don't like hard core pornography and obscenity, but a little erotica is good! It must be good, or God wouldn't have given it to all of us. He didn't give it to some of us. It's a blessing. It's a gift, just like intellect, like water, fresh air—sexuality."[9] The evidence indicates Otis made ample use of this gift during his years as an entertainer. As he wrote in his 1993 memoir, "Being popular and being onstage brought the young men and women in the bands unlimited opportunities to meet and be with attractive members of the opposite sex, or the same sex, for that matter, if that happened to be your persuasion."[10] Traveling on the road as a musician meant "swimming in a sea of adoring beautiful women," all vying for Otis's attention and company. Like many other men who gained fame as entertainers, Otis found pleasure and fulfillment through sexual conquests.

Otis was happily married to a beautiful woman, a person he deeply loved and admired, a person viewed by most of their mutual friends as one of the most appealing, loving, intelligent, and compassionate people they had ever encountered. He often told people that the best thing he ever did was to marry Phyllis. He missed her terribly during the hours, days, and months he spent on the road. He returned to his home in Los Angeles and became a disc jockey in the mid-1950s in no small measure to spend more time with her and their children.

For a man raised in a sexist and misogynist society, however, coming into a new town and finding more than a few of its most attractive women eager to make love was intoxicating. The frequency of these encounters between musicians and their fans made them seem routine, an expected fringe benefit of the job that offset the sometimes arduous conditions of constant travel, of a job that required the performers to be lively, enthusiastic, and self-confident every night. Probably very few men of that era (or today) would have refused such opportunities if they were offered to them.

Entertainers on the jazz, blues, and rhythm and blues circuits in the 1940s and 1950s inhabited a world characterized by positive attitudes about sexual pleasure and by comparative frankness and openness about it. Drag king Gladys Bentley performed wearing a tuxedo and top hat in Los Angeles lesbian bars while she sang bawdy songs she had written. Lillian Randolph sang similar fare for presumably heterosexual audiences at Lou's Swanee Inn at Beverly and La Brea. Exotic dancers with names like Lottie the Body and Titty Tassel Toni toured with rhythm and blues shows, and their provocative gyrations inspired more rhythmic innovations by drummers and bass players than many of the musicians might have been willing to admit. Yet breaking away from the dominant sexual mores proved easier said than done. Bentley took estrogen treatments, which she hoped would make her heterosexual and not so incidentally revive her career in the increasing sex-negative 1950s.[11] In a society that suppressed sex education and banned contraceptive devices, casual sexual encounters could produce not only pleasure but also exploitation, sexually transmitted diseases, and unwanted pregnancies.

Otis viewed sexual trysts between musicians and their fans as something that did not hurt anyone. Yet from the vantage point of contemporary times, we can hardly miss the context of unequal power that must have shaped relations between male artists and women spouses and fans in those days. Otis often explained with great discernment how relations between whites and Blacks in American society were never innocent or equal, how unequal power perverted even the best of intentions. Yet we have no record of him expressing similar insights about his privileges as a man interacting with women whose consensual relations with him and other men took place in a context of asymmetrical power. Sometimes these trysts had an illicit dimension. Preston Love's daughter Laura Love claims that when Otis and Preston Love talked about the women they slept with on the road, they described them using male names to protect their deception. If one of them spoke about having to go to meet Clark, for example, it signaled that he had a woman waiting.[12]

In a bitter memoir, Love writes about her feelings of abandonment as an outside-of-marriage daughter of Preston Love. Raised in dire poverty by her mother while Love's family enjoyed what she perceived to be a middle-class existence, Laura Love eventually tracked down her father and sought a connection with him. Her mother had never contacted the saxophonist about his daughter, so he did not know he had fathered her and was more than a little surprised to learn that Laura's mother had explained to her that her father, musician Preston Love, had died long ago. Laura Love appreciated his explanations, but after she challenged Preston about the behavior that had led to her birth, she reports that he replied sometime later by sending her a letter he had received from Johnny Otis claiming that their *liaisons* outside of marriage were actions that every man has the right to do.[13]

Johnny Otis and Preston Love were certainly not alone among entertainers of their era (or today) in their attitude about sexual encounters. Frank Sinatra bragged that men were animals and that he sought sex compulsively. "I'm just looking to make it with as many women as I can," he explained to a friend. The evidence indicates he had extraordinary success.[14] One of Sinatra's biographers reports that while making the film *Anchors*

Aweigh, the singer posted a list of women working in the MGM studio with whom he wanted to make love. By the time he finished the film, most of the names on the list reportedly had check marks next to them.[15] Elvis Presley routinely had his staff bring young girls to his hotel rooms, where, according to Albert Goldman, he generally commanded them to undress in front of him and wrestle each other.[16] Bobby Darin confided, "The sex element is the most important in this business."[17]

In an era in which nearly every social institution constrained the ambitions and talents of women, affairs with famous people offered an alternative to the anonymity of everyday life. As lead singer in the Impressions and as a solo artist out on his own, Jerry Butler was surprised to discover that "fine young ladies would do just about anything to share the spotlight with someone they considered a star."[18] Sam Cooke faced three paternity suits in his short career. Hank Ballard made it a point to sleep with schoolteachers, because he thought it would help him become better educated. Even within gospel music, sex between performers and audience members seems to have been routine. Lithofayne Pridgeon remembers having three-way sex in a Harlem hotel room one afternoon with another woman and a reportedly famous (although unidentified in her account) gospel singer. They had the radio on, and a news bulletin informed them that President Kennedy had been shot and killed. The singer grabbed one girl in each hand and led them off the bed, saying solemnly, "Let us all fall down on our knees and pray." When the prayer was over, he led them back to the bed and they continued their lovemaking.[19]

Sexual pleasures on the road had consequences, however. Otis fathered as many children outside his marriage as he did within it. He speaks affectionately and proudly about these children in public and accepts his responsibility for them. Phyllis Otis accepted them warmly as well, a stance consistent with her generous, compassionate, and loving demeanor. The dedication to his 1993 book, *Upside Your Head! Rhythm and Blues on Central Avenue,* is to his sons Shuggie, Nicky, Buddy, Robert, and Darryl Jon, to his daughters Janice, Laura, and Stephanie, and to eighteen grandchildren and two great granddaughters without separating them in any way. The extraordinary affection and romantic partnership that Johnny and Phyllis forged over more than six decades of marriage in every realm of their lives withstood whatever challenges his activities on the road might have posed to it.

Unlike many men of his generational cohort, however, Otis mixed heterosexual desire with deep respect and affection for women in nonsexual realms of endeavor. He was directly responsible for the professional success of an impressive number of extraordinary women singers and musicians. Of course, he profited from their successes as well, financially and artistically. Yet in a business dominated by males insistent on their privileges as men, Otis broke new ground in advancing the artistry of women performers. In addition to featuring the trumpet playing of Clora Bryant in his band, he provided her with ample opportunities to display her impressive gifts as a composer, arranger, and singer.[20] Otis maintained nonromantic and nonsexual friendships with women he admired, including newspaper publisher Charlotta Bass, choreographer Patsy Hunter, and singer–drummer Big Mama Thornton.

Despite his exuberant heterosexuality, Otis also evidenced respectful attitudes about gays and lesbians. His job put him in close contact with many of them whom he admired both as artists and as people. His long and close friendship with Willie Mae "Big Mama" Thornton exposed him to some of what it meant for her to live as someone perceived by others as a lesbian. Thornton sometimes wore men's suits and other masculine kinds of clothing. She held her own in fistfights with men and displayed a pistol prominently in front of her on the table when she gambled. People in the band thought of her as a lesbian, but Johnny says, "I could never get a handle on Willie Mae sexually and that's not a judgment. If you're a homosexual or whatever, it's nobody's damn business what you do in bed. . . . All I can honestly say is that she was a good, intelligent person. I personally never saw her with any men, but on the other hand, I never saw her with any women either."[21]

Gays and lesbians clearly influenced the careers of many of Otis's closest associates. Etta James acknowledges that she owes much of her success to "gay boys" who admired her self-assertion and artistry, and from whom, in turn, she derived clues about how to dress, how to wear her hair, and how to comport herself onstage.[22] Some men who seemed to be heterosexual in public turned out to be gay secretly. Reverend Clayton Russell, of the People's Independent Church of Christ, whom Otis admired tremendously, married a beautiful Black woman and was often seen in the company of some of the most attractive female members of his church. Yet according to pianist Hadda Brooks, who belonged to the church and had been the pastor's neighbor while growing up in Boyle Heights, "All the girls wanted him, but the hell of it is he was, the word is 'open' now—he was on the gay side. He didn't flaunt it. I don't think very many people knew."[23]

Singer and pianist Charles Brown often frequented local racetracks accompanied by attractive women who helped him make thousand-dollar bets on his favorite horses. He married fellow musician Mabel Scott in 1949 in an elaborate ceremony. Later he also wed a white woman, Eva McGhee. According to journalist R. J. Smith, however, Brown was also a gay man. Scott described Brown as the love of her life, adding, "But I wouldn't marry him again. That's for sure."[24] Brown described his marriage to McGhee as an alliance between "good friends." "It wasn't really love," he confided. "I learned to like her very much because she was a real great person. As you stay with a person, you learn to love 'em."[25] Some performers did not hide their desires for same-sex partners. Guitarist and composer Earl King remembers that Little Richard and James Booker frequently cruised up and down Canal Street in New Orleans in Richard's robin's egg blue Cadillac convertible, "hollering and carrying on like the two biggest sissies in the world."[26]

As a proponent of social justice, Otis did not think he should allow himself to become complicit in the dehumanization of any group of people. It bothered him when he heard anti-gay remarks. One day in San Diego, the connectedness of different struggles for human rights made itself evident to him. On the way to a performance, he rode with his band in a bus that moved slowly through traffic in downtown San Diego. Outside on the street, a group of marines were assaulting two men who appeared to be gay. Shouts of "stop this bus" and "open the doors" rang out from some members of the band. Otis was not sure if his band members wanted to stop the beating or join in on it. For years, he had heard them repeatedly insulting one another by using a term that signified that the target of the remarks was either gay or otherwise "unmanly." When they exited the bus and joined the fray, however, his musicians pulled the marines off their victims and sent them away. Then they stayed long enough to make sure that the victims of the beating did not need to be taken to a hospital for treatment. When his musicians boarded the bus, Johnny made an announcement. "First of all, I want to say that I have never been prouder of this band than I am right now. You did a wonderful thing. But second of all, I've got to know why you did it. I've never seen any of you care at all about what happens to people like that." There was a moment of silence on the bus as the musicians contemplated what they had done. Then one stood up and spoke out. "You don't understand, Johnny," he said, pointing to the Black skin on his arm, "that's what they do to us."[27] For one moment, at least, the fact of victimization had become more important to them than the identity of the victim. In the heat of the fracas, the sexuality of the victims seemed less important to the Black band members than their identity as other humans facing the kinds of brutality and hatred that Black people knew well. In that instant, the Black musicians in the band recognized that they were imperiled when the basic dignity of any other human was compromised. That recognition spoke to something very deep inside Johnny Otis. It was the kind of thinking that helped propel him toward an unexpected but deeply felt new identity: as a preacher in his own Holiness church.

Although the doctrine and practices of his family's Greek Orthodox faith had little appeal for him when he was growing up, Otis deeply valued the ethical grounding that his family's piety provided. "I was taught as a child that God was a just God," he told readers of his *Sentinel* column in 1960. "I believe that today as firmly as I did then."[28] When he visited his friends' sanctified churches, he heard the same message. As a working musician in Black bands, he could not help but see the religious underpinnings of the music he played. Yet Otis remained suspicious of organized religion, because he saw a huge chasm between the things that pastors said on Sunday mornings and the things that they and their parishioners practiced during the other days of the week. Moreover, many of the main enemies of his music had launched their condemnations from the pulpit. During one Sunday morning service at the Mount Sinai Missionary Baptist Church in Los Angeles, Johnny sat in a pew next to Sam Cooke. Before he began his sermon, Reverend H. B. Charles noted the presence of Cooke and Otis at the service. Pointing a finger at them, he expressed his prayer that one day they would give up the devil's music and return to the Lord. Sam whispered in Johnny's ear, "We've got to get out of here," and the two got up and walked quietly out of the church. When they stepped outside, Johnny remembers telling Sam, "Well, maybe someday we'll just have to form a church of our own."[29]

Otis found himself feeling more and more that many of the questions that concerned him were essentially matters of religion. He noted with approval that the Pilgrim Travelers gospel group sang benefit concerts for the Montgomery Bus Boycott and offered prayers at concerts for Autherine Lucy while she attempted to become the first African American to enroll at the University of Alabama.[30] Gospel singer Dorothy Love Coates (who sang with the Harmonettes) openly and enthusiastically supported the

Black freedom movement. The mother of trombonist Gene Connors, who played in Otis's band, was also a member of the Harmonettes. In an impassioned column in the *Sentinel* written as the civil rights struggle unfolded in Los Angeles, Otis recognized and saluted the "wonderful new kind of Negro ministers" emerging in the city. Identifying the militancy of activist pastors as "a product of the struggle for freedom," Otis observed that the scriptures authorize struggles for social justice. He insisted that "the Bible teaches us to be our brother's keeper and live according to the Christian concepts of the brotherhood of man." Yet Otis offered a more radical interpretation of the Bible than many of the ministers whom he praised. Noting that God was on the side of social justice and that the power of prayer was important, he added nonetheless, "I don't believe that God means for us to spend ALL of our time on our knees. He gave us ARMS, LEGS, EYES, EARS, VOICES and INTELLIGENCE and we should STAND UP AND USE THEM!! Right now, when there seems to be a national bid for Negro freedom, now is the time for us to move!"[31]

At the start of the 1970s, Otis juggled his ongoing career as a performer, producer, and promoter with activism on social issues. He worked on Mervyn Dymally's campaign to be elected to the office of lieutenant governor in California in 1974 and played a role in his old friend's victory. "When we were going around to the cities before I took office," Dymally remembers, "people would recognize him before they'd recognize me, because some of these big city managers were kids when Johnny was really big."[32] Otis stopped his work as a musician in 1978 to serve as chief of staff in Dymally's office and worked on the lieutenant governor's reelection bid that year. Dymally lost, and Otis believed that his race accounted for the reason why. When Dymally won office in 1974 as the first African American elected to statewide office in the Golden State, his picture appeared on none of his campaign literature, and he avoided photo opportunities so that voters opposed to Blacks would have less incentive to oppose him. During his four years as lieutenant governor, however, his racial identity became well known. In addition, days before the election, an opponent circulated a false report that Dymally was about to be indicted. Although the rumor was false, the damage was done. Dymally drew only 43 percent of the vote and was defeated for reelection by Mike Curb, a conservative Republican and record company executive. Dymally's running mate, Governor Jerry Brown, easily won reelection with 56 percent of the vote.

Dymally's defeat, the rightward drift of state and national politics, and the persistent refusal to enforce civil rights laws and court rulings by local, state, and federal officials soured Otis on politics. Yet when Dymally won election to the U.S. House of Representatives in 1980, Otis supervised constituent services in the congressman's Hawthorne office. He called what he did "social work," helping residents of the district deal with the bureaucracies at the Veterans Administration and Social Security Administration. On one occasion, representatives of the coalition seeking reparations for Japanese Americans who had been placed in internment camps met with Dymally and Otis. Miya Iwataki remembers that as she unlocked the door to the room where the meeting with Dymally was scheduled to take place, at the Japanese American Cultural and Community Center in downtown Los Angeles, the elevator doors opened and a man stepped out and said, "Hi, I'm Johnny Otis. I work with Congressman Dymally. He's on his way." Iwataki exclaimed, "THE Johnny Otis!" and sang his theme song, "Johnny Otis, Johnny Otis." Jim Matsuoka exclaimed, "Wow. Johnny Otis. Hey, I know you!" When Dymally arrived, Johnny proudly turned to the congressman and said, "Hey, Merv. They know me!" The meeting led to a long alliance between the congressman and the National Coalition for Redress and Reparations, which eventually secured a government apology and payments to people who had been placed in the camps.[33]

Otis viewed his work in Dymally's office as useful but limited. Increasingly, he turned his attention to religion. In 1974 Pentecostal evangelist Mother Bernice Smith suggested to Johnny Otis that he should become a minister. The advice struck him as humorous. He thought of preachers as solemn and sedate, as people capable of distancing themselves from earthly pleasures. Preachers were not people like Johnny Otis. He liked to sing, to play music, to make love, to cook, to tell stories, to use the language of the streets. "I should become a preacher?" he asked Smith, incredulously. "As what, Reverend Hand Jive?" Smith persisted, however, pointing out that Johnny took seriously the biblical commands to feed the hungry, to house the homeless, to visit people imprisoned, to clothe those who were naked. She reminded Johnny that Jesus came into the world to make one blood of all nations, that the Savior's most important injunction to his followers was "to love one another." She agreed with Johnny that too many churches were caught up in their own pride and vanity, what he often described as the "ain't nobody going to heaven but us nonsense." Mother

Smith introduced him to a different kind of religion. "She felt we should be dealing with things other than how to build a pedestal to stand taller than someone else, and maybe we should be reaching down to those folk who need help."[34] Mother Bernice Smith ordained Johnny Otis as a Holiness preacher, and soon he started his own sanctified church.

Otis's journey from his youth as a reluctant member of the Greek Orthodox Church to his young adulthood as a free thinker skeptical of all religion would not seem to predict his maturity as a member of the clergy and a pastor of a devout congregation in the Pentecostal faith. Yet his trajectory was not as strange as it seems. From the moment he arrived in Los Angeles, he had been moved by the activism of Reverend Clayton Russell, "the fighting pastor," whose People's Independent Church matched noble words with noble deeds, serving the community in many ways. He noted how Russell's church set up consumer buying cooperatives, provided relief for the unemployed, and established a home for orphaned and abandoned boys. Russell combined professions of faith with good works and activism, such as his efforts during World War II in creating the People's Victory Committee, an activist group that challenged racial and gender discrimination in employment and housing.[35]

In Holiness religion, Otis discovered a faith that spoke to his deepest concerns: his passion for racial justice, his commitment to egalitarian and democratic practices, and his belief in the centrality of music to the human spirit and soul. Pentecostals like Mother Bernice Smith traced their commitments back to the Azusa Street Revival, which began in Los Angeles in 1906. An interracial outpouring of faith that began in a Black church, the revival was propelled primarily by the faith of Black women working as domestics and laundresses. It transgressed the racial and class barriers of its day. White people of Russian, German, and Jewish ancestry prayed together with Chinese, Mexican, and Native American worshippers in services led by Black parishioners and preachers. Social distinctions seemed to disappear as men and women addressed each other as "brother" and "sister," spoke about their fellow congregants as "saints," and greeted one another with a "holy kiss" on the cheek.[36] W. H. Seymour played a key role in the revival. A Black preacher born in Louisiana to parents who had been slaves, Seymour dispensed with the practice of taking up collections during services. Yet participants left money for his Apostolic Faith Mission anyway.[37] At the revival's services, people with wealth and prestige welcomed the poor to worship with them in creative and productive fellowship.[38]

Early Pentecostalism challenged the power hierarchies of this world directly through its preferred worship practices. Breaking sharply with the segregated nature of churches of the time, Reverend Seymour insisted that people of all races would be welcome at his services, that women would be allowed to testify and preach, and that displays of status and wealth would have no place in his church. Seymour cited divine support for these views, noting, "The work began among the colored people. God baptized several sanctified wash women with the Holy Ghost, who have been much used of Him."[39]

Although white Pentecostal parishioners and congregations for the most part eventually broke away from their Black brethren to form their own segregated churches, Black Pentecostalism continued to serve as a crucible for democracy and social justice. In established denominations such as the Church of God in Christ (which today claims more than five million members), and in hundreds of humble store-front churches organized only at the local level, Pentecostal churches offered distinct alternatives to the practices and premises of materialism, hierarchy, and white supremacy so powerful in the rest of U.S. society. Belief in spirit possession and speaking in tongues often conveyed democratic principles, because church members presumed that the Holy Spirit could strike anyone in the congregation, even those who were least educated, undermining the authority of the specialized ecclesiastical language of the clergy. Pentecostal practices challenged the surface appearances of prevailing social conditions to posit a deeper reality of piety accessible through spirit possession, dances, songs, dreams, and healing and based on what theologian Harvey Cox calls "primal hope": a refusal to believe that the appearances and social relations of this world are all that exist.[40]

Otis started his own church in the building that had once been his home at 2077 Harvard, in the Sugar Hill neighborhood. He had moved out months before the 1965 riots because the old place had become too expensive to maintain as a residence, and he hoped he could defray its expenses by leasing it out as a business. City officials had rezoned the neighborhood for apartments and commercial businesses, which meant that the building's tax assessment increased. When the basement furnace failed, he could not afford to fix it. So he leased the property out as a home for the elderly, figuring that a business that made money from the building could pay for the necessary furnace repairs and the taxes. Now he decided to return to the building, to convert the property for use as a church.

The Landmark Community Church stood unobtrusively in the middle of a quiet, mostly residential street. Otis conducted church services on the very same property where years before he had written "Hand Jive" and recorded "So Fine." He established a gospel choir under the direction of David Pridgen and started to preach about love, forgiveness, and brotherhood. "I'm not a great Biblical scholar," he would tell his congregation. "But I know in my heart, when we take care of each other, we are pleasing God."[41] Two important messages of the church were "come as you are" and "no one turned away." There was no need to dress up, no pressure to compete with others over who had the fanciest clothes or the most money, and no reason to feel shame about having human problems, about being an alcoholic or having a drug habit: no one was turned away. Services were short and filled with music. The church collected money for itself and for programs to serve the public, but no direct spoken appeals were made for monetary donations during services. Unlike many churches, the doors remained open when the collection plate was passed, so people could leave if they so chose as the plate passed through the room unobtrusively. Pastor Otis also kept his sermons short. "I don't go around giving sermons or bugging people. In our church, we believe in witnessing by example, not exhortation. We believe in teaching by example, in treating other people right—that's the important thing," he proclaimed.[42] Otis encouraged the congregation to play a large and active role in worship. The congregation believed that one sign of God's grace is the ability to be possessed by the Holy Spirit and to speak in tongues, and sometimes during the services people displayed the Lord's presence in this way. Above all, the church focused on connecting with the community, on serving God by loving others.

In his sermons, Otis insisted on justice, love, and personal responsibility. He attempted to create a Christianity "in action" that motivated people to take steps in their lives away from the church building, out in the wider community. "Our church doesn't try to tie people up in knots by emphasizing that you can't do this, can't do that, and so on—we just try to love one another," he explained.[43] Otis tried to motivate parishioners to help feed the hungry, house the homeless, and visit those who were imprisoned, to forge a feeling of connectedness and common purpose, and to practice forms of love and acceptance of others that went beyond mere tolerance. Little Esther, by then known as Esther Phillips, became the first person to join the congregation. She had recorded a song titled "Wedding Boogie" when she was fourteen, as part of what the record label termed the "Johnny Otis Congregation." Now as an adult, she was part of another Johnny Otis congregation, this time a real one. Struggling with alcohol and drug addictions that would contribute to her death in 1984, Phillips's life came full circle in a way, as she spent her last years trying to heal herself close to the person who had set her on the road to stardom in her youth.

Like Clayton Russell's People's Independent Church of Christ thirty years earlier and unlike many of the Black churches in Los Angeles in the 1970s, Landmark welcomed people from show business as members of the congregation and participants in services. Otis attracted many performers to attend, sing, and play music at Landmark Community Church services. Church members included Etta James, Bardu Ali, keyboardist Jimmy Smith, comic actor Lawanda Page (best known for her portrayal of the ultrareligious Aunt Esther on the television program *Sanford and Son*), trombonist Henry Coker, and the jazz pianist known as King Pleasure. At one time, the church choir included Ketty Lester, the Three Tons of Joy, Delmar Evans, Harold Lewis (formerly of the Drifters), and Mary "Coco" Haynes (who was Bo Diddley's niece).[44] Despite the presence of these well-known artists, however, the church drew most of its membership from outside show business, from the working-class and middle-class Black neighborhoods that surrounded it. Some members of the congregation did not even know that Johnny Otis had been an entertainer, and many who knew did not care. Although the congregation was overwhelmingly Black and its services drew directly on long traditions of worship in Black communities, Landmark Community Church attracted members of other groups as well. Otis's ecumenicism was so pronounced that even three Jews and two Buddhists were members of the congregation.

Kim Hester-Williams, now associate professor and chair of the Department of English at Sonoma State University, grew up in a family that belonged to the congregation at the Landmark Community Church. As a child she did not know initially that Johnny Otis had come to the pulpit from a career in show business. To her, he was simply Pastor Otis. Hester-Williams's mother, Mary Hester, had previously been a Methodist and a Baptist but had not found any church up to that point that spoke directly to her spiritual needs and desires the way that Landmark did. She was what her daughter calls "a Matthew Christian," a pacifist who believed in a God that blessed the peacemakers, drove the money changers from the temple, and taught that "whatever you do to the least of my beings, you do to me." Hester-Williams remembers that one day when she was a child walking downtown with her mother, they came across a derelict on the sidewalk who had defecated on himself. Frightened and repulsed, young Kim frowned at the sight. "Don't do that," her mother warned, "don't judge. That could be Jesus."[45]

At the Landmark Community Church, Mary Hester found a theology that matched her own. In her view, a church that said "come as you are" and turned no one away practiced what many other Christians only preached. Hester appreciated the lack of pretense and the warm fellowship that discouraged status competition among members of the congregation. Most of all, Mary Hester appreciated the message that the pastor preached: that what counted was what was in your heart, and that the way you demonstrated your piety was to connect with the broader community and help people.

Mary's daughter Kim distinguished herself as a prize pupil in Landmark's Sunday school. She became a Sunday school teacher herself. Although initially she had wished that her family belonged to one of the big showy churches her friends belonged to, like the Cornerstone Baptist Church, presided over by Reverend James Cleveland, a preacher who gave the kinds of sermons Kim expected to hear in a church, she soon found herself persuaded and moved by Landmark's humble version of Christianity. Pastor Otis's sermons were short and plain spoken but extremely effective in their own way. Housed in an ordinary dwelling on a residential street, the church emphasized getting out into the world. Baptismal ceremonies were conducted in the Pacific Ocean. Excursions took the congregation to picnics all over the metropolitan area. These trips were ways to transcend the small size of the church itself, but they also reflected Otis's belief in a kind of Christianity that extended beyond the boundaries of the sanctuary to take action in the world. Members of Landmark's congregation passed out free food to about a thousand homeless people in downtown Los Angeles every Saturday for nearly a decade.

When he worked in his upstairs office in the church, Otis enjoyed the company of his pet African gray parrot, Jomo. The bird convincingly mimicked the voice of Otis's parishioner and friend Delmar Evans. On more than one occasion, Otis ran upstairs to his office because he thought he heard Evans's voice calling out "Hey Rev!" when in fact it was only the parrot. Jomo echoed the religious songs that the cleaning lady sang as she did her work in the church, exclaiming, "My soul is a witness!" in between verses.

Johnny Otis playing drums with Count Otis Matthews and his West Oakland House
Stompers, 1941.

Johnny Otis's twenty-first birthday party, 1942.

With Joe Louis at the Club Alabam, on Central Avenue. *Left to right:* Johnny Otis, John Thomas, unknown woman, Joe Louis, Leonard Reed, and Chalky Wright. Photograph by Tom Reed; reprinted with permission.

With Gerald Wilson in Los Angeles, 1946.

JOHNNY OTIS
and his ORCHESTRA

UNIVERSAL ATTRACTIONS
347 Madison Ave New York, 17, N.Y.

The Johnny Otis Orchestra, 1950. *Left to right:* Mario Delagarde, Pete Lewis, Lady Dee Williams, Don Johnson, Johnny Otis, Lorenzo Holden, Walter Henry, and Lee Graves.

The Johnny Otis Show in Atlanta with Little Esther, 1951.

Johnny Otis and Little Willie John, circa 1953.

Johnny Otis playing baseball with Little Arthur Matthews and Big Mama Thornton.

The Johnny Otis Show with Big Mama Thornton, El Paso, Texas, 1952.

Johnny Otis and Big Mama Thornton at the Apollo Theatre, New York, 1954.

Johnny Otis and "Handsome Mel" Williams.

Johnny Otis and Red Foxx, 1956.

Johnny Otis and Sam Cooke, 1957.

Johnny Otis and Shuggie Otis, circa 1957.

With the Three Tons of Joy. *Left to right:* Francielle Jones, Marie Adams, Johnny Otis, and Doris Easter, circa 1959.

Left to right: Bardu Ali, Ella Fitzgerald, Johnny Otis, and Shuggie Otis, 1962.

Picketing in support of southern lunch-counter sit-ins, 1960.

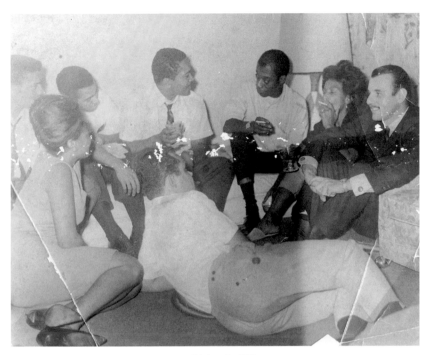

Discussion with James Baldwin *(center right)*, early 1960s.

On the set of the televised *Johnny Otis Show*, circa 1960.

Kim Hester-Williams with her Landmark Community Church Sunday school class.

Johnny Otis and Barbara Morrison, 1975.

Johnny Otis and Screamin' Jay Hawkins, 1984.

Little Milton visiting the Black Music Class at Club Ashkenaz, in Berkeley, California, 2001.

Even the conversations that wafted through the window on hot summer nights from the county home for developmentally challenged and developmentally disabled adults next door to the church became part of Jomo's repertoire. One elderly man howled like a wolf. He frequently sat outside with a companion who used an obscene phrase in telling him to keep quiet. This evidently made a big impression on the parrot. During one meeting in his office, Otis spoke with three church women to discuss an upcoming event. Jomo shouted out, "My soul is a witness!" The women laughed and one volunteered, "Ooh, Pastor. You've got a spiritual parrot!" Her exclamation "Ooh" evidently reminded Jomo of the two men from the home next door, because he then blurted out, "Shut up, mother––!"[46]

Otis devoted large segments of his services to the choir and the extremely skilled musicians who backed them up. The choir featured many superb singers, and the band included drums, brass, and reed instruments. People would get the spirit when the band played and the choir sang. Sometimes, some of them fainted, overcome by religious ecstasy. At the end of every Sunday service, Otis and the congregation walked out of the church singing "I Am a Soldier in the Army of the Lord."

As a teenaged Sunday school teacher, Kim Hester had the responsibility of preparing the younger children to appear in public. Her students stood before the entire congregation to present the lessons they had learned in her classes. The children learned to recite in public, put on plays, and perform music. When she was in junior high school, Hester was given the assignment of conducting an oral history interview with someone she respected. She chose Pastor Otis. When it came time for the interview, it became clear that she did not know enough about his life to know what questions to ask. Otis explained to her that she needed to do better preparation to conduct an interview. "He had faith in me, and I disappointed him," she remembers.[47] She made it a point to be prepared after that, a lesson that served her well as she went on to a distinguished academic career.

As a young parishioner, Kim noticed that the congregation was also remarkable for its diversity. Pastor Otis was white, but his family was Black. Blue-eyed, blond Mark Winship played the drums for a congregation that was mostly Black. In keeping with the church mottoes "come as you are" and "no one turned away," the congregation had gay and lesbian members. "Acceptance for differences in sexual orientation was something that I learned at Landmark," Hester-Williams recalls.[48]

Hester's experiences at Landmark Community Church played a vital role in shaping her success as an adult. She remembers in particular how the church helped her deal with one traumatic experience. Because her parents had high aspirations for her, they took advantage of the desegregation plan for the Los Angeles Unified School District that enabled Black students to be transported by bus to schools that offered opportunities not available in their neighborhoods. Her parents enrolled Kim in a program that took her to a school in a white neighborhood in the faraway San Fernando Valley. Before she arrived at school on the first day, the school building had been defaced by graffiti that read, "NIGGERS GO HOME." The treatment she received in her new school showed Hester that the sentiment written on the school's wall was shared by many of the students and teachers. She felt that if it had not been for her experiences at Landmark, she might have believed from the evidence available to her that all white people felt that way. The multiracial congregation she belonged to at Pastor Otis's church, however, had taught her otherwise. Armed with the self-confidence she had learned at Landmark, she went on to do undergraduate work at the University of California, Santa Cruz, and then to receive a doctorate in literature from the University of California, San Diego. Her pastor helped her see that education was important, that with discipline and hard work she could realize her potential. Today, as Kim Hester-Williams, she teaches these same lessons to her students of all races at Sonoma State University.

Others of Otis's parishioners also were unaware that he had been an entertainer before becoming a preacher. At some moments, however, his past and present lives came together. Big Mama Thornton asked Johnny to preside over her funeral if she died before he did. "Keep smilin' and keep it short," she advised. On July 25, 1984, Thornton suffered a massive heart attack and passed away at the age of fifty-seven. A few months before her death Thornton had walked into the studio to participate in Johnny's radio show, and he did not even recognize her because she looked so thin and drawn. She died penniless in the Los Angeles boardinghouse where she lived. Drinking Jack Daniels whiskey with her sister and a couple of friends, she put her head down on the table to rest and never got up. Gus Jenkins, who had often accompanied her on piano, told reporters, "Big Mama was angry to the end. She never made any real money. Not the kind of money she should have made. She was a legend. But the music industry used Big Mama. It is a disgrace—that she was never properly rewarded for her work."[49]

Otis conducted Thornton's funeral service at the Connor-Johnson Mortuary, on Avalon Boulevard. Looking down at her casket, where she lay in repose in a peach dress, Otis reflected on his deep admiration for his departed friend. When the service ended, Johnny had tears streaming down his face. A member of his congregation tried to comfort him, saying she knew how much Johnny loved Big Mama and how badly he must feel about her death. "Big Mama has gone to a better place," she said to console him. Johnny was not crying, however, because he was sad or because he missed Big Mama. In thinking about the life he had led, the friends he had made, the rich community that he got to be part of, his tears were tears of happiness. He thought, "I'm so lucky to be a part of this."[50]

Two weeks later, Esther Phillips died of liver and kidney ailments at the age of forty-eight. Once again, Pastor Otis led the congregation in saying good-bye to a dear friend, a magnificent artist who never received her just recognition or reward from the music industry. At the funerals of Big Mama Thornton and Esther Phillips, Pastor Otis carried out his biblically inspired obligation to comfort the afflicted. As he looked at the devastation that the Reagan administration and its policies enacted on the ghetto, however, he wondered if perhaps his work did not also require him to challenge the increasingly unjust, indecent, and racist social order he saw gaining strength around him every day. As Dr. King had observed decades previously, it is important to comfort the afflicted, but a just God would also want us to pursue social justice, even if that requires us to afflict the comfortable sometimes. Dissatisfied because he perceived that too many of his parishioners wanted to live more comfortably in a fundamentally unjust society, Pastor Otis disbanded Landmark Community Church and looked for other ways to carry out his mission.

He had started recording again in 1981, when he made *The New Johnny Otis Show* for Alligator Records. His return to performing surprised him somewhat. "I'd been immersed for years in trying to put that church together. I'd sold my tour bus. I'd really given up and I buried my disappointment. I just wouldn't think about it because it really hurt to think that I'd never be able to play again and that the stuff we did had no interest for anyone."[51] The new album sold well and earned a Grammy nomination. Yet music would never again fully consume Otis's energies. Over the next twenty-five years he would continue to perform and record, but he also devoted himself to radio work, creating visual art, and teaching the things he had learned over the years to new generations of listeners, fans, and followers.

$\mathcal{Six}$ PLAY MISTY FOR ME

 Johnny Otis's music and radio broadcasting endeavors owed their origins to one magic moment in 1970. A representation of that day has been preserved in a scene near the end of Clint Eastwood's 1971 motion picture, *Play Misty for Me*. The film's protagonist (Dave Garver, played by Eastwood) enters the grounds of the Monterey Jazz Festival while the Johnny Otis Show is performing onstage. The camera pans in on Gene Connors (aka the Mighty Flea) displaying his trombone talents on the song "Preacher's Blues."[1] When the selection ends, we hear Johnny Otis's voice (off-camera) asking for a round of applause for the Mighty Flea, saluting his triple-tonguing technique. "Let's give his tongue a hand!" Johnny implores. Clint Eastwood then re-enters the scene accompanied by his love interest, played by Donna Mills. The couple walk through the crowd, showing themselves at ease among Black people. A sound bridge introduces the first notes of "Willie and the Hand Jive," but we do not see the band until almost the end of the first verse. Instead, the camera focuses on Blacks joyfully dancing, clapping, and bouncing to the hand jive beat.

Eastwood's film is a remarkable cinematic triumph in many ways, but the brief snippet it presents of the Johnny Otis Orchestra also contains evidence of another triumph. The 1970 Monterey Jazz Festival contained a drama of its own. The performance by the Johnny Otis Show captured in *Play Misty for Me* launched a new and important direction in Otis's career, one that would have a lasting effect in shaping the meaning of Black music for millions of people. For the performance at Monterey, Otis assembled an all-star troupe of performers from the glory days of rhythm and blues in the 1940s and 1950s. With his old friend Preston Love playing alto and baritone saxophones, Otis brought together a band designed to demonstrate the difference between popular music's shunned, neglected, and ignored Black originators and its celebrated, prosperous, and successful white imitators. The band that performed at Monterey featured the blues singing and playing of Esther Phillips, Pee Wee Crayton, Roy Milton, Eddie Cleanhead Vinson, Joe Turner, and Ivory Joe Hunter, backed by a roster of instrumentalists and vocalists from Otis's old and new ensembles. In addition to the talent of Gene "Mighty Flea" Connors on the trombone, the performance displayed the singing of Delmar "Mighty Mouth" Evans and the virtuosity of instrumentalists Clifford Solomon on tenor saxophone and Big Jim Wynn on baritone saxophone.

The performers spanned eras and ages. Artists in their late fifties and early sixties, including Roy Milton, Big Joe Turner, and Pee Wee Crayton, played the music that had made them famous in the 1940s, and sixteen-year-old Shuggie Otis played blistering blues guitar to demonstrate a new generation's interpretation of this rich tradition. It was one of those days in which everything worked; each musician gave a superb performance and inspired others to reach new heights. Released as an album on Epic Records as *The Johnny Otis Show Live in Monterey!*, the performance announced a new direction in Johnny Otis's career, one that would consume a significant part of his energies for the next thirty years.[2]

At a time when clever promoters recognized that "golden oldies" from the 1950s had nostalgic appeal for baby boomers entering their young adult years, Otis tried to offer an alternative understanding of the music that so many people loved. He wanted to challenge nostalgia and promote a deeper historical understanding. Onstage at Monterey, in a series of recordings that he produced for his Blues Spectrum label, and on weekly broadcasts on public radio, Otis identified popular music unambiguously as the creation of Black people. He played music and interviewed musicians to demonstrate the blues, gospel, and jazz roots of rock 'n' roll, placing in front of the public the artistry of singers, musicians, and composers who by that time had become largely neglected by the commercial music industry.

During the 1960s, the success of the Beatles and the Rolling Stones included the rediscovery and repackaging of musical forms, devices, and styles from 1940s and 1950s blues, country, and rhythm and blues music. The Beatles covered songs by Little Richard, the Isley Brothers, and Carl

Perkins. The Rolling Stones took their name from a Muddy Waters song and recorded "2120 South Michigan Avenue," a tribute to the Chess and Checker record studios at that street address in Chicago. As the huge cohort of baby boomers, born between 1945 and 1960, grew up, the rock 'n' roll music they knew as children grew up too, evolving into a music for young adults marketed as rock. The Beatles and the Rolling Stones made overt political statements in the lyrics of their songs. Multitrack recording and elaborate studio productions brought a wide range of special effects, orchestral harmonies, and guitar-based power chords into popular music. Sales of recorded music increased dramatically during these years, enabling Elvis Presley, the Beatles, the Rolling Stones, the Beach Boys, Janis Joplin, the Jefferson Airplane, and others to reap a rich harvest from seeds sown by Little Esther, T-Bone Walker, Big Mama Thornton, and Bo Diddley. The emergence of rock as the industry's dominant commercial form seemed like a generational victory to many consumers, a validation of their childhood tastes and preferences. They had little incentive, however, to recognize the racial origins or social implications of the music they loved.

Promoters of rock 'n' roll revival shows stepped up to meet consumer interest in the origins of the musical forms that had become triumphant and dominant. On October 18, 1969, promoter Richard Nader staged a rock 'n' roll revival show at Madison Square Garden. The evening's entertainment celebrated the golden age of 1950s rock 'n' roll. The show staged performances designed to evoke nostalgia among members of the baby boom generation, emphasizing the audience members' memories of their teen years. The event sold out. Nader's production proved so popular that he repeated it over and over again in the years that followed. His "Rock 'n' Roll Revival" became the longest-running continuous event in the history of Madison Square Garden, eventually attracting four hundred thousand customers to twenty-five different performances. Nader then took the show on the road for performances in municipal arenas, on college campuses, and in Las Vegas nightclubs. A representative performance is captured in the 1973 documentary film *Let the Good Times Roll,* featuring Little Richard, Chuck Berry, Bo Diddley, Fats Domino, Chubby Checker, the Five Satins, the Shirelles, and Bill Haley and His Comets. Recognizing the demographic bulge that gave the baby boom generation disproportionate market power, some radio programmers started to adopt "oldies" formats designed to make nostalgia for the 1950s and early 1960s a marketable commodity in the 1970s and 1980s. The television shows *Happy Days* and

Wonder Years followed this pattern, as did a series of Hollywood films, including *Grease, Hairspray,* and *Dirty Dancing.*

This revival did important work in honoring and augmenting the commercial viability of great artists who had not placed hits on the best-seller charts in years. It reacquainted music fans with the consummate artistry of performers like Little Richard, Bo Diddley, and Chuck Berry, and it introduced these artists to a new generation of listeners. The revival genre, however, marketed the music through the eyes of its target audience, affluent white suburbians, evoking nostalgia for their youthful innocence and consumer memories. It privileged the experiences of the music's 1950s' teenage suburban consumers over those of its adult inner-city producers, gesturing toward malt shop jukeboxes, after-school dance parties, car cruising, and AM radio stations rather than the atmosphere at inner-city bandstands, dance halls, and nightclubs. It especially promoted the artists who had broken through to white audiences, not those validated by Black dancers and listeners. Dick Clark's *American Bandstand* television program and the artists it endorsed—Chubby Checker, Frankie Avalon, and Bobby Rydell—became the remembered pinnacle of popular music history in this framework. Young white consumers congratulated themselves for their triumph as a market segment, for the victory of 1960s rock over 1950s pop, without taking stock of the struggles, suffering, and sacrifices of the Black artists who produced the music in the first place.

The rock 'n' roll revival circuit provided lucrative opportunities for veteran artists willing to sing their old hits in nostalgic settings, and it opened up new streams of revenue for 1970s artists whose performances campily reenacted elements of the 1950s. Producers of rock 'n' roll revival shows onstage, in television, and in film, musicians like the group Sha Na Na, and the producers, actors, singers, and dancers in films like *Grease* profited greatly from this trend. Yet these successes did nothing to right the wrongs done to the original rhythm and blues artists who made the music popular initially, who had been systematically cheated out of royalties by unscrupulous record companies, and whose skin color and phenotype prevented them from playing in the venues that welcomed the Beatles and the Beach Boys. While the revival circuit boomed in the 1970s, Pee Wee Crayton drove a freight truck, because he could no longer make a living from his music. Big Jay McNeely stopped playing music and started work at the post office. Charles Brown, whose hits "Drifting Blues" and "Come Home for Christmas" greatly influenced the singing style of balladeers and doo-wop groups alike on the revival circuit, spent his days in the early 1970s working as a window washer and a janitor. He lived in a tiny apartment rented for eighty dollars per month, even though he had lost none of his musical talents. Brown's professional career had been interrupted in the late 1950s when an engagement near Cincinnati at a gambling club owned by a racketeer turned into a period of involuntary indentured servitude. When Brown informed the club owner in 1961 that he wanted to go on the road to tour with Dinah Washington, the mobster replied that of course Brown *could* leave but noted that he would receive a bullet in the head if did. Brown decided to stay on as a regular entertainer in the club.[3]

Johnny Otis's friend Preston Love found himself scrambling for music jobs during most of the 1960s, ending up as a member of the band that accompanied Motown artists on their West Coast tours. Love genuinely admired and respected the talents of Marvin Gaye, the Temptations, and the Four Tops, but he wondered why music by other artists with lesser talent outsold works of art by gifted originators. It amazed Love to see how association with the Jefferson Airplane enabled the modestly talented Papa John Creach to earn large sums of money playing his violin with rock musicians. Although happy for Creach's success, Love recoiled at the stage image the Airplane assigned to Creach as "Papa John," more of a minstrel-like mascot than a valued member of the band.[4]

Johnny Otis had seen white artists and entrepreneurs derive disproportionate rewards from Black music all his life. He remembered wondering as a youth how Paul Whiteman could be billed as the King of Jazz when Louis Armstrong played the real thing, or how Benny Goodman could be known as the King of Swing in a musical universe that included Fletcher Henderson, Count Basie, and Duke Ellington. As a producer, Otis watched as the "cover" system combined with censorship to enable inferior recordings by Georgia Gibbs and Pat Boone to outsell the vastly superior originals by Etta James and Little Richard. As a disc jockey, he saw Dick Clark become the national arbiter of which records got played on radio and television, when Black disc jockeys Jocko Henderson, Spider Burks, Martha Jean the Queen, and Tom Reed clearly knew more about music and programmed their shows accordingly. Moreover, it was not just a matter of the embodied identities of individuals. These issues raised questions about justice and culture to him, not just questions about color. Otis respected the white musicians who had mastered Black styles, such as drummer Dave Tough, pianist Mose Allison, and saxophonist Zoot Sims. He felt that whites had valuable roles to play as interpreters and promoters of Black music, but only if they acknowledged and honored the community that had created it in the first place.

With his band's performance at the 1970 Monterey Jazz Festival, Johnny Otis launched a campaign to right the wrongs that he had seen committed by the music industry throughout his life. Otis used performance venues, recording studios, and radio broadcasts as his preferred sites for an extended exercise in adult education, for one long, continuous, entertaining, and impassioned seminar about Black music and Black culture. Otis felt that it fell to him to tell the story correctly, because the commercial music industry and the music journalists who depended on the favor of that industry for their own professional advancement had told the story mistakenly and even dishonestly. On records and in live appearances, Otis especially featured the artistry of Roy Brown, Charles Brown, Eddie "Cleanhead" Vinson, Joe Turner, and T-Bone Walker. "These men are national treasures," he told a British writer, "and the way they've been treated is a national disgrace."[5] Throughout the 1970s, Otis produced and played on a series of recordings titled *Great Rhythm and Blues Oldies* for his Blues Spectrum Record label, featuring Charles Brown, Pee Wee Crayton, Louis Jordan, Joe Liggins, Amos Milburn, Roy Milton, Gatemouth Moore, Joe Turner, and Eddie "Cleanhead" Vinson. For some of these performers, the new opportunity came too late. Milburn recorded his album while suffering from the effects of his second stroke in two years. He could play the right-hand parts on the piano but needed Johnny to sit next to him and play the left-hand parts to make the record. The Blues Spectrum oldies records introduced a new generation of consumers to the artistry of early rhythm and blues, creating a market segment below the radar of the major recording company executives and radio and television programmers. Otis's efforts brought belated recognition and reward to underappreciated artists. He made it possible for music listeners to appreciate the blues origins of much of the music made popular by the Beatles, the Rolling Stones, Janis Joplin, and Jimi Hendrix.

John Otis Jr., better known as Shuggie Otis, played an important role in the bridge between generations that Johnny constructed during the 1970s. At the age of four, Shuggie had started playing on a miniature, white pearl, three-piece drum set that his father bought him for Christmas. One day, T-Bone Walker came over to the house and announced that he felt the Otis family had enough drummers already and recommended that they find Shuggie a guitar. Shuggie soon found his own guitar, watching Don Harris and Dewey Terry rehearse with his father's band. Dewey played a shiny, red-glitter, telecaster guitar that captivated Shuggie. He learned the instrument quickly, for the most part teaching himself to play by imitating the sounds that Jimmy Nolen and Johnny Guitar Watson made with the Johnny Otis Show. Johnny contacted a guitar teacher in Hollywood and asked him to give lessons to Shuggie, but when the teacher heard the child play he demurred. "I can't teach him anything," the instructor said. "I teach beginners and he's way advanced."[6] Shuggie played so well that he made his recording debut when he was twelve, backing Ethel Fort recording as Lily of the Valley on the song "I Had a Sweet Dream," produced by Johnny Otis for his Eldo Records label.[7]

A public television producer asked Johnny to stage a performance of his rhythm and blues review in 1971. Contacting "all the people we love," he arranged for a lineup that featured T-Bone Walker, Charles Brown, Little Esther Phillips, Eddie "Cleanhead" Vinson, Joe Turner, and Roy Milton, backed by a band that included Preston Love on alto saxophone, Wilton Fender on bass, and Shuggie Otis on guitar. During rehearsal they decided to conclude with a performance by T-Bone Walker. When his moment arrived, however, Walker played a short number and then turned around and asked Shuggie to come up front and play a duet with him. Knowing how shy his son could be, Johnny was not sure if Shuggie would leave his chair to join T-Bone up front or quietly walk offstage. Shuggie ambled slowly and seemingly reluctantly toward the front of the band as precious television minutes ticked away. Soon T-Bone had Shuggie trading licks with him, with T-Bone calling out on his instrument and Shuggie responding. The pair played beautifully together, showing that in the blues a sixty-year-old and a sixteen-year-old could speak the same language. Even more impressive to Johnny and Shuggie was T-Bone's generosity, sharing a spotlight he had worked his whole life to achieve with a newcomer.

Shuggie became a regular in the Johnny Otis Show almost as soon as he became a teenager. He sometimes wore dark sunglasses onstage so that nightclub owners would not realize that he was too young to perform in such venues.[8] Shuggie recorded his first solo album, *Here Comes Shuggie Otis!*, on Epic Records when he was only fifteen years old. A consummate virtuoso on the guitar, he also played five other instruments. He took the advice of saxophonist Benny Carter to undertake the formal study of composing and arranging.[9] While playing songs he had composed and arranged, Shuggie also proved to be an innovative rhythm box and synthesizer player. He showed himself to be steeped in the idioms of the blues on numbers like the electrifying "Shuggie's Boogie," but his tastes and abilities revealed an open-minded and eclectic approach to a broad range of musical figures, devices, and styles. His second solo album, *Freedom Flight,* contains an oboe and guitar duet, and his 1974 masterpiece, *Inspiration Information,* draws perceptively on the innovations of Sly Stone and P-Funk while anticipating some of the fusions later made famous by Prince. He played a guitar "duel" with heavy metal virtuoso Steve Vai in the motion picture *Crossroads,* but the footage did not make the final cut of the film.

Three of Shuggie's albums placed among *Billboard*'s Top Two Hundred best sellers, and his single release "Inspiration Information" reached number 56 on the top 100 chart in 1975, remaining on the chart for ten weeks. His composition "Strawberry Letter 23," which he originally recorded in 1970, became the number-one song on the charts in 1977 in the version released by the Brothers Johnson. Yet these successes do not begin to describe the breadth and depth of his ability.

Shuggie displayed the talent, but not the temperament, required to be a major star. He went for long periods without performing or recording, retreating into private life with his wife, Terry, daughter of jazz trumpeter Gerald Wilson.[10] Several attempts at comebacks faltered when Shuggie could not produce in front of live audiences the kinds of intense and original music that he played in the studio. His seeming indifference to stardom has hidden the fact that his recordings and compositions remain archives of some of the most extraordinary achievements in the blues, rhythm and blues, and rock idioms.[11]

Through his collaborations with Shuggie and other family members during the 1960s and 1970s, Johnny continued to meld his biological family with his musical family. During the 1950s Phyllis sang the duet with Marie Adams that became the theme for his radio show. Johnny also produced a recording session for his teenage daughter Laura in 1961, which resulted in "I'm Gonna Make You Love Me" and "Bye Bye Soldier Boy," by Laura Otis and the Satinettes, on the Mexie label (named after Preston Love's mother). Shuggie played guitar behind the singing of Barbara Morrison on the Johnny Otis Orchestra's *Back to Jazz* album in 1977 and contributed a scintillating version of the guitar solo on Freddie King's "Hideaway" to the band's 1984 album *Otisology*. Shuggie also played acoustic guitar and arranged many of the songs on Johnny Otis and His Orchestra's big band–styled 1992 *Spirit of the Black Territory Bands,* and his brother Nicky joined the ensemble, playing drums while Johnny played piano. They were soon joined in performances by bass player Lucky Otis, Johnny's grandson.

Otis made two attempts to resume his career in television broadcasting during the 1970s. With the help of producer Bill Griffith, he taped episodes of a new *Johnny Otis Show* for local broadcast and syndication in 1974 and 1975. Recorded before a studio audience sitting at tables on a set that resembled a 1950s nightclub, the program featured live performances by Johnny and his band, Marie Adams and the Three Tons of Joy, Mighty Mouth Evans, the "foxy Otisettes," and Shuggie Otis. From 1975 to 1977 Otis attempted another show, *Johnny Otis's Golden Oldies.* On this program, 1950s and 1960s stars, including Bob B. Soxx and the Blue Jeans, the Penguins, Gene and Eunice, and Vince Howard, lip-synched the words to recordings of their old hits. Johnny introduced the musical selections and chatted with the performers in addition to contributing his own playing and singing.

Although he enjoyed the television medium, Otis found himself out of step with commercial trends. He turned his attention increasingly to noncommercial radio broadcasts on public stations. For more than thirty years, he hosted a weekly program that presented music and commentary virtually unavailable elsewhere. Tapes of these shows, archived at Indiana University, reveal them to be an extraordinarily knowing, insightful, and passionate history of Black popular music. With a showman's flair, a musician's timing, and a teacher's dedication, he used these programs to present an astoundingly rich chronicle of popular culture but also a compelling counterhistory of race and racism in the United States. *The Johnny Otis Show* on public radio ran first in Los Angeles on stations KPCC and KPFK as *Blue Monday* and later in Berkeley on KPFA. It was syndicated on affiliated Pacifica nonprofit stations in Fresno, New Orleans, and Fairbanks, Alaska, as *The Johnny Otis Show,* providing diverse audiences with sustained amusement, humor, and nostalgic reminiscence. Yet these shows also involved a detailed analysis of the role of race in the music business in particular and in the broader U.S. society in general. Remaining on the air for more than thirty years, Otis's radio show constituted one of the longest-running continuous public discussions of Black culture and Black history presented anywhere.

The Johnny Otis radio program exposed listeners to a playlist they could not hear anywhere else. Otis insisted on mixing blues, gospel, and jazz records on the same show to illuminate their similarities as well as their differences. Billie Holiday's sprightly jazz vocal "Nice Work If You Can Get It" might be followed by southern soul balladeer Toussaint McCall's sensual "Nothing Takes the Place of You." Then Otis might play gospel shouter Dorothy Love Coates's exuberant "Get Away Jordan." Jazz and blues and gospel were related, Johnny insisted, because they were all cultural products of the Black community, branches on a tree growing out of a common trunk. Otis programmed his radio show the way he decided the lineups for his caravans and reviews back in the 1950s. "People would tell me," he remembers, "you can't take Big Mama Thornton to New York because she's too rough and too bluesy, and you can't take Sallie Blair to the Apollo because she's not bluesy enough. Well, bulls— on both counts. The people just—if it's really strong and it has artistry, they liked it."[12] Singer, songwriter, disc jockey, and music historian Billy Vera appeared on the show one day to talk about a record he had purchased as a youth in North Carolina. It was a Little Esther–Johnny Otis recording of "Better Beware" on the Federal label, featuring sequential solos by jazz saxophonist Ben Webster and blues guitarist Pete Lewis, who blended their styles seamlessly. Johnny observed that when Webster first heard Lewis play his amplified hollow-body Gibson, he remarked that it reminded him of the way his grandfather played the guitar. Even though Webster came from the world of jazz while Lewis played straight blues, they played together perfectly.

In an era in which shrinking top-forty playlists had given way to top-twenty and even top-ten playlists, radio audiences heard the same songs over and over again all day. Even worse, despite a brief efflorescence of mixed programming on FM radio in the 1960s, the dominance of "narrowcasting" in the industry relegated different types of music and their different audiences to different stations. The genre boundaries that divided rock, country, blues, and pop into discrete and separate worlds made little sense musically and never encompassed the range of interests demonstrated by most artists and most listeners. Programming based on genres primarily served the interests of marketers, however, delivering clearly defined demographic market segments to advertisers. Johnny Otis's programming broke all the rules of radio in that era, not only by blending blues, jazz, rhythm and blues, and rock, but also by using categories other than market success to determine what he would play. As a result, listeners of his programs heard Obie Jessie's original 1955 version of "Mary Lou," not the more commercially successful 1959 cover by Ronnie Hawkins. Obie Jessie (aka Young Jessie) had been a member of the Flairs, a local vocal group that included Richard Berry. Moreover, when Johnny played "Mary Lou," he asked Obie Jessie to call in and let the people of Los Angeles know what he was doing now.

On another program, a caller asked if Otis was going to play anything by white blues singer Janis Joplin. Otis politely said no, but then volunteered that he *would* play songs by Etta James, Lavern Baker, Dinah Washington, Billie Holiday, Big Mama Thornton, and Aretha Franklin.[13] It was not that Otis thought whites could not play Black music. His own artistry disproved that supposition, and he often acknowledged that many white musicians could play the music with technical proficiency. He did believe, however, that whites generally only interpreted Black music, without making original contributions to it. Benny Goodman and Eric Clapton were skilled technicians on their instruments, but if neither one had ever been born, jazz and blues music would not be any different from what they are today. Louis Armstrong and T-Bone Walker, however, made original contributions that changed the way everybody played—and still plays. Otis had less optimism about the ability of whites to sing the blues, not because their racial makeup prevented them from having the vocal ability to do so, but because the blues was a cultural product of the Black community, and immersion in that community had proven itself to be the best training ground for blues singers. Otis frequently employed whites other than himself to play in his band, and he frequently praised white musicians that he liked. He made sure, however, that no discussion of popular music omitted confronting what he often described as "that racism that's so deeply woven into the fabric of American society."[14]

In his radio programs, Otis highlighted and explained the artistry of individual performers whom the commercial music industry and music journalism largely ignored. On his show he saluted Richard Berry, Barbara Morrison, Charles Williams, Margie Evans, Don "Sugarcane" Harris, and Dewey Terry as great artists, and he explained carefully the exact nature of their achievements. He delineated the ways in which the music industry had hurt their careers: how record companies cheated Richard Berry out of royalties due him for composing "Louie Louie," how Alligator Records refused to release Charles Williams's version of "Every Beat of My Heart," which Johnny had produced for him knowing it would be a hit, how radio disc jockeys played only the up-tempo songs that Don and Dewey recorded (like "KoKo Joe" and "Farmer John"), not their beautiful ballads like "Soul Motion" and "Don't Ever Leave Me."

Otis directly challenged the choices made by the music industry in respect to which artists they recorded and promoted. In one characteristic show in 1982, he played a song he liked by Bettye Swann, "Make Me Yours." Bettye Swann was the stage name of Betty Jean Champion, born in Shreveport, Louisiana, in 1944. She had moved with her family to Los Angeles when she was a teenager and recorded as a member of the Flairs as early as 1964. As a solo artist, Swann released nearly twenty singles between 1964 and 1975, half of which landed on the rhythm and blues or pop best-seller charts. She did the original version of "Victim of a Foolish Heart" (covered in 2003 by Joss Stone) and recorded exceptional soul versions of country songs, including Merle Haggard's "Today I Started Loving You Again" and Tammy Wynette's "Till I Get It Right." She scored her last hit in 1975 with "All the Way In or All the Way Out" and left the music business shortly afterward. Johnny Otis wanted to know why. "When you hear these beautiful things like Bettye Swann singing 'Make Me Yours," he observed, "it makes you kind of sad. Because where is Bettye Swann? Why isn't she a big star today? What a gorgeous singer! Where is she? If she's around, we want to contact her, because somebody ought to record that child."[15]

The personalities and life experiences of the artists that Johnny Otis played and interviewed on his show took center stage in his broadcasts as part of a strategy to illustrate that Black music emerged from complex and complicated networks of apprenticeship and instruction, not simply from the innate skills of individual artists. On-air interviews treated listeners to the ebullient cheerfulness of Pee Wee Crayton, the gentle good humor of Lowell Fulson, and the creative intensity of Bumps Blackwell. Rather than simply honoring the history of recorded music, Otis evoked the origins of the music that he had heard played in dancehalls and taverns and town squares by inviting his guests to perform live with members of his band, accompanying them himself on piano, drums, vibes, or tambourine. These sessions produced some astounding artistry and offered opportunities for performers to show previously hidden sides of themselves. For example, listeners who knew Ted Taylor as a member of the rhythm and blues groups the Cadets and the Jacks or as the solo artist who recorded "Stay Away from My Baby," "Something Strange Is Going on at My House," "It's Too Late," and "Pleading for Love" may have been surprised to hear the breathtakingly beautiful live a capella version of the gospel tune "Never Grow Old" that Taylor performed on the show.[16]

At a time when the five firms that dominated the production and distribution of recorded music kept old records out of circulation so that they could pressure the public to buy their new products, *The Johnny Otis Show* played song after song that listeners could probably not purchase for themselves. When callers inquired where they could purchase the music he played, Otis usually explained that they could not, that many of these recordings were not available. He suggested, however, that while it would violate copyright laws for listeners to tape songs off his show rather than trying to purchase the recordings themselves, listeners might have their tape recorders running "accidentally" during his show and wind up with copies of the songs they wanted.[17] Contemporary readers who have access to a much broader range of music via the Internet and releases by small companies might not realize how important it was in the last three decades of the twentieth century for Otis to preserve and promote the recordings he played on his program against the grain of business practices by the oligopoly that dominated the music industry.

Otis took special pains in his radio broadcasts to teach listeners about the nature of different musical instruments and the roles they played in songs that listeners already knew. His conversations with producers and players revealed why a celesta appears on Professor Alex Bradford's "Too Close," why a piccolo graces Bobby Day's "Rockin' Robin," and why the electric violin dominates Don and Dewey's "Soul Motion." Bumps Blackwell explained that market considerations and the need for product differentiation shaped his decision to order a studio musician to accompany gospel singer Professor Alex Bradford on the celesta, a keyboard instrument that produces tones like chimes when its keys strike metal plates. Blackwell reasoned that many good gospel groups sounded alike, so the ringing tones of the celesta would make "Too Close" stand out as something different.[18] Perhaps best known for his memorable saxophone introduction to Henry Mancini's theme for the motion picture *Pink Panther*, Plas Johnson played saxophone on many Johnny Otis recordings, including "Willie and the Hand Jive" and "Big Time Scoop." When Johnson visited the radio program, Otis called attention to his work for other artists, especially the piccolo solo Johnson played on Bobby Day's "Rockin' Robin." Johnson provided that recording with much of its distinctive sound through an unforgettable solo evoking the chirps of a robin. He revealed to Johnny that he had not expected it to work out that well, because the piccolo was an instrument that he had been playing for only about six months. On another show, Don "Sugarcane" Harris described how he created and deployed the electric violin as a blues and rock instrument. Frustrated because amplified electric guitars generally drowned out the sounds Harris coaxed from his violin onstage, Sugarcane took a crystal from the cartridge on the arm of a record player, connected it to an amplifier with a wire, and taped it to the wood of the violin. On some occasions, Otis foregrounded the felicitous surprises that multi-instrumentalists could provide. In a discussion with Don and Dewey about their great ballad "Don't Ever Leave Me," Otis pointed to the playing of Johnny Guitar Watson on the piano rather than the guitar on that recording and noted that Don Harris moved away from his customary violin to play electric bass. On the twosome's "Soul Motion," Johnny called attention to Sugarcane's virtuosity on the violin but noted that Dewey Terry added a wonderful dimension to the recording with his playing on organ and bass.[19]

Songs that had entered the pantheon of Golden Oldies took on new meaning for listeners as Otis and his guests explained the hidden history behind them. He played Etta James's version of "Roll with Me Henry" and explained how Richard Berry had provided the accompanying vocal as "Henry" answering her invitation. He identified Berry as the composer of the original version of "Louie Louie" and decried how he had been cheated out of the royalties the record earned when it became a hit by the Kingsmen. An appearance by music producer Dootsie Williams traced the authorship and origins of the popular Penguins' song "Earth Angel." Williams produced the recording at a session in Ted Brinson's garage studio, at 2190 W. Thirtieth Street. Johnny Otis was the first disc jockey to play the song on the radio, putting it on the air as soon as Dootsie Williams brought a copy to Otis's live broadcast from the window of Conley's Record Rack, right next to Smith's Bar-be-cue, on Wilmington near 112th Street. The Penguins' Curtis Williams had actually written the song, but Jesse Belvin was listed as the composer on the initial recording. Curtis Williams had signed away the rights to his composition to another company, so Dootsie Williams could not release the song with the actual composer's name on it.

Taking a gamble, Dootsie Williams listed the composer as Jesse Belvin, who was under contract to him. Curtis Williams and his publisher subsequently took Dootsie Williams to court but lost their suit, even though Curtis Williams had indeed written the song. When Dootsie Williams re-released the record (after Belvin's death), however, he listed Curtis Williams as the composer.[20]

One of the most important themes of Otis's broadcasts entailed tracing the networks of apprenticeship in the Black community responsible for the success of individual artists. Johnny asked nearly all his guests to explain how they had got started in music, how they got launched in their professional careers. Pee Wee Crayton had a particularly revealing story about how he had developed his unique style on the guitar. For listeners who might have been convinced by music biographies, Hollywood films, and public relations hype that only inspiration and innate musical gifts lead people to careers in music, Crayton carefully delineated the help he had received that enabled him to learn, refine, and master his instrument. Crayton had been a fan of the guitar playing that Charlie Christian contributed to the Benny Goodman Orchestra, so he bought a twelve-dollar guitar to see if he could duplicate the sounds he liked. His early efforts did not succeed, but a visit to Oakland by the great T-Bone Walker led to a conversation between the two. Walker advised Crayton to buy a better guitar and tutored him on the instrument. He showed Pee Wee the three-finger style that Walker favored. When they discovered that Crayton could not master playing in time, Walker accompanied him on the piano and told him when to change chords until Crayton could make those decisions for himself. Later John Collins expressed amazement that anybody could play the guitar with three fingers (T-Bone Walker notwithstanding) and showed Crayton how to play with four fingers, a change that enabled him to learn to play "the big chords."[21]

Listeners were probably not surprised to learn that a great blues guitarist had been influenced by Charlie Christian and T-Bone Walker, but Red Holloway's account of how important the guitar had been to *his* development as a saxophone player revealed another dimension of those networks that shaped great Black music. Holloway loved Charlie Christian's playing but could not afford a guitar. A friend gave him an old banjo, and Holloway tried to mimic Christian's solos on that instrument. He could not find anyone to teach him how to play the banjo, however, so he traded it for a guitar. Listening to Lester Young one day, Holloway heard echoes of Christian's guitar playing on Young's saxophone, and, as he explained it, "that was the end" of his days as a string musician. It happened that his mother's boyfriend played the saxophone, but badly. Frustrated by his inability to play the instrument well, the man gave his saxophone to the youth. Holloway started playing it in 1942. By 1943, he had earned a slot in bassist Gene Wright's big band as a featured musician. Wright later played bass with pianist Dave Brubeck's group. Holloway went on to become a jazz and blues virtuoso who recorded duets with Sonny Stitt, played with Jack McDuff and George Benson, and backed up many great rhythm and blues artists, including Lloyd Price.[22]

By placing Black music within the context of Black life and culture, Johnny's radio broadcasts called attention to the allure that careers in music held for Black people facing limited employment opportunities in a racist society. Red Holloway explained to Otis's listeners that his motivation to be a musician came mainly from the narrow range of jobs open to Black men in the 1940s. He did not want to be a barber or a Pullman porter, so he worked at making a living as a saxophone player. Don Wilkerson, Ted Taylor, and many of the guests on the radio show began their "professional" careers by winning talent show contests that Johnny had organized at the Largo Theater and the Little Harlem Club.[23] They performed for the small amount of prize money that the contests provided but also in the hope that they would not have to take low-paying, unchallenging, nine-to-five jobs. When Johnny asked blues singer Long Gone Miles what got him started in music, the singer replied, "the cotton sack."[24] Otis remembered that Preston Love used to joke, "My mother's name was work, and I promised never to hit her."[25]

Drumming virtuoso Earl Palmer may have surprised listeners when he explained that becoming a drummer was his second choice as a career. He had started out in show business as a child tap dancer in his family's vaudeville act, turning to drumming only when the demise of vaudeville compelled him to find a new source of employment.[26] Songwriter and band manager Ernestine Rounds did not originally intend to pursue a career in music, either. She became interested in the field only after she saw how little money she could make in her chosen profession as a writer. Rounds loved to write and aspired to become a journalist. She had some success writing fiction, even selling a story to Johnson Publications about a woman who fell in love with her own father. When Rounds discovered, however, that she would be paid only twenty dollars for that effort, she concluded that writing would never provide her with an adequate income. Rounds composed a song for the Jayhawks, a music group that she managed. They had a minor hit with the tune, but when it was covered by the Cadets, it became a smash hit. The song was "Stranded in the Jungle," a bizarre narrative replete with playful (yet still embarrassingly primitivist) imagery about an explorer captured by cannibals in Africa. Otis knew Rounds in the 1950s but had lost touch with her. One day at his bank he had to speak with the manager about a financial matter. She asked if he remembered her, and Otis realized that the vice president of the branch of the Security Pacific Bank where he deposited his money was none other than Ernestine Rounds. He brought her on his show and had her describe the origins of "Stranded in the Jungle," which he hailed as an innovative work of dramatic art.[27]

Clora Bryant told Otis's listeners that she chose to become a musician simply to get out of the house. Bryant grew up in Dennison, Texas, where the Red River divides Texas from Oklahoma. Her mother passed away when Bryant was quite young, and her father was very strict with her—so strict, in fact, that she could not leave the house unless it was for a school function. Her brother left a trumpet behind when he went into the military, so Bryant took up the instrument mainly in order to go to football games and other after-school events with her father's permission. She built on that foundation to become a great virtuoso on her instrument, a good singer, and a consummate entertainer. Otis also informed his listeners that Bryant had been one of the most responsible and reliable musicians who ever played with him, someone who showed up on time and in shape to play, a member of the band whom Otis viewed as a model for the other musicians to emulate.[28]

Otis used the platform that his radio program provided to contest the practices, premises, and prejudices of the people in charge of the music industry. When major festivals and awards shows minimized or entirely neglected the contributions of Black artists to popular music, Otis informed his listeners of these actions and roundly condemned their injustice. He upbraided the 1982 US Festival, one of the most widely publicized popular music events of its era, for not including even a single Black artist in its lineup. The annual Grammy Awards shows, organized by the National Association of Recording Arts and Sciences, drew special derision on his show for their marginalizing of Black music and demeaning presentations of

Black musicians. The Memphis Blues Festival came in for particular scorn from him one year when it invited mediocre white artists to perform but failed to contact local stars Rufus Thomas and his daughter Carla Thomas.[29]

Otis championed the virtues of Black music against its critics inside the Black community as well. He directed special attention on the air to the preachers who condemned the kinds of music he played. "It's a big lie to call this the devil's music," he opined. "Nothing as beautiful as Black music could be from the devil."[30] "It's a blessing from God. It's beautiful, and if it's beautiful, it comes from God."[31] On one show, a caller related that he had encountered a former member of the Five Royales, who lived in Los Angeles. When Otis encouraged the listener to have the man contact him to appear on the show, the caller explained that the musician was now a preacher who was ashamed of having been a rhythm and blues singer in his previous professional life. "I don't know what his problem is," the listener volunteered. "I do," replied Johnny contemptuously.[32]

Otis drew on his extensive experience as a producer to help his listeners learn how artists were discovered and how recordings were made. A visit from legendary producer Bumps Blackwell enabled Otis and his listeners to explore the legacy of Sam Cooke. Blackwell had been so devoted to advancing Cooke's career that he actually delayed his own honeymoon to accommodate Cooke's recording schedule. Producing a session for the singer on December 16, 1956, Blackwell took a break, left the studio, and got married. Then he came back to the studio immediately to finish the recording session. Blackwell and his wife, Marlene, spent their wedding night in a hotel while Cooke spent the night sleeping on the floor of their as-yet-unfurnished apartment. Blackwell also took his new wife with him when he approached the manager of the Oasis Club in Los Angeles in an effort to secure an engagement for Cooke. The club manager was not interested in reserving a slot for an unknown singer, but, impressed by Marlene Blackwell's beauty, he asked her, "Do you sing?" Bumps nudged her and whispered, "Say yes." But then piping up himself before she could answer, Bumps enthused, "Yeah, she can sing; put *her* on your show." Marlene had never done any performing as a singer, but Blackwell figured out a scheme. He told her to step up to the microphone as though to do her first number, but instead introduce her "special guest," Sam Cooke. Bumps figured that Cooke's artistry would so captivate the crowd that Marlene could just leave the stage to him. Sam broke up the audience with his music, so the plan worked, but not before Marlene spent some anxious moments wondering what she would do if she actually had to sing.[33]

Otis's conversations with Blackwell on his show offered extraordinary insight into the difference a good producer can make on a recording. In an era when most producers sought to have artists conform to their arrangements, Nelson Riddle's productions made Frank Sinatra and Nat King Cole sound the same. Riddle enjoyed great commercial success with this format, but Bumps thought it preferable to shape the arrangement to the artist. He tried to bring out the distinctive personality of each singer he recorded, producing songs for Sam Cooke, Jesse Belvin, Thelma Houston, and Billie Holiday that sounded very different from one another. He related his belief that each artist conveys a particular attitude responsible for his or her success. "The same black and white keys that play Bach, play rock," Blackwell rhymed, so to sound different a producer has to respect the artist, create a concept appropriate for him or her, and unleash the singer's unique "attitude." Blackwell pointed out that once Sam Cooke or Billie Holiday or Jackie Wilson sang a song, everyone who followed them sang it the same way, because they had inscribed their "attitude" on it.[34]

Blackwell also disclosed some of the politics of the record industry during his appearance. He revealed that he had bought the contract of Little Richard from Don Robey in 1953 but could not record him for a year, because Specialty Records label owner Art Rupe doubted that Richard would be successful and procrastinated before agreeing to arrange a session for him. Johnny Otis had produced sessions with Little Richard for Robey's label and had not had any hits. The blues ballads that Richard brought to the Specialty session disappointed Blackwell, because they did not seem like hits either. During a break, however, Little Richard kidded around by singing an earthy song that he used to sing to entertain nightclub audiences. Blackwell liked the song but thought the lyrics had to be cleaned up. Dorothy LaBostrie took on that task. A young Black woman who had quit her job cooking for a white lady the previous day with the declaration, "I have to go write a hit record," LaBostrie hung out at Cosimo Matassa's recording studio, hoping to break into the business. She rewrote Little Richard's song as "Tutti Frutti," which became the hit she said she was going to write.[35] That session also produced "Long Tall Sally," one of Specialty's best-selling records ever. The session seemed to prove that Art Rupe had been wrong about Little Richard.

Rupe's judgment was no better by 1957, however, when Blackwell produced Cooke's great hit "You Send Me" at the Radio Recorders studio. Bumps broke many of the rules of rhythm and blues in that recording session. He omitted the full combo sound that usually accompanied R&B singers, deleted saxophones and baritone voices, and used only two guitars and a drum. Even more daringly, he hired the Pied Pipers, a white vocal group known for their sweet harmonies and backup work for Frank Sinatra and Jo Stafford, to sing behind Cooke. When Rupe came into the studio and saw five white singers behind Cooke, he fired Blackwell on the spot, replacing him with white producer (and later Republican mayor of Palm Springs and member of the U.S. House of Representatives) Sonny Bono. Blackwell had spent forty dollars to rent the studio; his arrangement and orchestration of "You Send Me" went on to make millions for Art Rupe, who got to keep the money Blackwell and Cooke made for him, even though he had fired the producer for making a record that in Rupe's judgment would not sell.[36]

Otis worked tirelessly to create a community out of his listening audience. He invited listeners to join his Blue Monday Club, which entitled them to discounts at live blues shows. He asked them to donate food and join him and his congregation in handing out food to homeless people camped out on Skid Row. He requested that listeners send him tapes of good music so that he could play them on the air, that they come forward and be interviewed on the show about their memories of the music scene in Los Angeles in the 1940s and 1950s, and that they participate in the red beans and rice cooking contests and picnics that he staged annually.

Otis's programs promoted shared enthusiasm for the blues among his listeners. Many telephoned or wrote letters expressing what his shows meant to them. He read one letter from two fans who related they had been listening to Otis's show on the car radio as they drove to a motel after their wedding to start their honeymoon. According to their letter, when they arrived at their destination, they did not want to stop listening to the music, so they turned up the volume on the radio and danced in the parking lot instead of entering the motel. "Now you talking about some fans," Johnny exclaimed. "Stayed out in the parking lot and danced. I have no further comment."[37]

For all the attention Johnny Otis paid on his radio show to the continuity of Black culture in the United States, he also treated Black identity as a point of entry into a global sense of citizenship. One interview with Ed Soesman, a parishioner at Landmark Community Church and an old ally from Johnny's civil rights days, led to a discussion of the music of Suriname, Soesman's native land. Johnny remarked on the significance of the survival there of African customs, languages, and beliefs in village communities in the countryside. Soesman in turn introduced Johnny's listeners to the sounds of Lieve Hugo, the "king" of Surinamese creole Kaseko music.[38] The same cosmopolitanism led Johnny to compliment one of the other disc jockeys on his station for playing some good Greek music. "Not that Lawrence Welk–styled Greek music," he specified. "I mean that good oriental Greek music."[39]

Johnny insisted that the blues was a living, vibrant, and ever-evolving form, a music with something to offer all people. He delighted in introducing his listeners to harp player Zaven Jambazian, an Armenian born in Jerusalem who migrated to the United States and became a deputy sheriff in Temple City, California, where he also assisted his wife in running a Mexican restaurant. While on patrol one night, Jambazian heard a blues song by Little Walter on the radio and became captivated by it. The blues reminded him of the Greek and Arabic music that he loved in the Middle East. Jambazian started buying recordings by Jimmy Reed and Sonny Boy Williamson, listening to them over and over. He purchased a harmonica and practiced playing it in his patrol car. Jambazian sought out teachers, eventually taking lessons on his instrument from Kid Thomas (Tommy Lewis) and Big Walter Horton. He teamed up with African American guitarist Johnny Turner to form the group Blues with a Feeling.[40]

Otis presented his show in the performing style of Black vaudeville and the chitlin' circuit nightclubs and theaters to a new audience on the radio. Old jokes and patter permeated his conversations. When discussing why Black musicians liked Los Angeles even though they found very few good-paying jobs in the city, Otis explained, "You can do badly more comfortably out here than in other places."[41] On one show, he described Pee Wee Crayton as a man who grew up so far south in Texas that when his father bought him a two hundred dollar bus ticket to go north, the fare ran out in Austin. When Crayton asked Otis if he knew the guitarist John Collins, Otis quipped, "No, but I know his brother Tom." Another time saxophonist Chuck Higgins revealed that he had been married four times. Otis asked, "All at once? I knew you were a big-a-man, but I didn't know you were a big-a-mist."[42]

When the mood struck him, Otis related stories that he had heard over the years by great Black comics on nightclub stages, like the one about a husband worried that his wife was cheating on him. The man routinely answered the phone, hoping to catch his wife's lover attempting to make a date with her. He related that his effort proved unsuccessful, however, because most of the calls were just wrong numbers seeking the weather report. The man knew that the caller was seeking the weather bureau, the joke goes, because the voice on other end of the line kept asking if the coast was clear.

A scheduled appearance on the program by blues singer Blind Joe Hill had to be delayed when Hill did not show up on time. When the visually impaired singer finally arrived, he explained that his entourage had started out for the station early enough but had trouble locating the address. Without missing a beat Johnny asked, "Was you driving?" Yet the joke took an odd turn later in the conversation when Hill related that he had served a term in prison for automobile theft. Two of his friends told him to wait in the car when they went into a store, planning to rob it unbeknownst to Hill. The two fled when the store owner confronted them with a gun. The police arrived to find Hill in the car parked outside. They could not charge him with robbery, since he had not been in the store, but when he could not produce the title and registration for the vehicle, they charged him with auto theft. Hill served a term in prison for the offense, even though he could not have driven the car. "I've heard of police brutality," Johnny remarked, "but charging a blind man with auto theft is just police stupidity."[43]

Otis also related quips he had heard in the industry over the years to accent and illustrate the music history he related to his listeners. Discussing Sam Cooke's tragic shooting at the door of the office of a cheap L.A. motel late in 1964, Otis remembered Hal Zeiger's wry and sardonic summation of the lesson to be learned from the sordid incident: "Never park a ten-thousand-dollar sports car in front of a four-dollar hotel."[44]

These moments of humor, however, could not hide the serious aims and achievements of *The Johnny Otis Show* on the radio. Through this work, Otis carved out an unexpected space in popular culture for education, engagement, and moral instruction. Forty years after his radio and television broadcasts first introduced Los Angeles teenagers to Black music, his Saturday-morning broadcasts on KPFA, in Berkeley, California, in the 1990s attracted more listeners than any other show on the air in that time slot, according to the industry's Arbitron ratings.[45] Johnny Otis earned plaudits from the musicians whose work he championed, not only for exposure of their work, but also for his sincerity about social justice. A case in point is T-Bone Walker's comment when he learned that Johnny Otis had asked Bob Hite, of the white blues group Canned Heat, "Can't the Black man have any game of his own?"[46] When Walker's friend and biographer Helen Oakley Dance related Johnny's comment to the guitarist, T-Bone chuckled and said, "Johnny tells it like it is. Jumps in with both feet."[47]

Seven THE WATTS BREAKAWAY

 Throughout his life, visual art played a special role in Johnny Otis's world. The California School of Fine Arts offered him a scholarship when he was a teenager. Before he painted the portrait of Nat Turner that won a citywide Black History art contest in 1965, he had entertained fellow band members and friends with deftly drawn cartoons while working on the road as a traveling musician in the 1950s. After his sixtieth birthday he immersed himself in art, turning parts of his home and backyard into a studio for mixed-media assemblages and sculptures.

"Art is an act of love," Otis maintains, and like so many things in his life, his engagement with drawing, painting, and sculpture emerged from his love of and immersion in the vitality of the Black community.[1] He started drawing seriously on bus rides as his band made its way from job to job in the early 1950s. This reconnection with visual art started when Little Esther pestered him to make pictures of the sites that caught her eye as they moved along through the countryside. He began making sketches of cows, horses, and barns to keep her entertained. On one trip, Esther got into an argument with Little Arthur Matthews, a member of the band who also drove the group's tour bus. Her older antagonist got the better of the exchange, and a frustrated Esther stalked to the back of the bus indignantly. Seething with anger, Phillips took the empty seat next to Johnny. She asked him to draw a picture of Little Arthur that would make him look really ugly. When Johnny demurred, Esther picked up a pencil and started to do it herself. She filled the center of the page with a big box decorated with windows and wheels to represent the band bus with the words "The Johnny Otis Show" across it. She placed a grotesque image of Little Arthur behind the steering wheel in the driver's seat, with the words "evil little ugly motherf——" underneath. The figure behind the wheel did not actually look anything like Arthur Matthews, but the drawing and its caption struck Johnny as very funny. After persuading Esther to change the caption to the less obscene but still insulting "L'il Booger," Johnny showed the drawing to the other members of the band, who found it riotously amusing. Even Little Arthur found himself laughing at the over-the-top caricature of himself.

Almost immediately, members of the band came up with more ideas for cartoons. They requested images to settle private scores, reenact funny conversations, and record memorable events from their tours. Little Esther's inspiration ebbed, however, once she had vented her feelings about Arthur Matthews. The group elected Johnny to be the band's official cartoonist. He started frequenting art supply shops to obtain drawing pencils and sketch pads. The beautiful colors of oil paints caught his eye, leading him to purchase a canvas and try his hand at painting. Years later, Otis's discovery of the similarities between the paintings of Pablo Picasso and traditional African wood sculptures struck him as extremely significant.[2] He began to create in that style. Conversations with friends, especially Los Angeles–based African American artists Charles Dickson and John Outterbridge, educated Otis about the possibilities of sculpture in plaster of paris and Ultracal 30. When he moved from the big house on Harvard Boulevard to the suburban city of Altadena, he became a neighbor to Charles White, John Outterbridge, Noah Purifoy, Curtis Tann, and many other Black artists who made their homes along the tree-lined streets of the suburb.[3]

Otis perceived strong affinities between visual art and music. In many ways, his drawing, painting, and sculpting are more extensions of his musicianship than distinctly different endeavors. "I'm not a visual artist," he insists, "but I consider myself very lucky to have other ways to express and interpret what I see in the world."[4] The color wheel in painting reminded him of the basic triad in music. In painting, the primary colors of red, blue, and yellow form the base from which secondary tints can be created. In music, a major chord consists of the tonic, a third, and a fifth. Just as variations on the triad produce minor, augmented, and diminished chords, different mixes of primary colors produce subtler and more complex shadings. Moreover, communication by both sight and sound is made possible by the movement of waves, light waves in painting and sound waves in music.[5]

Like his music, Otis's artwork draws upon the everyday life of the Black community for its content. Many of his sculptures consist of found objects and rubbish. Tools once used to enhance beauty, such as discarded lipstick tubes, plastic curlers, and mirrors, become revived for a different kind of beauty as raw materials in the installations he creates. Otis favors remnants of containers like broken glass, metal cans, and bottle tops to serve as vessels of a different sort in his works of sculpture, evoking the West African artistic emphasis on using containers as metaphors. Tiny chairs that proved to be too small and uncomfortable for use by the students at Landmark Community Church's Sunday school became the basis for his Chair series, made up of surrealistic sculptures that evoke the African ideal of a chair as a symbol of power.[6] His sculpture *Mom and Pop Store* re-creates a neighborhood candy store he remembers from his childhood. In that work, a clock advertising 7-Up soda is set at 3:20, the time when classes ended at his elementary school.[7] In creating mixed-media assemblages, Otis followed the lead of local Black and white artists who found beauty in the discarded ephemera of consumer society in Southern California. Noah Purifoy and Judson Powell made artworks out of nearly three tons of charred wood and fire-molded debris left behind from the 1965 Watts Riots.[8] Critics hailed mixed-media assemblage as the key art form for many artists in the area.[9]

The paintings in Otis's Rhythm and Blues series depict scenes of the night life he viewed directly from bandstands in thousands of clubs and dance halls over the years, images of a world that existed only in his memories at the time that he painted them. The bold images he presents of musical instruments, clothing, microphones, and neon signs highlight the dramatic lines of dancing bodies in motion, all clearly conveying the bold and fiercely theatrical sense of the self-assertive display that Otis witnessed in his audiences over the years. Otis's art has enjoyed both commercial success and plaudits from his fellow artists. John Outterbridge, once a bus driver and vocalist in Chicago but subsequently director of the Watts Towers Arts Center, hails the stories Otis tells in his art as "the dominant sounds and motions of our lives, from the small accounts of each day's events to the vast incommunicable sagas that beset us all."[10]

Art historian Mary Lovelace O'Neal wrote the key essay in *Colors and Chords,* a book featuring Otis's artwork. While still a student at Howard University in the 1960s, O'Neal distinguished herself as one of the founding activists in what would become the Student Nonviolent Coordinating

Committee. She went on to a distinguished career as an abstract expressionist painter and critic. Her skilled use of color and her aesthetic and social concerns come to the fore in magnificent works such as *Set Them Wings on That Table* and *Racism Is Like Rain: It Is Raining or It Is Gathering Somewhere.*[11] O'Neal sees Otis's art as an expression of the major cultures that have shaped his life: Mediterranean, African, and American. She finds the ultimate contribution in his work to be the honor it does to the Black community, explaining, "The power of the people he is depicting—the presence of the subjects themselves—forced onto our consciousness—is what gives the work its significance."[12]

Otis's commitment to his art expanded when he moved to a farm in Sebastopol, in northern California, in 1991. On a property covered with apple orchards, he had plenty of room for art and music studios. It did not take long before he dotted the grounds with dozens of sculptures of people of various sizes, shapes, and colors, surrealistic animals, deities, demons, and other installations. The sculptures were interspersed among bird coops, tool sheds, and an assortment of old cars, tour buses, and fishing boats.

After nearly fifty years in Los Angeles, Johnny and Phyllis moved to Sebastopol intending to retire to a leisurely life in one of the rural areas that Johnny used to see as a child out the window of his father's car. "When I was a kid during the Depression," he recalls, "my daddy would put a few bucks of gas in the Tin Lizzie and we'd drive up here, past those little farms with the white picket fence. I've been trying to get back here ever since."[13] Yet the move to Sebastopol hardly led to a life of leisure. Invigorated by his new surroundings, Otis threw himself into a broad range of activities as a visual artist, organic farmer, composer, community activist, educator, and musician.

Although he departed Los Angeles physically, Johnny Otis left a legacy that lived on in that city through the activities of the many musicians he had influenced. Blues and gospel singer Margie Evans combined her experiences and principled commitments as a socially conscious Black woman with the lessons she had learned as a member of the Johnny Otis Orchestra, to fashion a unique role for herself. When Otis moved back to northern California, Evans rose to prominence as a Los Angeles artist-educator dedicated to preserving knowledge about and building respect for the blues. Born in Shreveport, Louisiana, in 1940, Evans had moved to Los Angeles in her early twenties. Raised in a strict church background that did not allow her to drink, smoke, or gamble, she grew up listening to her mother sing gospel songs in church and around the house. Evans became a great gospel singer herself, but she also displayed exceptional talent for singing jazz and the blues. She secured work as the featured vocalist in the Ron Marshall Orchestra and attracted a devoted following while singing in shows at the Tikis show room and entertainment complex in suburban Monterey Park. Musician, manager, and union officer Hector Rivera liked her performances and suggested that Evans go see if Johnny Otis could use her services as a vocalist in his band. She tracked him down at the Eldorado Recording Studio and asked if she could audition for him. Johnny had no need for another female vocalist at the time. In fact, he was not sure if he could support the band members he had already hired. Evans's personal enthusiasm and presence impressed him, however. He asked her if she knew anything about the blues, wary that most young singers he encountered had little knowledge of and even less respect for that tradition. "Yeah, I like the blues!" Evans answered. Johnny started playing a few notes on the piano. Evans responded by singing a wonderful version of Dinah Washington's "Evil Gal Blues." Johnny said, "You better wait awhile; we want to talk." He later recalled, "At that point I knew she was a great singer."[14] Otis brought Evans into his band and featured her singing in the Johnny Otis Show's memorable performance at the 1970 Monterey Jazz Festival.

Evans attracted attention for her fine performance on "Margie's Blues" on the *Live at Monterey* album in 1970. She went on to a career of singing with blues artists Willie Dixon and Pee Wee Crayton. Later, she produced recording sessions for Bobby "Blue" Bland. Evans never left her gospel roots, however, sometimes introducing sacred songs like "We've Come This Far by Faith" to her performances at dances. She appeared frequently as a welcome guest on Otis's radio programs. He often lauded her as one of the great singers in gospel, an artist whose virtuosity placed her in a category with the great Mahalia Jackson. Through her activism on behalf of the heritage of the blues, Evans also demonstrated that she shared some important values with Johnny Otis. As a new member of Otis's band in the early 1970s, Evans did more than sing and perform well. She also used her position to help organize the community and build progressive institutions inside it. At a moment when blues music had all but disappeared from commercial radio, Evans played a central role in establishing the Southern California Blues Society to promote blues education in the schools, to sponsor performances in public spaces accessible to listeners of all ages, and to preserve the heritage of the blues and the artistic, social, and political spaces from which it emerged. In the early 1990s, Evans spearheaded efforts to preserve the 5-4 Ballroom in South Central Los Angeles as an institution devoted to honoring the greatness of Black culture. Working with a sympathetic officer from the Los Angeles Police Department, Evans founded the 5-4 Optimist Club, an organization established to provide music, art, and recreation opportunities for children in the neighborhood.

Evans minces no words in describing her work as part of the Black freedom struggle. "It's bad enough to live in a country where everybody hates you," she explains. "People like me who travel a lot, everywhere we go we have to explain to people why they hate us so [much] here in our own country. It's a hard life in the blues, and too often, because of the hardship of our race, we argue and fight instead of working together." The blues, she argues, can nevertheless help address these somber realities. "The blues is the *cry* of my people. It grew out of our suffering from the slavery times. We are still suffering. *That* is the blues *tradition.* I have been trying to tell this to people all over the world, and they seem to understand this better in Europe than here in our own land. We have got to get the word out about these things or they will be forgotten. And when you forget your culture, how can you understand *who* you are? You can't. And we cannot *sit back* and depend on others to tell the truth about us. They *won't!*"[15]

Like Margie Evans, Brad Pierce also learned some important musical and life lessons from Johnny Otis. Pierce spent his childhood years in South Central Los Angeles and later in the mostly Black city of Compton. He learned to play piano when he was seven years old but took up the guitar six years later. As a teenager, he lived across the street from Marie Adams and the Three Tons of Joy and often heard them rehearsing. He saw Johnny Otis on television but never in person. Seriously injured in an automobile accident when he was sixteen, Pierce attended Widney High School for the physically handicapped, graduating in 1969.[16]

As a young guitarist playing in Los Angeles area bands, Pierce encountered an impressive array of musicians, including keyboard specialist Rudy Copeland (who later performed with Solomon Burke and Johnny Guitar Watson), saxophonist Danny Flores, who had recorded with the Champs under the name Chuck Rio, singer Rosie Hamlin of "Angel Baby" fame, and the great Richard Berry. Shortly after Pierce learned to play guitar, he secured a job in a band that backed the legendary Coasters at an oldies show in the Alpine Village shopping and entertainment center in suburban Torrance. On that job, he met saxophonist Clifford Solomon, who often played with the Johnny Otis Orchestra. Solomon had worked as bandleader for Ray Charles and shared many of Pierce's attitudes, opinions, and passions about the music they played. They had exceptional chemistry together as musicians. In 1989, Johnny needed a replacement for Shuggie on one of the occasions when he was off doing his solo work, and Solomon recommended Pierce for the job.

Knowing full well the extent of Shuggie's artistry on the guitar, Pierce wondered if he was up to the challenges that would face him in the Otis aggregation. Johnny and Clifford Solomon conducted an audition by playing and inviting Pierce to play along. After a few numbers, Johnny asked, "Do you want to be in the band?" Amazed and delighted that he had won the approval of his new boss so quickly, Pierce replied, "Hell, yeah." He started with the band that weekend without the benefit of rehearsal. Even so, everything went so smoothly that Pierce remembers thinking, "I've arrived in musical heaven." Brad went on to play a central role in the band's music for the next two decades, playing lead and rhythm guitar, building the band's core sounds, and even taking over responsibilities as driver of Nellie Belle, the band bus.[17]

In the Otis ensemble, Pierce used the stage name of Brad Pie. The name had been given to him as a nickname by other musicians, perhaps in tribute to famed Black sportswriter Brad Pye Jr. He became accustomed to the handle and liked it. Like most guitarists of his generational cohort, Pierce had learned to play using a complicated array of pedals and amps, but Johnny told him to "lose all of that," to "start clean" and imitate the way Freddie Green played in the Count Basie Orchestra. Pierce discovered that it took real discipline to play the big band style. A guitarist working for Otis had to think in terms of the needs of the entire band and could not get too far out in front of the other musicians. Pierce adapted his tone to Otis's preferences, eschewing the metallic sounds of rock 'n' roll for almost an acoustic sound. Playing as a supportive section musician meant that Pierce had fewer opportunities to be recognized as an individual player, yet he still played impressive solos, as evidenced by his scintillating work on the sensuous "Hey Mister Bartender" on the Johnny Otis Show's 1990 album *Good Lovin' Blues*.[18]

Pierce discovered that playing with Johnny Otis posed unique challenges. Johnny has never performed with a preplanned set list. He improvises according to the mood of the crowd and his musicians. A song comes to him like a vision. He plays a few notes to signal the rest of the band and expects them to respond appropriately. Not every musician is ready for this kind of challenge, but those who are value it highly. As singer Jackie Payne once observed about this regimen, "I had to adjust to Johnny, but it was one of the greatest experiences of my life."[19] Those who played with him through the years have explained that for all the emphasis on teamwork and section playing, everyone in the band still had an opportunity to display his or her skills and enjoy the spotlight. Pierce describes Johnny's bands as "horizontal," by which he means that everyone remained on the same level. Unlike "vertical" bands, in which one or two stars predominate, the Johnny Otis Show created an egalitarian community. Each musician had different skills and a different level of ability, of course, but Pierce felt that in Johnny's bands these differences were like fingerprints: marks of individuality that expressed differences without necessarily creating a hierarchy of the members' worth as musicians or people. The key rule in the band was that the rhythm section had to be tight. That was the part of the band that Johnny kept closest to himself. During the years when Pierce played lead guitar, Johnny often made sure his piano and vibe playing was backed up by his son Nicky on drums and his grandson Lucky on bass. Because of the congruence between these family ties and their playing together as musicians, Otis began to refer to Brad Pie as his "nephew."[20]

Playing with the Johnny Otis Show for Pierce meant immersing himself in the traditions that Johnny referenced in the music. Acting on his own rather than in response to any request from Johnny, Pierce began attending Otis's public radio broadcasts in person every Monday night, whether Johnny wanted him to perform or not. He felt that listening to the music Johnny played and paying attention to the people he interviewed would give him the qualities that he knew he needed to become the kind of musician, and the kind of person, that he had to be to play well in this setting. Pierce's wife, Brooke, also found her life enriched by Brad's participation in the Otis aggregation. She had grown up listening to the swing music that her jazz drummer father preferred, so she felt right at home with the music Johnny played. Intimidated at first by his manner, she soon began to treasure the ways that Otis enabled the different personalities in his band to both stand out and come together through their playing. Being behind the scenes attending the shows as Brad's partner, she came to feel that music has a spiritual dimension to it, that the Johnny Otis Show was so much more than one person; it was a product of the magic that happens when people come together in mutual respect and fellowship.[21]

For Brad, playing with the Johnny Otis show entailed all the hardships that come from life in a band: frequent and difficult travel, unpredictable playing conditions, and audiences with uneven levels of interest. Yet Pierce relished being among musicians who just loved to play, who felt grateful for every opportunity because they believed working with one another was like "magic." On one tour of Japan with Buddy Guy and Albert Collins, the band played an outdoor venue. The Japanese audience loved the music so much that at the end of the gig no one wanted to stop playing. On a "blues cruise" featuring Johnny Adams, Luther Allison, and Albert Collins, the musicians would play their contracted shows until two in the morning, but then find a place on the boat to jam with one another until dawn. "It was like dying and going to blues heaven," Pierce recalls.[22]

Brad felt that he shared more than music with Johnny Otis. Growing up in South Central Los Angeles and Compton, he experienced firsthand the racial realities that commanded so much of Johnny's attention and passion. He felt camaraderie with the views that Otis expressed and honored the scars the bandleader had picked up along the way because of his militant public stands. "I have never in my life met anybody that loves to live like Johnny does. He inspires me to do things and experience things I would never do on my own, because he has no fear of trying something new. A challenge for him is like an adventure." Many people daydream about doing things, but Johnny has actually done the things he imagined, whether it was making sculptures, raising birds, or starting an organic farm.[23]

Otis became like a second father to both Brad and Brooke, inviting them to move up to northern California and live on his property alongside Johnny and Phyllis. Brad and Brooke liked being part of the extended Otis family. They especially enjoyed keeping company with Phyllis while she shopped for antiques. But they had a life in the Los Angeles area as well. When Brooke explained she could not leave her job, Johnny offered her one with the band. Although Brad and Brooke decided to stay in Southern California, they remained part of Otis's extended network of close friends and family members. During one performance backing Rosie Hamlin at San Diego's Barrio Station, Pierce realized that these opportunities would not last forever. Tears welled up in his eyes as he thought about all he had experienced in the band. When the last note died down, Brad walked over to Johnny, hugged him, and said softly, "I just want to say thank you."[24]

Singer Barbara Morrison also cherishes her interactions with Johnny Otis. She first met him in 1977, while performing at the Marlton Building in the Crenshaw District in Los Angeles. Her piano accompanist asked if she had ever made a record. When Morrison replied that she had not, he explained that Johnny Otis was looking for a singer and suggested she call him. Morrison doubted that she could actually get the job, so she threw Otis's number away. Soon Otis called her and made an appointment to record the next day. When she did not show up, Otis phoned her back and asked with his characteristic playfulness if "she had a screw loose." It was not an auspicious start for Morrison. Once she arrived in the studio, however, nearly all of the songs they were scheduled to record were familiar to her because of her father's extensive record collection. Otis released their record and remained a devoted promoter of Morrison's career, singing her praises in interviews and recording with her whenever he could. She felt honored that the person who had discovered Esther Phillips and Etta James had so much faith in her, and she learned from him to trust her own artistry, to stop trying to sound like Barbra Streisand or other popular singers, and instead to be herself.[25] Morrison also admired the way Johnny Otis demanded that his musicians be treated with respect. After one long rehearsal at the Santa Monica Civic Center, the stage manager ordered Otis's tired and hungry band members to clean up the stage before leaving the building. Johnny looked the manager square in the eye and asked, "Would you make the Rolling Stones clean up the stage?" Then he turned to the band and said firmly, "If anyone in this band picks up anything in the way of trash to clean up this stage, you're fired." The regular custodial staff eventually cleaned up the stage.[26]

Otis had other attributes that amazed Morrison. She had never seen a man cook for his family and take care of children the way Johnny did. He displayed his love for them openly and looked after Morrison and other members of the band in much the same way he looked after Janice, Laura, Shuggie, and Nicky. "He would hug his sons and kiss them too just like he did his daughters," Morrison recalls. "You were even lucky if you were his dog," she quips, "because he loved all his animals with that same intensity."[27] Even after the Otis family moved north, Morrison remained a close friend. She feels that Johnny treated her like another one of his daughters, and his respect and attention meant a great deal in her life. "I've known this man for over thirty years now, and the warmth of his love for me as a daughter has matured my whole being. He and his wife sent flowers to my mother's and father's funerals, they have loved my sisters and brothers and their children. They have paid my rent, recorded me, and tried to make me a star. They have tried in every way to support me throughout those thirty years. If that's not love, I don't know what love is."[28]

As Johnny Otis started his new life in Sebastopol, his restless and creative nature soon disrupted his plans for a leisurely retirement. He formed a corporation to market juice made from the organic apples in his orchards and harvested grapes from his fields to make two brands of Johnny Otis Wine: Rhythm Red and Do Right White. He opened the Johnny Otis Market/Deli in downtown Sebastopol to sell organic produce from his fields. When Otis found he could not make a profit solely selling organic produce at that location, he began promoting musical shows in the store at night. He arranged for many of his old rhythm and blues friends to play evenings at the site but also opened the stage to a Scottish-Irish band, to spoken word artists, and to a Jewish klezmer band that played a rollicking version of "Hand Jive," renamed "Meshugana [crazy person's] Hand Jive" for the occasion.[29]

The Johnny Otis Show performed on weekends at the market/deli during its entire fourteen months in business. The band's performances were sold out three weeks in advance, and their performances kept the market afloat financially. Jim Kohn, who fronted the klezmer band that performed "Meshugana Hand Jive," handled bookings for shows during the week. Yet despite quality acts, ticket sales were slow on weeknights, and Otis eventually decided to close the business.

In "retirement," Otis created the same kinds of communities he had always built throughout his life as an artist, business executive, media personality, preacher, and community activist. Johnny's sons Nicky and Shuggie moved their families onto the property. They helped renovate some small cabins to serve as venues for art and music classes for children from the area. Otis recruited musicians and artists he knew to give these lessons for free or at minimal cost. He worked with local civic leaders, educators, and physicians to form the Johnny Otis Center for the Arts, an unusually ambitious and visionary project aimed at addressing the needs of children in Sonoma County. The JOCA offered free lessons in music, dance, and art, homework help and tutoring, information on nutrition, exercise, and sexuality, as well as health screening, counseling, and care by nurse practitioners, pharmacists, psychologists, and physicians. Otis served as guest preacher in some local churches and for a brief time led a congregation of his own that met in Santa Rosa at the Luther Burbank Center for the Arts. He switched the base of operations for his weekly radio program from its Los Angeles home at KPFK to the studios of KPFA, in Berkeley. Every Saturday morning, he drove the 120-mile round-trip from Sebastopol to Berkeley to do the program live until health considerations compelled him to do remote broadcasts from Sebastopol and then to give up the show altogether.

As he farmed, ran his businesses, hosted his radio program, and promoted the arts, Otis continued to perform, tour, and record with his band. He started to write a new book, tentatively titled *Rhythm and Blues on Central Avenue,* as a way of recording his impressions of the people, places, and music he had encountered in his life. He was able to look in retrospect at a life lived well and a successful career while continuing to do the creative and community work that he loved. Then Watts burned again.

On April 29, 1992, a jury in suburban Simi Valley returned a "not guilty" verdict in the trial of four Los Angeles police officers who had been captured on videotape brutally beating Rodney King, a Black motorist they had arrested allegedly for speeding. The verdict culminated a long history of insults and deprivations experienced by African Americans in Los Angeles. It proved to be the spark that ignited a riot that was even more destructive and bloody than the 1965 Watts uprising. The 1992 riot left fifty-eight people dead and more than two thousand injured. Police officers and National Guard troops made more than seventeen thousand arrests. The violence destroyed or damaged more than a billion dollars worth of property, leveling some twelve hundred buildings.[30] It took twenty thousand law enforcement officers and soldiers to suppress the insurrection.[31]

Otis felt once again that systematic police brutality had set the stage for the riot. "Many LA cops seem to feel," he observed, "that their gun and badge give them license to apprehend AND mete out punishment. They are judge and jury squads. Never mind that some of the men they nab are innocent of any wrongdoing—UPSIDE YOUR HEAD, anyhow!"[32] He made that capitalized phrase the new title of his book in order to underscore how the relentless deployment of unwarranted force by police officers in the ghetto sowed the seeds of the insurrection, stoking the rage of a community that finally fought back by burning buildings, looting stores, and attacking outsiders who occupied or wandered into the ghetto. Johnny felt that the riot underscored how little had changed and how little had been won from the struggles in which he participated. He wrote in his new book, "Sometimes I wonder, what the hell good it is if nothing has changed in over fifty years. I mean nothing of any real consequence where black people are concerned. . . . Could I have even dreamed back in the forties that half a century later my people would still be trapped and oppressed?"[33]

Upside Your Head! Rhythm and Blues on Central Avenue displays many of the features of Johnny's previous book and radio programs. He turned over three of the first four chapters of the book to oral testimony by community members. Taken from transcripts of *The Johnny Otis Show* radio programs, these chapters present memories of the glory days on Central Avenue in the 1940s by attorney James Tolbert, theatrical agent and journalist Lil Cumber, bail bondsman Bob Barber, artist Cal Bailey, saxophonist Buddy Collette, trumpeter and record label owner Dootsie Williams, dancer Frenchy Landry, choreographer Patsy Hunter, and vocalist Caroline Harlson. He followed those transcripts with a series of short sketches. These range widely, offering Otis's observations about music, politics, and art. They describe the secret language of Lester Young and the secret sorrows of Esther Phillips, the little-known political interests of Count Basie and the diverse approaches to drumming taken by Roy Milton, Kid Lips Hackett, Gus Johnson, and Art Blakey. Otis presented vivid vignettes from his life, tales about growing up in Berkeley and going on the road with the territory bands, about the destructive drinking habits that undermined the careers of Big Joe Turner and Eddie Cleanhead Vinson, about his days as a Holiness preacher, and about his activism and artistic efforts.

Once again Otis had produced a book that plays with history, that moves back and forth inside it, that leaps from decade to decade to summon up some illustrative anecdote or adopted ancestor from the past to shed light on the problems of the present. The book also contains the same sense of mourning and loss that pervades *Listen to the Lambs,* from Jimmy Witherspoon's sad lament about how "crack and hardship" now define the Central Avenue that he once knew as a vibrant site of creativity and mutuality to Buddy Collette's complaint that young musicians no longer force themselves to expand artistically, as the members of his generation were compelled to do by the veteran musicians they played alongside.[34] Most somber of all are Johnny's concluding passages. He explains that having reached his seventies he probably should be cutting back on his work and settling into a life of comfortable retirement. "But it's not that simple," he continues, "because the same old hypocritical All-American white man's hypocrisy is still stuck in my throat and I can't spit it out."[35] He cautions readers that if he seems angry to them, they should imagine how the millions of people trapped in poverty must feel. He concludes the book with a poignant sentence fragment that ends in an ellipsis and speaks volumes, "I'd like a little peace of mind, but no . . ."[36]

Upside Your Head! Rhythm and Blues on Central Avenue received rave reviews in *Publisher's Weekly,* the *Village Voice, Library Journal, Booklist,* and the *Boston Globe.* In 1993, it introduced Otis to a new generation of readers unable to access the by then long out of print *Listen to the Lambs.* As a text frequently assigned in college and university courses, it has performed important work in publicly connecting Black music to the lives of Black people. The 1992 riot, however, made Johnny Otis feel that he still had urgent educational and political work to do beyond writing this book. His career continued unabated and even prospered in unexpected ways. The album *The Spirit of the Black Territory Bands,* by Johnny Otis and His Orchestra, received a nomination for a Grammy Award in 1993. Otis was inducted into the Rock 'n' Roll Hall of Fame in 1994 and into the Blues Hall of Fame in 2000. Yet he found savoring his personal success difficult when Black people still faced such dire conditions in America. When administrators in the extension division of the University of California, Berkeley, and Vista College asked him to teach a course in Black music for them, he jumped at the opportunity, hoping that he could accomplish in a classroom setting some of what he felt he had been unable to succeed at completely with his books and radio programs.

Otis ran his college courses the way he ran his reviews and caravans as an entertainer. Each weekly three-hour meeting of the class was like a carnival coming to town. Otis moved the site of instruction off-campus so that he could include live music performances in the curriculum. He first conducted the class at Kimball's East nightclub in Emeryville, then at the Berkeley Repertory Theatre, and eventually set up shop in the alcohol-free Club Ashkenaz, in north Berkeley. Each session began with presentations about musical forms and music theory by Otis's trumpet and flugelhorn player Larry Douglas or by Vista College music instructor Albert Yamanoha. Then class coordinator, Carlos Zialcita, would take over as master of ceremonies. Johnny would come to the microphone and make a presentation about some aspect of the history of Black music, followed by a guest speaker. Each class ended with a concluding "show" by a musical act. Otis treated his classes to live performances of rhythm and blues by great artists, by

Sugar Pie DeSanto, Barbara Morrison, Little Milton, and the Johnny Otis band. He illustrated his lectures on gospel music with live performances by the Clara Ward Singers, on jazz with playing by Karlton Hester and Larry Douglas, on acoustic blues with performances by Clarence Van Hook. Guest speakers included activist–scholar Angela Davis, producers Bob Geddins, Chris Strachwitz, and Tom Mazzolini, hip-hop deejay Davey-D, and a varied and stellar group of journalists, academic researchers, and spoken word artists. Each semester ended with a "Red Beans and Rice Night" that featured Johnny cooking his specialty dish and feeding the entire class.

Otis recruited Carlos Zialcita, a teacher in the Oakland school system and a blues harmonica player he had come to know well, to be the coordinator of the Black music course. Zialcita became Otis's latest protégé as they worked together to teach the class and play music. Born in Manila, in the Philippine Islands, where his family lived upstairs from a nightclub named El Sotano (which means "the basement"), Zialcita included among his earliest memories the smells of stale beer and the sounds of rhythm and blues and rock 'n' roll records on the downstairs tavern's jukebox. He became a fan of Elvis Presley at an early age, largely because of the popularity in Manila of Presley's films *King Creole* and *Jailhouse Rock*. Yet while Zialcita liked Presley, the music that really moved him came from his exposure to Black entertainers, to Ray Charles, Fats Domino, the Coasters, the Platters, and others. "I had never heard of slavery. I had not seen many Blacks. But this music just spoke to me," he remembers.[37]

Zialcita had moved to San Francisco's Bernal Heights neighborhood shortly before his tenth birthday. In that neighborhood, his classmates and friends included Mexicans, Blacks, and Filipinos. Carlos made his performing debut on his school's stage singing the bass part on the Coasters' song "Charlie Brown" as a member of a vocal quartet made up of Blacks and Filipinos. His real passion, however, was jazz. As a teenager, Zialcita liked listening to music by Miles Davis, George Shearing, Cal Tjader, and Wynton Kelly. Frustrated because he was too young to get into most nightclubs where jazz musicians played, he was overjoyed to discover that the Both/And Club on Divisadero Street roped off a section where minors could drink soft drinks and listen to the likes of Pharoah Sanders, Jon Hendricks, Joe Henderson, and Bobby Hutcherson. After his high school graduation he took a trip to New York's Greenwich Village, mainly to listen to jazz, proudly wearing a polka dot tie decorated with a facsimile of the cover of Miles Davis's album *My Funny Valentine*.[38]

His aspiring immigrant family encouraged Zialcita to associate exclusively with whites and to date blond-haired women, but Carlos identified himself as a proud person of color. As a student at the College of Marin, his roommate was the head of the Black Student Union. Zialcita participated in the activities of the campus Third World Liberation Front. He remembers taking up the blues harmonica at the same time that he developed his political consciousness, becoming aware of the Black Panther Party, the United Farm Workers union, the Brown Berets, and the Red Guard at the same time that he became aware of Junior Wells and James Cotton. He had seen Paul Butterfield in concert many times and was impressed that someone who was not Black could learn and seemingly master the blues idiom. These new elements in his life seemed to blend together perfectly.[39]

Zialcita's performing career began in an unusual venue: the prison band at San Quentin. He was not an inmate, but some youthful indiscretions had resulted in his classification as a potential offender in need of constructive activity, and a counselor directed him toward playing music with and for inmates in the prison system. The lead guitar player in the San Quentin band also doubled as the heavyweight boxing champion of the prison. The rest of the musicians were drawn from the penitentiary population, its staff, and participants in work furlough programs. The group played mainly in prisons, jails, and youth reformatories. This band enabled Zialcita to sharpen and refine his skills on the harmonica so thoroughly that he soon secured a regular job with the Chico David Blues Band. Zialcita chuckles now when he recalls thinking as a member of the celebratory and self-conscious youth culture of that era that it was amazing that David could *still* play well even though he was *thirty-eight* years old! Eventually the Chico David Blues Band became the backup ensemble for singer–pianist Charles Brown at the Zanzibar Lounge. Zialcita and his band mates wore dashikis as their band uniform and played mostly at clubs serving a Black clientele in Marin City and Oakland. For a time they worked as the house band at the Colorado Negro Voters Club in Denver and later backed up Lowell Fulson at the Mr. Major's nightclub in east Oakland. By that point, Zialcita felt that he had come a long way from Manila.[40]

Playing blues harp in different bands led Zialcita to experience dimensions of Black life and Black culture that he valued greatly. He learned to make cornbread in the kitchen of bandleader Eddie Ray's east Oakland home. Ray regaled him with stories about taking breaks from picking cotton as a youth so that he could play the harmonica. Carlos collaborated with Joe Louis Walker, sometimes playing after hours at a club called 1-2-3 Look at Mr. Lee under a freeway near Sausalito. Years later, Walker often came to hear Carlos play. He always brought along his mother, a woman who stood out in a nightclub crowd because she wore a blond wig, kept her sunglasses on at night, and sipped drinks from a bottle that she kept hidden in her cleavage. His friendship with Walker led Carlos to a stint in the gospel group Spiritual Corinthians, with whom he made two records. Carlos toured with guitarist Sonny Rhodes and played in bands backing up a long list of blues stars, including Charles Brown, Big Mama Thornton, Pee Wee Crayton, and Lowell Fulson. He also played on a rap album by the Coup, one of Oakland's most politically conscious hip-hop groups, an album with the unforgettable title *Kill My Landlord*.[41]

Zialcita's immersion in Black culture did not prevent him from branching out to other cultures or delving more deeply into his own identity as a Filipino American. He married the talented vocalist Myrna Del Rio, a bilingual Afro-Honduran who grew up listening to her dark-skinned Carib grandmother speak a language of African derivation. The couple made records together and performed as a duet in clubs in Chiapas, Mexico. Zialcita originally encountered Johnny Otis largely because of a connection with another Filipino. His skills as a blues harmonica player led Carlos to a steady job with the band Domingo and Friends, fronted by Sugar Pie DeSanto's brother Domingo. The journey Carlos had started as a child in Manila, listening to Black blues songs on a jukebox, now led him to playing in a band with an Afro-Filipino whose sister was one of the great artists of rhythm and blues. Born in 1935 as Umpeylia Marsema Balinton, Sugar Pie was raised to respect the cultures of both her Filipino father, a merchant seaman, and her African American mother. She grew up in San Francisco in a family of ten children who spoke both English and Tagalog at home. Her mother played the piano, but Sugar Pie found her passion mostly in dance and song. She took five years of ballet lessons and enjoyed singing with her friends in their sanctified churches (even though she was a Catholic), as well as out on the street corners of the Fillmore District in San Francisco. Sugar Pie's sister occasionally backed up Etta James as a member of the Peaches, and James's success stoked Sugar Pie's ambitions. Johnny Otis first saw and heard her in a talent show at the Ellis Theatre in San Francisco in 1955. She did so well, he brought her into the studio to record. Otis thought that the given and family names she carried would be too hard for fans to pronounce and remember. He searched for a nickname that could be used to package her, just as he had when he changed Esther Mae Jones's name to Little Esther, Jamesetta Rogers's name to Etta James, and Willie Mae Thornton's name to Big Mama Thornton. Balinton's big voice contrasted with her petite body. She was five feet tall, weighed only eighty-five pounds, and wore a size three shoe. In those days microphones could not be adjusted to the height of the singer, so in order to record, Balinton had to stand on a box to reach the microphone. Seeing her standing on that perch, straining her body so she could project her music into the microphone, Otis said, "You look cute, like a little old sugar pie." In an industry that included artists named Butterbeans or Hambone, Sugar Pie seemed an appropriate handle. Don Barksdale, Johnny's old neighbor then a popular disc jockey and club owner, decided, however, that Sugar Pie alone was too informal, so he came up with DeSanto for her last name.[42]

Whatever fears Sugar Pie might have had about a career in show business dissipated when she learned the ropes from Johnny Otis. "He was real nice to work for," she told a reporter years later. "He's a real easy person."[43] Eventually, DeSanto would tour with James Brown, Willie Dixon, Lightnin' Hopkins, and Howlin' Wolf, scoring hit records on the charts, including "Slip-in Mules" and a duet with Etta James, "In the Basement." A diminutive person with great stage presence, a wonderful voice, and an attractive face and body, DeSanto became a target for nearly every romantic (or lecherous) musician she encountered. She held her own, however, proudly recalling, "I refused all those old goats."[44] She got her own way onstage as well, insisting that club managers set up the venue correctly and requiring her musicians to join her in giving their best effort for every show. Maurice White, of Earth, Wind, and Fire, played with her at one time and remembers that Sugar Pie ordered band members around using "cuss words that hadn't been invented yet."[45]

DeSanto recorded songs for many of the major rhythm and blues labels: Federal, Aladdin, Chess, and Veltone. She enjoyed success as a live performer, recording artist, and songwriter. In the early 1960s, she made records with her then husband, guitar player and singer Pee Wee Kingsley. While on the road promoting their Veltone hit, "I Want to Know," DeSanto and Kingsley encountered an exceptionally ugly instance of white supremacy. Near Tupelo, Mississippi, a police officer who doubled as the local judge stopped the couple, allegedly for exceeding the speed limit. The contrast between DeSanto's light skin and long straight hair and Kingsley's dark skin led the officer to conclude that he had nabbed an interracial couple—a Black man and a white woman. He impounded their car and incarcerated Kingsley in the local jail. Sugar Pie and her husband protested that they were a married Black couple and had broken no laws. The officer demanded to see a copy of their marriage license, forcing Kingsley to spend two weeks in jail while DeSanto waited nearby in a local hotel. When their marriage certificate from Nevada arrived, the authorities reluctantly let them go, offering no apology for their arrest and confinement.[46]

In 1997, Otis invited Sugar Pie to perform at his country store and nightclub in Sebastopol. To back her up, she brought along her brother's band, featuring Carlos Zialcita playing blues harmonica. Sugar Pie and Carlos had actually met before, back when he was a member of the Eddie Ray band in the 1970s. Later he played behind her as a member of Domingo and Friends. Carlos and Sugar Pie hit it off well right from the start, musically and personally. She asked Carlos if he was a Filipino. He replied that he was and, trying to connect with Sugar Pie, said he knew that she was a Filipina. In her characteristically feisty fashion, DeSanto replied, "I'm not just a Fil-ipina. I'm a spook-ipina."[47]

Sugar Pie was sixty-one years old at that time. She had lost none of her vocal skills, however, and was as dynamic onstage as ever, kicking her legs high in the air, moving sensuously in a tight pants suit, and instructing her musicians to stand up, turn around, and shake their rear ends for the audience. Johnny enjoyed the entire show, but he especially appreciated Carlos's playing. The two of them got a chance to talk, and Johnny found that they shared many ideas and attitudes about music, culture, race, and social justice. When he discovered that Zialcita held a day job as a teacher in the Oakland school system, he invited him to help plan and teach the class on Black music. As they worked together on the class, Otis and Zialcita found that they were kindred spirits. The course drew huge enrollments and enthusiastic responses from students. Some of those enrolled, however, complained that material about white racism had no place in a Black music course, maintaining that it was "divisive" to bring up the history of racism in the class. Like Johnny, Carlos found it was impossible to understand Black music without studying the social and historical contexts out of which it had emerged. Even a small number of student complaints needed to be listened to and respected, of course, but in most cases these statements simply meant that the covers had been pulled off, that individuals with merely consumer attachments to Black culture did not enjoy being reminded of the unequal conditions, opportunities, and life chances that gave the music its determinate tones and textures. During one class, a student asked why they couldn't just enjoy the music without being troubled by the history that surrounded it. Carlos found himself answering before Johnny could. "I've played this music for years with some of the most brilliant musicians and most wonderful people I've ever had the privilege to meet. Many of them became musicians as an alternative to sweating in the fields picking cotton. They created great music and never got credit or compensation for it. Some did not even own a suit to be buried in when they died, but they made millions of people happy. I can't teach the music without teaching what I know about why it exists." The class gave him a standing ovation, and Carlos noticed Johnny standing and clapping as well.[48]

Zialcita asked Otis to produce his blues album *Train through Oakland* in 2000. Otis not only agreed but also insisted on providing his own band as backup musicians. They recorded the album in Otis's home studio for no charge. Carlos stayed at Johnny's house while they worked together on the project, and he learned a great deal about music and about life from that sojourn. Johnny worked hard at music, but he had fun too. If Carlos had difficulty mastering a song, Johnny might tell him to take a break and help himself to the pot of red beans and rice Otis kept simmering on his stove. Somehow, Carlos's playing improved upon his return. One night Zialcita could not sleep and heard music coming from the hallway. He left his room and found Johnny in a bathrobe playing the same vibraphone he had played on Johnny Ace's "Pledging My Love," not really practicing, just enjoying himself. Carlos pulled out his harmonica and accompanied him. When they finished, Johnny said gently, "I wish I had met you years ago."[49]

From Otis, Carlos learned how to assess and cope with his own limitations as an artist. Johnny would deprecate his own musical abilities, especially as a singer, to prove to Zialcita that good records could be made without having overwhelming vocal talent. "Neither one of us is really a great singer," Otis would advise, "but we can still sing. Just know thyself." Otis also made his signature move in giving Zialcita a new name, dubbing him the "Thrilla from Manila" in the liner notes for *Train through Oakland*. Zialcita is proud of the album they made together but also treasures how the process of making it enabled him to grow as an artist and as a person. "Johnny could always say something that was not only kind," he recalls, "but really went straight to the heart of who you were."[50]

Eight MIDNIGHT AT THE BARRELHOUSE

 One of the most important symbols in West African culture, which shapes so much of Johnny Otis's aesthetic, political, and moral understandings of the world, is the crossroads. Crossroads are places where different paths come together, sites where strangers meet, and locations where choices have to be made. Crossroads can be confusing. The right path can look like the wrong path, and the wrong path can look like the right path. Crossroads can be dangerous. Collisions occur at crossroads. People lose their way at crossroads. Yet the great challenges of life often come in the form of decisions that have to be made at different kinds of crossroads. At a crossroads one can see in more than one direction. At a crossroads it is possible to leave behind the narrow road one has been traveling and strike off in a new direction. In the West African tradition, Robert Farris Thompson explains, a crossroads is "the point where doors open or close, where persons have to make decisions that might forever affect their lives."[1] Creative action at the crossroads makes all the difference in the world.

Johnny Otis has lived his life making choices at many different crossroads. In his childhood home above the grocery store on the corner of Dohr and Ward streets in Berkeley, California, his immigrant parents' memories of life in Greece collided with the demands of their existence in the United States. The folk Greek that Johnny spoke at home conflicted with both the formal Greek spoken in church and the English-language lessons he received at school. Music that Otis heard emanating from his neighbor's windows and at services in his friends' churches blended African call-and-response practices, five-tone scales, and polyrhythms with the musical practices of European tonal functional harmony. In the playground and the park, at school and on the street, he discovered similarities that enabled him to compare his own family's journey from Greece to California with school friends' stories about their families' journeys to California from Poland, Russia, Germany, Japan, and Mexico, as well as from Texas, Louisiana, Oklahoma, and Mississippi. When Otis went on the road as a working musician, he brought the things he had learned in Oakland with him to Denver and Omaha. When he arrived in Los Angeles with Lloyd Hunter's band, locals viewed him as a migrant from the Midwest.

In traditional West African societies, crossroads concern time as well as space. The burial ground connects the past with the present, the dead with the living. Decorations on grave sites create conversations with ancestors. Rivers and vessels that hold water serve as symbols of continuity between generations. No part of the past is lost forever. Even the sorrow of death can serve as the basis for creative transformation in the present. The humiliation of dying prepares the spirit for an honorable return in the form of "talkative" ancestors who serve as helpful guides in the future long after their own personal departure. The West African way does not turn mourning for departed people or lost ways of life into the pleasures of nostalgic reminiscence, but instead promotes creative appropriation and redeployment of past memories as part of solving problems in the present.[2]

Johnny Otis's pronounced commitments to preserving the past and learning from its lessons have evidenced this African approach to time and history throughout his life. Because he could not count on temporal continuities in his own experience, he learned how to keep parts of the past alive in performance, memory, and reflection. These creative moves often emerged out of profound pain and deep suffering, out of the many times in his life that he found himself at temporal crossroads, in places where the past would not quite die but the future could not quite be born.

Migration to America removed Alexander and Irene Veliotes from the social world that had shaped their early lives in Greece. The hate-filled nativism of 1920s politics and culture put the Otis family on the defensive. Like other immigrant parents and children, they clung to members of their own group for mutual aid and self-defense. This lovely solidarity emanated from ugly realities, from the humiliating indignities that flowed from their designation as foreign, un-American, and outside the Anglo-Protestant mainstream. The Great Depression of the 1930s eclipsed the separate worlds of different ethnic groups with a pan-ethnic culture of unity that embraced a new inclusive and democratic vision for America. This was the era that saw John Alexander Veliotes become Johnny Otis, a successful swing musician. Yet World War II channeled that culture of unity into a militaristic nationalism that countenanced the Japanese internment, the segregation of Blacks in the armed forces, and violent attacks on Mexican American zoot-suiters. Postwar urban renewal and suburbanization dramatically transformed the Black communities that sustained the big band sound. Otis responded creatively by turning his big band into a rhythm and blues ensemble, by opening up the Barrelhouse nightclub, and by promoting and producing live performances and radio and television broadcasts. Yet when social upheavals of the 1960s exposed the true dimensions of racial inequality and polarization, they destroyed the world of the 1950s. The radical movements of the 1960s and 1970s produced important and lasting improvements in society, but they also provoked a repressive counterrevolution that rolled back many of the era's gains and worked relentlessly to distort and suppress the memory of the movements and their achievements.

Otis did some of his best work during these years of reactionary politics in the four decades that followed the 1960s, using his art to keep alive parts of the past that contained enormous relevance to the present. His preaching, publications, paintings, and performances served as repositories of collective memory, as sites of moral instruction, and as mechanisms for calling communities into being. They exemplified the creative conflict at the heart of the epistemology of the crossroads, blurring the boundaries between culture and politics, recreation and education, and the secular and the sacred.

Making the right decisions at the crossroads, however, is not a simple matter. In the cultures of the African diaspora, a trickster stands at the crossroads, ready to challenge those who come along. This trickster is not God or the devil, but rather an embodied contradiction, an intermediary between the human and the divine. The trickster presents people with challenges, riddles, problems, insults, jokes, diversions, and evasions, yet his mischief has a positive purpose. It compels those he meets to make difficult choices, to use intellect and imagination to solve vexing problems, to make decisions in time before doors that may open briefly close shut forever. Most of all, the trickster at the crossroads demands action. He compels people to do work in the world that makes a difference. As Haitian *rara* musician Moris Moriset explains, "To get anywhere in life you have to follow a road. . . . To make anything happen, you have to walk through the cross-roads."[3] Yet it is not so much the path one *takes* as the path one *makes* that matters in this tradition. It is the work you do that speaks for you.

The metaphor of the crossroads bears a resemblance to the *pharmakon,* the symbol involving a stick with a snake curled around it that is displayed in pharmacists' windows. This image emblematizes the discovery by the physicians of antiquity of the close connection between poison and medi-cine. Substances that kill can also cure if taken in the right ways and in the correct doses.[4] Much of African American history and culture has revolved around these kinds of inversions, around efforts designed to turn humilia-tion into honor, refuse into treasure, dehumanization into rehumanization, and poison into medicine. Enslaved Africans took the Christian Bible that their owners used to legitimate their bondage and turned it into a tool for emancipation. In their hands the coping religion imposed on them by their oppressors became transformed into an enabling religion that justified rebellion by appealing to a divine master with power and authority greater than those of the slave master.[5] The nonviolent civil disobedience cam-paigns waged by Dr. King and his followers in the mid-twentieth century used the epistemology of the crossroads by provoking violent repression that was designed to silence them but that ultimately publicized their cause and disgraced their enemies, establishing their own cause as worthy. In a form of moral jujitsu, they used their positions as victims to provoke un-earned suffering that won sympathy from bystanders and transformed the oppressors of Black people into unwitting accomplices of Black liberation.[6]

Johnny Otis has drawn deeply on the West African epistemology and cosmology of the crossroads throughout his life. Of course every ethnic and racial group has its own valuable traditions of fighting for social justice. Black culture in the diaspora has never been completely isolated; indeed, it has grown and developed through constant contact, conflict, cooperation, and coalescence with others. The word *pharmakon* and its concept come from Otis's own Greek heritage. His youthful rebellions notwithstanding, Otis's parents' piety and the moral teachings of the Greek Orthodox Church helped shape his sense of right and wrong. His intellectual curiosity, cosmo-politan social interactions, and political experiences exposed him to diverse currents of sacred and secular thought and action, all of which no doubt informed his thinking and guided his actions. Yet it was the ability of Afri-cans in America to make a way out of "no way" that did the most to arm Johnny Otis intellectually, spiritually, and politically for the challenges he faced. He attended services at Black Christian churches, where the crossroads took material form in a cross that compressed the greatness of God and the lowness of man into one image. In those churches, people cut off from connections to their African origins "adopted" ancestors from the Bible by naming their children after flawed heroes who fought for freedom, such as Moses and David. Worshippers in those congregations recited verses and sang songs about healers like Ezekiel, who took the shattered and scattered bones of an oppressed people and brought them to life again.

Otis learned to play music inside networks of apprenticeship and instruction that stretched back centuries, networks in which lessons in music played only one small part of a broader aesthetic and moral education. From the Basie band's guitarist Freddie Green he learned about creative uses of time, about how to keep a steady beat while expressing motion and change through chord modulation. Long before he became a visual artist himself, Otis saw Black people create works of art in their yards by turning tires, wheels, hubcaps, and oil drums into stationary symbols of movement, art that used the discarded ephemera of everyday life as raw materials for demonstrating the power to give new life to things that have been forgotten.[7] He witnessed entire communities turn the segregation imposed on them by housing discrimination and brutal police practices into joyful congregation that used their linked fate as the basis for cultural affirmation and political mobilization.

Making choices at the crossroads, however, proved to be no simple matter for Johnny Otis. At the crossroads, the right thing can look like the wrong thing, and the wrong thing can look like the right thing. Embracing one path uncritically can obscure the virtues of the road not taken. The epistemology of the crossroads requires respect for both sides of a contradiction. It necessitates building a unity of opposites by synthesizing the best of both sides. Many of the personal anecdotes Otis has related over the years in his books, on his radio programs, and in interviews revolve around the importance of finding balance, reconciling opposites, and living with contradictions rather than suppressing them.

In *Upside Your Head! Rhythm and Blues on Central Avenue,* Otis relates that while first making his mark as a swing musician with the George Morrison, Lloyd Hunter, and Harlan Leonard bands, he gradually developed a condescending disdain for the music he had learned from Count Otis Matthews and other blues-based performers in Oakland. Otis thought of the sounds that he liked, those produced by the bands of Count Basie, Duke

Ellington, and Jimmie Lunceford, as advanced and modern, and he dismissed Bessie Smith, Jelly Roll Morton, and George Vann as relics of the past. When a new generation of bebop musicians, led by Charlie Parker and Dizzy Gillespie, came along to challenge swing, Otis reacted defensively and condemned the new music. Eventually he saw that his perspective had been flawed in both cases, that he had wrongly rejected the blues simply because musically sophisticated people disdained it, but that he had also wrongly resisted bebop merely because it brought something new to a world in which he was already comfortable. In discarding the blues because its time had passed and resenting bebop because it threatened to change the present, Johnny Otis found himself on the wrong side of history each time. To put things right, he embarked on a sustained project of listening to old blues and jazz recordings, reacquainting himself with "ancestors" whom he had rejected. This training saved Otis's career and shaped his future. His immersion in the blues paid off artistically and commercially when the big bands became too expensive to maintain. Rather than remain mired in melancholy sorrow about the demise of swing and the social world it served, Otis helped create the rhythm and blues genre. Years later, he reflected, "Dropping all the pseudo-elitist notions about what was 'best' in music, and who was modern and who was dated, helped to prepare me for my role in rhythm and blues."[8] Otis's understandable devotion to swing enabled him to become a successful musician. Carrying that devotion too far, however, impeded his ability to see other paths. Through self-criticism, flexibility, and adaptability, he found the balance that made it possible for him to see the many different kinds of artistry that occur in the world and the many roles that he could play.

In his evaluations of musical performances, Otis also insisted on balance, on reconciling virtuosity with feeling and emulation with originality. In his judgment, no amount of harmonic sophistication could outdo the music that John Lee Hooker could create using just one chord. Otis found that conservatory musicians often hindered rather than helped the sound of his band. Their strengths could become weaknesses in that setting. He explains, "Some of them, in addition to the academic background, had perfect pitch—and that made it even worse. Every two minutes, they wanna tune up. They're distressed. They want it to be perfectly on pitch, I can't understand it because I don't have perfect pitch. I'd rather have somebody with relative pitch, with a lot of feeling."[9] Yet no amount of feeling could overcome the problems caused by musicians who could not play essentially in tune, could not keep to the beat, lacked the technique to execute their ideas, or failed to understand their obligations to contribute to the overall sound of the band rather than merely show off their own playing. Otis disapproved of both extremes and instead sought to balance the conflicting qualities of feeling and virtuosity.[10]

Tensions between the need for both skilled emulation and inventive originality also require balance. Otis treasured the things he had learned through emulation. He picked up valuable knowledge playing alongside Lester Young and Ben Webster. He used arrangements borrowed from Count Basie when he formed his big band. He patterned his revues and caravans in emulation of traditional African American tent shows, caravans, and carnivals. Yet he condemned the cover system in rock 'n' roll that enabled imitative "cover" recordings by Georgia Gibbs and Pat Boone to outsell the originals by Etta James and Little Richard. The commercial and industrial practices that channeled monetary rewards along racial lines bothered him, of course, but Otis also objected to the failure of the cover artists to bring anything of their own to the songs. His opposition to the cover system never stopped him from praising the "cover" music made by country and western singer Hank Williams or by Chicano rhythm and blues bands from Los Angeles such as Thee Midniters. He perceived important differences between the two kinds of covers these musicians created. Gibbs and Boone, in his judgment, watered down the vitality and complexity of Black music and then profited from presenting it as their own creation. Hank Williams and Thee Midniters openly acknowledged their debts to Black artists but also added things from their own musical backgrounds to enhance their interpretations.[11]

Otis eschews abstract definitions about what makes music good, because so much depends on context. Art Blakely was a better drummer than Kansas City Bell, but for the music the Johnny Otis Show made in the late 1940s and early 1950s, Bell was the better choice. By the late 1950s, however, the music industry changed. Even rhythm and blues and rock 'n' roll musicians needed to read music and master more complex challenges, so Otis found that he had to fire Bell and replace him with a musician capable of playing the new music.[12] The sounds that Brad Pierce coaxed from amplifiers and wah-wah pedals in rock bands might have enabled him to make valuable original contributions to rock 'n' roll, but they were out of place in the Johnny Otis Orchestra, in which imitating the playing of Freddie Green did the most good.[13]

A commitment to balance through self-reflexivity and even self-deprecation permeates Otis's accounts of sex and violence. In a chapter in *Listen to the Lambs* devoted to his youthful attraction to a slightly older woman on his paper route, Otis tells about bragging to his closest friend, Rudy Jordan, that he slept with her. Because of Johnny's disheveled appearance, his friend believes that he has just come from a sexual tryst. The claim makes Johnny feel grown-up, powerful, and manly. Yet it is a lie. The woman is lonely and sad. Otis is frightened and ashamed when they are together. He did enter her home and thought about propositioning her, but a neighbor knocked on the door. Otis ran from the woman's bedroom in panic, fearing that her boyfriend had arrived and would beat him up. Even worse than having told a lie, Otis sees that the bragging that makes him feel better makes Rudy Jordan feel worse. So he tells the truth, realizing that the actual affection and support he feels from and for his friend is worth more than the fantasy of male sexual conquest that absorbs him. Together Johnny and his friend Rudy set their sights on romantic attachments with girls their own age whom they know and like. Once again, balance is the issue. Sexual desire is not wrong, but it can be distorted into something negative when used in the wrong way. The young Johnny Otis sees that the question he must answer is not whether he will have sex but rather what kind of sex he will have and what it will mean to him.[14]

In the same chapter of *Listen to the Lambs* in which he relates his education about sexuality, Otis offers a brief aside about a violent fantasy. He describes the incident of the Greek Orthodox priest rapping his knuckles for not paying attention in Greek school and emphasizes the traumatic effect the event had on him. Otis imagines that when he is older, he will return to the school and enact his revenge on the cleric by beating him up. A chance encounter with the priest on the street a few years later, however, changes his mind. He sees that the man is not the giant that he remembered but rather a small wizened figure, elderly, bent over, and wobbling as he makes his way slowly, inching along the street. Otis feels sorry for him and embarrassed by his hatred. "I decided to close the case," he writes.[15]

His other recollections about violence follow a similar pattern. Otis leaves his seat in the band to attack a white racist heckler at the Club Alabam who called the Black master of ceremonies a nigger. Another member of the band, however, restrains Otis, infuriating him. He believes, "I had had a chance to give vent to my pent-up, brutal aggressions about white racists and act like a hero in front of the chorus girls in the show."[16] But later Otis learns that his action might have brought down legal repression on the club, jeopardizing its municipal license and threatening the livelihood of everyone working there. Some ten years later in a Los Angeles picket line protesting employment discrimination, a white police officer kicks Otis hard in the behind to humiliate him and perhaps to bait him into reacting violently. Otis takes off after the officer, but publisher and civil rights activist Leon Washington restrains him, explaining, "We can't win that way... they'll kill us, baby."[17] In both cases, Otis imagines himself playing a heroic role for a good cause. Both times, however, what looks like the right thing turns out to be the wrong thing. He justifies his desires to be violent but sees that the price of violent, heroic male masculinity is too high. In these cases, it would have hurt the causes it purported to help. In both instances, Otis's public humiliations serve honorable purposes. Restraining his violent desires proves more heroic than indulging them.

The cosmology of the crossroads shaped Otis's frequent practice of renaming people. He started of course with himself, turning John Alexander Veliotes into Johnny Otis. From the late nineteenth century through the 1950s, immigrants and their children frequently shortened or changed their names to make them more easily pronounceable by native speakers of English and to escape anti-foreign, anti-Catholic, and anti-Semitic persecution. As late as 1952, civic officials throughout the United States handled fifty thousand requests for name changes that year.[18] During the late nineteenth century and through the 1920s, nativist attacks on "hyphenated Americans" demanded that immigrants conform to Anglo-Protestant norms, that they shed all signs of allegiance to their cultures and countries of origin. Michael Denning demonstrates, however, that this persecution ultimately backfired in the 1930s. In his view, casting off foreign-sounding names played an important role in inventing a new American people proud of their common egalitarian goals and shared proletarian identities. Consistent with the epistemology of the crossroads, name changing originated with a bad thing, with the shame and self-hatred created by vicious exclusionary prejudice. Yet aggrieved white ethnics turned this hegemony on its head by viewing their new "American" names as a ticket for entering a newly democratized nation. At the same time, they defended themselves from prejudice and exclusion while putting their oppressors on the defensive about the ownership of the term *American*.[19]

Changing John Veliotes into Johnny Otis, however, was not exactly the same thing as the writer Itzok Granich calling himself Mike Gold or the trombonist and bandleader Muni Zudekoff becoming Buddy Morrow. The homonymy of Otis with the last two syllables of Veliotes enabled Johnny to keep half of his Greek name. In the context of Black performance, the name Otis read not as ethnically unmarked and Anglo-Protestant but rather as Black. Nearly all white ethnics who changed their names did so to move up in status and improve their chances of acceptance by Anglo-Protestants. Otis's choice went in the opposite direction in one respect: he chose to identify with a group certain to be treated even worse than white ethnics. In his opinion, however, he had moved up. He became more connected to and accepted inside the community he respected the most, a community, moreover, with a rich tradition of naming and unnaming.

The native names and languages of enslaved Africans in America were stolen from them. Slave owners controlled everything about the humans they held in bondage, even their names. Some slaves tricked owners into speaking African languages by adopting names that seemed funny to whites but had serious connotations for Blacks. They invited their owners to call them names that seemed silly, like Quacky, hiding the truth of their African name, Kwako. After emancipation, whites assumed that Blacks had no last names, so they tagged them with the names of their former owners. Here again, some resisted by calling themselves Freeman to celebrate their newfound liberty or by adopting names like Washington and Lincoln to legitimate themselves as Americans. In the late nineteenth century, a Black general named Antonio Maceo rose to prominence as a leader of the Cuban struggle for independence from Spain. Some Blacks named their sons Maceo, not only in tribute to a Black hero, but also as a way of forcing white bosses and police officers to speak his name. Inside the Nation of Islam, Blacks renounced their slave names and used the letter X as a last name to mark the theft of the African name and language stolen from them in America. Great works of fiction by Black writers, including Richard Wright and Toni Morrison, revolve around issues of naming, misnaming, and unnaming. As literary scholar Kimberly Benston reminds us, "For the Afro-American, then, self-creation and reformation of a fragmented familial past are endlessly interwoven: Naming is inevitably genealogical revisionism."[20]

John Veliotes entered Black culture with the name Johnny Otis, only to encounter a community with a rich tradition of wordplay that included the adoption of dramatic and descriptive names. In New Orleans, musicians had names like Nookie Boy, Hold That Note Sam, and Half-a-Hand, and disc jockeys called themselves Ernie the Whip, Poppa Stoppa, and Doctor Daddy-o. As a bandleader, producer, promoter, and mentor, Otis displayed an exceptional talent for giving people new and memorable names. We've seen that he turned Jamesetta Rogers into Etta James, Leard Bell into Kansas City Bell, Willie Mae Thornton into Big Mama Thornton, and Umpeylia Balinton into Sugar Pie DeSanto. Names that disc jockeys could remember and pronounce improved the artists' chances of being heard on the radio. At the same time, name changes helped produce a festive and creative culture in which artists left their family names behind for new identities that marked their confidence about meeting the challenges of the moment. Years later, in a flamboyant effort to fashion a new reality of their own making, young people in hip-hop followed the standard practice of adopting new names to cast off the constraints they believe that history has imposed on them. The names that Johnny Otis gave to artists involve a *pharmakon*-like paradox. In some ways they capitulated to the bigotry of the culture industry by selecting easy to pronounce names, some of which had resonances of minstrelsy through their focus on body types (Big Mama Thornton, Little Esther, Mighty Mouth Evans). Yet in other ways, these new names announced a break in time, the arrival of a new generational cohort with its own style and self-confidence.

Otis found himself challenged by a need to strike a proper balance in many areas of his life. His presentations of music from the past could connect audiences successfully to cultural treasures that might otherwise have been ignored. Yet too much reverence for the past could discourage creativity in the present. Otis viewed his efforts to counter the shame and guilt that surround sexuality in this society with positive and pleasure-affirmative attitudes, ideas, and descriptions as part of a progressive step toward a healthier society. Yet these same representations might serve different purposes for audiences. His frank language and overt descriptions of sexual behavior might seem oppressively sexist to some and at the same time titillating and arousing to others. Otis's preaching promoted the importance of faith in the lives of oppressed people, but too much reliance on faith could lead to fatalism and resignation about the affairs of this world. The bold and biting criticisms that he mounted against inequality and injustice could motivate some people to try to change society, but they might cause others to conclude that evil is so entrenched it cannot be challenged. His insistence on a Christianity that actively serves the needs of the poor might do too little to challenge the conditions that produce poverty in the first place, but criticisms of major social and political institutions might overlook the necessity of personal kindness and respect. Every area of his life required the artful negotiation of complex contradictions. The problems he faced could not be solved by following inflexible rules that ignore the competing possibilities latent in any single action.

At the crossroads, the right thing may not simply *look* like the wrong thing. When one loses balance or conditions change, the right thing can *become* the wrong thing. Yesterday's solutions can become today's problems. The struggle does not end when a decision is made at the crossroads. Each decision that enables one outcome inhibits others. Past decisions can haunt the present because they contain unintended and unexpected consequences. For example, at times in his writings and radio broadcasts, Otis has referred to Black people as "naturally" less repressed and more in tune with their emotions than whites. Enlightened contemporary readers and listeners understandably reject the idea that race gives individuals any innate personal characteristics or qualities. Otis's claim sounds essentialist to them, like an inversion of the white supremacist belief that Blacks naturally possess rhythm or are superstitious and happy-go-lucky. Yet in making his claims, Otis has drawn on a political stance that was important to him and others in the 1930s and 1940s. Anthropologists in that era, claiming to have observed relative freedom from sexual repression among so-called primitive peoples, seemed to reveal the neuroses and rebuke the pretentions of privileged members of modern "civilized" societies. In writings by that era's intellectuals from aggrieved communities of color in the United States, Mexico, and Cuba, celebrations of "primitivism" functioned as mechanisms for fusing solidarities across ethnic, linguistic, and racial lines. As literary scholar David Luis-Brown notes, "Writers on race in the 1920s would portray members of the so-called primitive races as having developed ways of life that stood in protest against unjust, undemocratic, and racially oppressive neocolonial regimes."[21] For Otis and the intellectual tradition upon which he has relied, these celebrations of primitivism were comments about culture rather than about color. They provided mechanisms for turning hegemony on its head, for turning negative ascriptions about Blacks into positive affirmations. Yet they also ran the risk of becoming unbalanced, of unwittingly strengthening the racial assumptions they intended to undermine.

In *Listen to the Lambs,* Otis relates his resentments when white men approach him in nightclubs and on ghetto streets, asking him to provide them with Black women on the assumption that his light skin identifies him as a pimp.[22] He condemns whites who seek escape from the limits of their own lives by attempting to live out fantasies of crossing the "exotic" color line. Yet he also describes himself as someone captured by Black culture and enriched in every way by that captivity. When conducted in a respectful manner, cross-cultural contact can augment and enrich people. Once again balance remains the crucial element for him. Honoring rules that divide the races is wrong, but so is crossing the racial line selfishly and uncritically, with all the assumptions of white supremacy left intact.

Otis's struggles to balance antagonistic contradictions appear most evidently in his embrace of Black Power as a political strategy. Why would a white man endorse race-based mobilizations around the shared sign of Blackness? If white people cannot understand white supremacy or fight effectively against it, how is Otis authorized to speak? Once again, the issue is a matter of facing antagonistic contradictions directly and fusing them into a new synthesis. For Johnny Otis, the criticism of the U.S. racial order articulated by the adherents of Black Power in the 1960s remains accurate and relevant today in most respects. White supremacy still protects the group position of whites at the expense of communities of color. White property still commands more respect than Black humanity. The problem of prejudice pales in comparison to the problems caused by unequal power relations. Moreover, writings like those by Johnny Otis helped the idea of Black Power serve important strategic purposes. Building solidarity around the linked fate of Black people served indispensable ends. It addressed the destructive divisions within the Black community caused by racial and class oppression, by white control of the institutions most important in the lives of Black people, and by manipulative strategies of "divide and conquer," deployed effectively by white supremacists. Black Power encouraged Blacks to think freely without fear of offending powerful whites, to affirm that Black lives are as important as white lives, to insist on the right of self-defense, to demand freedom and justice now. It countered the negative stigmas associated with Blackness, positioned the Black national minority as part of the global majority of nonwhite people, and rendered the pathologies of white racism in the United States as relative, provisional, and contingent aspects of Black existence rather than as inescapable dimensions of Black identity. Most important of all, Black Power helped constitute Black people as a collectivity, as an aggrieved and insurgent people with mutual obligations and responsibilities.[23]

When *Listen to the Lambs* was published, in the year that Dr. King was murdered, Blacks held almost no elective offices, controlled few businesses, and appeared only sporadically in print and broadcast media. Fortunately, these realities have changed dramatically over four decades. Black culture dominates popular music and plays a prominent role in many other areas of popular culture. Black people have held important appointed and elected offices. In 2008, voters made Barack Obama the forty-fourth president of the United States. Yet the distribution of opportunities and life chances in the nation remains drastically skewed along racial lines. Race still exists because racism persists. Race remains the most important variable determining which families own assets that appreciate in value and can be passed down to subsequent generations, which people breathe polluted air, and which children attend underfunded and inadequate schools. The words that Dr. King wrote in his final book, *Where Do We Go from Here: Chaos or Community?*, regrettably still ring true today:

> Every civil rights law is still substantially more dishonored than honored. School desegregation is 90 percent unimplemented across the land; . . . open occupancy laws theoretically apply to population centers embracing tens of millions, but grim ghettos contradict the fine language of the legislation. Despite the mandates of law, equal employment still remains a distant dream.[24]

Black Power solved some problems, but it exacerbated others. In the face of the neoracism of the decades that followed Dr. King's death, Black Power proved to be a necessary but insufficient weapon in the struggle for racial justice. Although race-based mobilizations will always make sense as long as racism persists, by themselves Black Power and other one-race-at-a-time nationalist approaches serve different purposes today from those they served forty years ago. By putting so much emphasis on solidarities of sameness, racial nationalism can undermine constructive efforts at racial unity with destructive demands for racial uniformity. Racial nationalism can fuel democratic mass-based mobilizations, but it can also degenerate into the politics of ethnic brokerage, which serves mainly the interests of elites rather than the interests of the masses.

Otis anticipated some of this in his earlier writings, observing in *Listen to the Lambs* how the "well-intentioned (and well-fed)" leaders of the civil rights movement had failed to involve the Black poor in the struggle.[25] Black Power to him did not entail uncritical support for leaders on the basis of their skin color, but rather served as a political concept designed to promote radical democracy, economic justice, and anti-imperialism. It tried to use the linked fate of Blackness to hold elite Blacks accountable to those poorer (and often darker) than themselves. Black Power sought bargaining power inside the system, but to Otis it was not so much a mechanism for "buying in" as it was a means of "branching out" to other aggrieved and oppressed people, even poor whites. As administrative aide to Congressman Mervyn Dymally, he saw no contradiction between the goals of Black Power and enthusiastic support for reparations to be paid to those Japanese Americans who had lost their property and liberty during World War II because of white supremacist, anti-Asian hatred. His goal has been never simply to desegregate the ranks of the pain inflictors of this world but rather to use the situated knowledge and experiences of Black people as the basis for creating a world without brutality, exploitation, and hierarchy.

Johnny Otis's efforts to find balance and reconcile seemingly opposite positions into a unified totality express an important part of his personal makeup, but they also evidence his deep immersion in the culture of the crossroads that permeates African American communities. Throughout his life, Martin Luther King Jr. preached about choices at the crossroads. He told his followers that "life at its best is a creative synthesis of opposites in fruitful harmony."[26] King's sermons championed the need to blend a tough mind with a tender heart, to build on the best insights of both religion and science, to pay attention to the earthly world of time as well as the divine world of eternity.[27] He argued again and again that what seemed like the right thing could easily be the wrong thing. King saluted sincere altruism, especially the kind extended to members of social groups unlike one's own, but he warned that altruism can easily degenerate into prideful self-congratulation, finding pleasure in pitying others and refusing to challenge the social conditions that make charity necessary in the first place.[28] As a Christian he condemned communism because of its anti-religious materialism, but he also warned that uncritical anti-communism blinded people to the faults of capitalism. It led them to evade responsibility for the reason that communism thrived in the world: precisely because capitalism had failed to produce justice, dignity, and equality.[29]

In what might well have been the most important sermon he ever delivered, "The Drum Major Instinct," King identified how the desires to surpass others and receive recognition and praise serve as central sources of evil in the world. King explained that everybody has some version of this vanity, some hope of standing at the head of the parade like a drum major in front of a marching band. He claimed that in trying to make ourselves greater we often hope for others to become lesser. King condemned the ways in which this "drum major instinct" fuels the creation of class hierarchies, racial oppressions, and imperial conquests. Yet in a typical turn for the epistemology of the crossroads, King claimed that this source of evil can become a good thing if people use it correctly. Instead of advising people to eschew aspirations to be important, King asked them to channel those aspirations in a new direction. He explained that Jesus wanted his followers to be important and significant, to be first. Yet if everyone tries to be first in power or wealth or status, nearly everyone will lose. The only way for everyone to be first is to seek to be first in other ways: not first in earthly distinction or possessions, but first in love, first in generosity, first in moral excellence. Transforming the drum major instinct into an impetus for serving others can take a destructive thing and make it into a constructive thing.[30]

Just as Johnny Otis based his ministry at the Landmark Community Church on the need to "love one another," Dr. King grounded his appeals for "a world-wide fellowship that lifts neighborly concern beyond one's tribe, class, and nation" in a key passage in the first epistle of Saint John: "Let us love one another; for love is God and everyone that loveth is born of God and knoweth God. He that loveth not knoweth not God; for God is love. If we love one another God dwelleth in us, and his love is perfected in us."[31] Yet true to the epistemology of the crossroads, King noted how hard it can be to love and be loved in a world ruled by hate, hurt, and fear. "Evil in all its ugly dimension" permeates everyday life, he observed. "We see it expressed in tragic lust and inordinate selfishness," he complained, adding in words that seem as apt for our own time as for his: "We see it in high places where men are willing to sacrifice truth on the altars of self-interest. We see it in imperialistic nations crushing other people with the battering rams of social injustice. We see it clothed in the garments of calamitous wars which leave men and nations morally and physically bankrupt."[32]

King pointed to what he called the dark midnight within the social order. He felt this darkness in the social order is paralleled by an attendant midnight within the inner lives of men and women. King saw people plagued by pervasive fear, anxiety, and depression, disillusioned by their experiences with what G. K. Chesterton called "cures that don't cure, blessings that don't bless, and solutions what don't solve."[33] Dr. King sought to build a social movement capable of transforming both the inner and the outer lives of humans. He sought to change our society, not simply to desegregate it.

The metaphor of midnight appears recurrently in Dr. King's writing, as it did in his preaching. The moment when one day ends and another begins holds special significance. It entails the death of one reality and the simultaneous birth of a new one, a turning point, a meeting of opposites, a crossroads with contradictory possibilities. "Even the most starless midnight may herald the dawn of some great fulfillment," King contended at one of those dire moments in the 1950s when white supremacist violence may have made it seem as if Jim Crow segregation would last forever.[34] On the night of November 12, 1956, the Montgomery Bus Boycott, which King had been leading, had lasted almost a year. Although the determination and discipline of the Black community had held firm through months of attacks and provocations, it now seemed as if the city had the upper hand. The mayor requested an injunction from a local court that would end the boycott and defeat the movement against segregation on the bus system in that city. At a public meeting the night before the city's motion was to be adjudicated, King could feel pessimism sweep through the audience, and even he feared that the struggle might be over. "The night was darker than a thousand midnights," he observed.[35] Proceedings in court the next day confirmed the Black community's fears. It seemed certain the judge would rule against them. In the middle of the hearing, however, they received word that the U.S. Supreme Court had ruled that segregation on Montgomery's buses violated the law. King immediately saw the connection between their moment of despair and their ultimate triumph: "The darkest hour of our struggle had become the first hour of victory."[36]

Today, we find ourselves facing another dark midnight. In some ways our problems seem even more painful than they did four decades ago. The "Second Emancipation," in which Dr. King played such a large role, turned out to be very much like the first emancipation: a victory without true victory. In the nineteenth century, sharecropping and Jim Crow segregation replaced racialized chattel slavery when the nation abandoned its commitments to racial justice and ended radical Reconstruction. In the twentieth century, mass refusal to desegregate schools, jobs, and neighborhoods despite the passage of strong civil rights laws combined with neoliberal economic restructuring at home and abroad to produce a reracialization of opportunities and life chances in today's world. Just as the betrayal of the first Reconstruction was a defeat not only for Black people but also for democracy itself, the betrayal of the social warrant won by egalitarian social movements of the mid-twentieth century has exacerbated inequality, austerity, and insecurity for the majority of the world's population, reinforcing old forms of dehumanization, exploitation, and oppression while bringing into being new ones.

Today too, midnight in the economic order has its corollary in the inner lives of men and women, in wounded psyches, blasted hopes, and broken hearts emanating from the calculated cruelty of economic and social policies imposing the most arduous costs of social change on the most defenseless groups—on the poor, on aggrieved racialized groups, on women, on children, and on criminalized nonnormative populations. For African Americans the devastation has been particularly severe, in part because anti-Black racism is the ideological linchpin of neoconservative and neoliberal attacks on public education, public housing, public health care, and public employees, but also because Black people and Black communities have suffered most from the unraveling of the social wage and social services. The abandonment of efforts to enforce civil rights laws and the subsequent green light given to discriminators and haters have exacerbated inequality and severely impacted the social distribution of suffering, pain, pleasure, and joy. This midnight in the economic order and the political order influences every seemingly private and personal aspect of our lives. It promotes disillusionment, despair, and internalized self-hatred. As George Rawick used to say in another context, in its final stages, genocide starts to look like suicide.

Dr. King used the metaphor of midnight deliberately. He often spoke about the passage in the Thirtieth Psalm that explains that weeping might last for a night, but joy will come in the morning. At midnight, that morning might seem far away. Midnight was the hour when Africans enslaved in America in the nineteenth century used to slip away for meetings in brush arbors, where they could pray in the African way. In the tradition of the crossroads in West Africa, they knew that midnight could be a propitious time for action, because it is a moment of liminality, a time when the end of the old day and the beginning of the new come together in both peril and promise. The famed Montgomery Bus Boycott that propelled Dr. King to prominence did not start the very moment that Rosa Parks refused to give up her seat. It took a meeting at midnight, when Joanne Robinson and other activists met to discuss their response to what happened to Mrs.

Parks, to launch the dynamics that gradually led to the boycott. Months later when ferocious repression made some of his parishioners wonder if they should give up the struggle, Dr. King reminded them that committed Christians always face moments of danger, that we stand in this life at midnight.

As Johnny Otis has surveyed the world late in life from his farm in Sebastopol and later in the dwelling in Los Angeles, to which he and Phyllis moved in order to be closer to their daughters Laura and Janice and their families since their health has declined, the dark midnight that Dr. King described has seemed all too visible to him. The state of the world, the state of the nation, the state of the cultures and communities about which he has cared most, have all offered ample reason for despair. He has spent much of his time reading science fiction stories and books, immersing himself in alternate realities, which, however painful, cannot match the sense of disappointment he feels about the world around him.

Yet memories of other midnights continue to console him. Sixty years ago, he wrote "Midnight at the Barrelhouse," an instrumental number dedicated to the slow dancing that couples performed as the lights dimmed at the end of performances at the Barrel House club in Omaha and at his own Barrelhouse in Watts. Originally released as a single on Leon René's Excelsior Records in 1947, "Midnight at the Barrelhouse" appears on many Johnny Otis albums, including one named after the song, a re-release of his sessions for Savoy. The song is a favorite of many of Johnny Otis's fans. Its slow, sensual beat, ringing chords, and funky one-string runs played by Pete Lewis on guitar, trumpet solo by John Anderson, and piano accompaniment by Lady Dee Devonia Williams combine to evoke the aura of an era of unlimited possibility. At midnight in the Barrelhouse and in many other nightclubs, dance halls, and taverns around the world, Johnny Otis delved deeply into the traditions of African American artistry to try to make the world better. He wanted to entertain people, to be sure, but he also hoped to educate and agitate, to change his listeners into better people. The large body of recorded music he leaves behind will carry on that work for as long as people will listen to it. Whether they will recognize the power and possibility encoded in songs like "Midnight at the Barrelhouse" is an open question.

The life that Johnny Otis has led has been a life of extraordinary successes in many different arenas. He has savored the joy of a long and loving marriage, known the warmth of a close and supportive extended family, and experienced the companionship of loyal and devoted friends and admirers. He has reached heights of fame and fortune that few people ever attain. He has made extraordinary contributions to Black culture and to Black people in his multiple roles as a performer, promoter, preacher, arranger, artist, entrepreneur, and activist. Johnny made music with Lester Young and Count Basie, launched the careers of Little Esther, Etta James, Little Willie John, Hank Ballard, and Jackie Wilson, secured enormous success as a radio and television personality, composed and produced some of the most popular songs ever recorded, and made dozens of hit records of his own. He has influenced music across genres and generations. His composition "So Fine," for example, has been recorded by Ace Cannon, the Chambers Brothers, the Fiestas, the Mugwumps, the Newbeats, the Oak Ridge Boys, Paul and Paula, Paul Revere and the Raiders, Sonny and Cher, Ike and Tina Turner, and the Ventures. Johnny Otis has published four books, taught college courses, written a weekly newspaper column, and even consulted with leading avian biologists about the birds that he bred in his backyard. Otis has encountered a broad range of people along his life journey, forging personal friendships with many famous and talented writers, artists, activists, and politicians. He has helped make history as a participant in nonviolent direct action protests for civil rights, saved souls as a pastor in a Holiness church, and late in life continued to launch programs designed to feed the hungry, bring health care to children, and involve more people in the arts.

Although considered to be a white man by the standards of a white supremacist society, Johnny Otis chose to become "Black by persuasion." His decision to embrace and inhabit an identity rooted in the collective, cumulative, and continuing struggles of Black people has enabled him to live a life replete with moral purpose and profound connection to others.[37] In this society, however, racial identities are not so easily taken on and cast off. Many times, Johnny Otis has been forced to face this reality in stark and unmistakable ways, to confront the limitations and contradictions of the choices he has made. He has lived almost all of his life as a white man who is completely comfortable inside the Black community. But is there a place for a life like his in this world? Do even the best of personal intentions mean anything in the face of the hate, hurt, and fear that systemic structural racism and enduring injustice and inequality perpetually produce? Is it possible for any white person to be genuinely anti-racist as long as the privileges and advantages of whiteness persist? In the wake of the

1965 Watts Riots, Otis decided it was not enough simply to oppose white racism, that he had to declare himself an advocate of self-determination for the Black community, of the entire revolution in values and practices demanded by the adherents of Black Power. He has never wavered from that belief, and he has used all the means at his disposal to advance those ideas in the United States and around the world.

Clearly, Johnny Otis has paid a price for the life he has chosen to lead. He has attempted to defy the racial order of the United States, not just to criticize it, challenge it, or condemn it, but actually to live a life in defiance of it. His longtime friend Hal Kronick has seen Johnny Otis pay a price many times for trying to live that way. Thinking about Otis's battles with white supremacy in the music industry and politics, about Irene Veliotes's rejection of her son's Black wife, about the millions of dollars Otis denied himself because he refused to exploit Black musicians for his own gain, and about the scorn and threats he routinely received in response to his civil rights activism, Kronick contends, "If there's anybody who has suffered from this society, it's Johnny Otis."[38] Many times Otis has found himself concluding sadly that all of his efforts have been in vain, that racism runs so deep in this society and this world that opposition to it is futile.

Yet Otis's life also demonstrates the power of a good example. Hal Kronick feels that his own life has been graced and greatly improved because of the things he has learned from Johnny. "He taught me a few things that took a long time to learn," Kronick muses appreciatively.[39] Japanese American author Hisaye Yamamoto also expresses gratitude for the things she has learned from Johnny Otis, albeit in a different way. In her remarkable 1985 short story "A Fire in Fontana," Yamamoto's narrator describes Johnny Otis's life as a triumph. Told from the vantage point of a Japanese American woman whose family members were put into internment camps during World War II, Yamamoto's tale revolves around a fictionalized portrayal of an actual incident that took place in 1945. A Black man named O'Day Short tried to move his family into a white neighborhood in the city of Fontana, in San Bernardino County. Vigilantes burned down the house. The fire killed the entire family. Yamamoto's narrator is a Japanese American writer working on the staff of an African American paper in Los Angeles. A "Mr. Short" visits her and relates threats that his family has received, designed to intimidate them from moving into a white neighborhood. The narrator brushes him off by claiming that his account contains too little actual information to qualify as a news story. A few days later, she discovers that a fire in Fontana has destroyed Short's house and killed his family. Police investigators cover up the crime by contending that Short probably set the fire himself and killed his own family. A local priest writes a play about the incident and finds himself transferred to a remote parish in Arizona as punishment for challenging the racial status quo.

The narrator feels guilty for not doing enough to help the imperiled Black family. She compares her inadequate response to the fire in Fontana to the life of Johnny Otis, whom she describes as a white musician who played in Black bands, a man who overcame white racism and its pernicious privileges to seek solidarity with African Americans. The respect Otis earned as a white musician in Black bands and as pastor of a church that she locates in "Watts" (actually the Sugar Hill section) strikes the narrator as a successful negotiation of the U.S. racial order. Her own life, however, is something she portrays as far less than a triumph. Yamamoto's narrator makes mild gestures intermittently toward support for racial justice but ultimately retreats into the safety of suburbia and the life made possible for her there by her marriage to a white man. Twenty years later, when the Watts Riots erupt, the narrator links the fire that killed the Black family in Fontana in 1945 to the fires now raging in South Central Los Angeles. From her safe vantage point in the suburbs, the narrator feels an unexpected thrill and a vicarious identification with the rioters, asserting that maybe she was "burned Black" in the fire in Fontana. Her excitement makes her uneasy, however, because she cannot find the clarity and commitment in herself that she projects onto Johnny Otis.[40]

The fires that made Yamamoto's narrator feel as if she had been "burned Black" had literal rather than figurative meaning for Johnny Otis. The hate crime that killed O'Day Short and his family in Fontana seemed like merely one example of an endless series of assaults on Black dignity and Black lives in Los Angeles during Otis's formative years in the city. The Watts Riots of 1965 and the Los Angeles rebellion of 1992 represented only the most visible and violent responses to the slow strangulation of the Black community in the city over the second half of the twentieth century. Discrimination and disinvestment combined to lock in advantages for whites while locking out Blacks from opportunity and upward mobility.

The decision by a Japanese American writer to have her narrator affirm the life of Johnny Otis as a good example for people concerned with combating the evils of racism testifies to his ability to make creative and honorable decisions at many different kinds of crossroads, to balance the claims of self and other, family and humanity, the local and the global. Dr. King's call for "a world-wide fellowship that lifts neighborly concern beyond one's tribe, class, and nation" describes some of the most important dimensions of Johnny Otis's life. Incorporating diverse currents of Black and white cultures inside himself, he had a special affinity with others who bridged cultural boundaries, including his Afro-Filipina life partner Phyllis Walker, his Caribbean–South Asian ally Mervyn Dymally, and his African American and Arab business partner Bardu Ali. His life has been neither color blind nor color bound, but profoundly principled in both its color consciousness and its clear commitment to a worldwide fellowship.

Otis's life of unusual accomplishment and success has taken place in the context of the pernicious pathologies of white supremacy and anti-Black racism in U.S. society. The fact that he has been at war with those pathologies and the policies that stemmed from them does not lessen the agonizing contradictions of his life. "America has let our people down," he told artist and art historian Mary Lovelace O'Neal.[41] Old age has brought him neither peace nor rest, because he sees the nation as further away than ever before from addressing the unjust conditions that Black people and Black communities face. He wonders how the United States could not be grateful for the African presence in this land, why the nation has used and abused people who have given it so many gifts. "That's the big question in my life," he once said in an interview. "I've got to figure that one out."[42]

When O'Neal interviewed Otis about his art in 1995, the well-being of Black people was in the forefront of his concerns. "When I had my church in the late '70s and '80s," he told her, "our parishioners were always going to downtown LA to give away food to the homeless and the hungry. You could see that things were getting worse; it felt like the bread lines during the depression. It wasn't just black folks down there—it was some of everybody being represented. It really upset me, because we could do much better than that."[43] As the nation's politics drifted rightward during the Nixon, Ford, Carter, Reagan, Bush I, Clinton, and Bush II presidencies, Otis witnessed relentless and systematic reversals of the gains made by the culture of unity that had nurtured the democratic idealism of his youth and the Black freedom movement that won his allegiance during the 1950s and 1960s.

In some ways, his greatest accomplishments lie in what he did *not* do. His unique role as a white man immersed in Black culture remains largely unknown to the general public because he refused to exploit his identity and the opportunities it offered for selfish gain. He did not pass off the things that he learned from Black musicians as his own creations in the ways that produced so much success for Paul Whiteman, Benny Goodman, and Elvis Presley. He did not ride to success as a disc jockey and television host by watering down Black music and making it safe for consumption by white audiences, as Dick Clark did. He did not use the privileges of whiteness and relative financial advantages to make millions from a music he barely understood and then keep most of the rewards for himself in the process of cheating Black musicians, composers, and singers, as Syd Nathan and Herman Lubinsky did. He did not turn his back on the community that gave him his first professional successes and become a political ally and representative of its enemies, as Sonny Bono did. Otis did not use his interactions with Blacks as a platform for creating a self-indulgent image as an exotic border-crosser yet downplay the material realities of white supremacy, as jazz musician Mezz Mezzrow did.[44] He did not use a purported love for rhythm and blues music as a screen for concealing vicious acts of racism in the manner of Republican Party operative Lee Atwater, who supervised the deployment of the despicable "Willie Horton" ad promoting George H. W. Bush's candidacy during the 1988 campaign. When Bush won, Atwater invited blues artists to perform (without pay) at the 1989 festivities celebrating the victory made possible in part by Atwater's own racist moves.[45]

The ideas, actions, life, and legacy of Johnny Otis all contrast radically with dominant norms in the United States. This is why his story remains virtually unknown, even to many who have been touched by his life and his art. Our society's educational, political, and media institutions practice selective deafness about race and racism, often complaining that too much time is spent examining something that is actually hardly discussed at all. As Claire Jean Kim notes, "In American society, radical dissenters can indeed speak truth to power, but power garbles the message, rendering it harmless."[46] Even beyond issues of race, however, the truth of Johnny Otis's life has been scarcely understood because it conflicts so thoroughly with the prejudices and presumptions that permeate the national culture of the United States. Writers, readers, and music fans rarely face the harsh truths about the business that distributes the music they love. Books, magazine articles, movies, and music album liner notes routinely celebrate white identifications with Black music, saluting rock 'n' roll as a major force in making desegregation possible during the 1950s and 1960s.[47] These accounts never acknowledge how racist the music industry, and indeed the whole society, remains. Writers who make their living catering to the people who control the music industry cannot bring themselves to tell the truth about the corruption and exploitation that rule the business. They do not wish to alienate the executives who control the rights to the recorded music they love; as a result, they depict musically illiterate label owners as wise rather than lucky, forgetting the endless stream of evidence of how artists had hit records with songs that people such as Syd Nathan, Herman Lubinsky, and Art Rupe ridiculed and denigrated. When musicians like Johnny Otis and Preston Love write their own books that tell the truth about the industry, they seem sour and bitter to readers who do not understand the sources of their dissatisfaction.[48]

Equally important to the marginalization of Johnny Otis's identity in popular culture, journalism, and music history has been the simple fact that his life and the values by which he has lived it depart so significantly from the central myths of our society. In our culture, a supremely talented person is supposed to be a rugged individualist who surpasses others, not a compassionate and caring person whose connections to others become his most prized "possession." Our society craves stories about benevolent white people who have sympathy for Blacks, but it cannot fathom a story about a white person who casts his lot with Black communities and their struggles. Many writings about racism exert a great deal of effort to save white souls, when the real need is to save Black lives.

Our nation is populated by many people who proclaim their deep devotion to Christianity, but we have precious few examples of preachers or their parishioners working tirelessly to feed the hungry, house the homeless, bless the peacemakers, and drive the money changers from the temple, as Pastor Otis and his Landmark Community Church congregation did. The world in which we live bombards us with messages about "love," but it remains ignorant of what someone like Johnny Otis means when he embraces Jesus' admonition to "love one another."

The last chapter of Toni Morrison's great novel *Beloved* contains a sentence that exemplifies the contradictions of the crossroads. After devoting nearly three hundred pages to the tale of a Black woman escaped from slavery who kills her own daughter rather than letting her child be returned to bondage, Morrison writes, "This is not a story to pass on." The sentence relies on the dual meaning of "pass on" as an idiom. The first meaning conveys the idea of transmitting a story from one person to another. As public articulations, all stories are designed to be passed on to someone else. Morrison's statement seems like a complete contradiction. It stems, however, from her often articulated belief that when historical practices like slavery and genocide become translated into prose they become sanitized, domesticated, and smoothed over. Revealing the crimes and hurts of history may be the "right thing," but it can become the wrong thing, unwittingly enabling people to speak the unspeakable and tolerate the intolerable. Yet the sentence "This is not a story to pass on" has another meaning as well. In this sense, to pass on a story is to pass it by, to let it go, to choose not to hear it. Morrison argues that the story she tells is not a story to be avoided. This requires balance, grace, and reconciliation of seemingly incommensurable realities. We cannot pass on the story by simply retelling it, because that leaves us too passive and reduces the struggles of life to mere entertainment. Yet we cannot pass on or avoid the story altogether, because it has a great deal to teach us.[49]

In a much lesser way than *Beloved* but with some points of affinity and connection to it, the life of Johnny Otis is not a story to pass on. We cannot run the risk of complicity with the cruelties and corruptions of white supremacy by turning the collective struggles of an oppressed people into merely dramatic background and local color in an exceptional life history. On the other hand, neither can we "pass on" the story, avoid it or neglect it, because it has too much to teach us. We need a third approach beyond simply repeating the narrative or avoiding it. We can pass on this particular story by participating in it, by confronting the moral challenges that appear at the crossroads in our lives while armed with the power of the good example provided by the insight and artistry of Johnny Otis. At this dark midnight in the moral order, the political order, and the social order, it is still always Midnight at the Barrelhouse.

Acknowledgments

Thanks to Johnny and Phyllis Otis for their kindness and generosity in sharing their story with me. Props to them as well for the example they set as people who imbue the world with the potential to make right things come to pass.

I am grateful to Johnny's business manager, Terry Gould, for the countless hours he devoted to helping this book come into existence, and to Nick Veliotes, Brad Pierce, Brooke Pierce, Carlos Zialcita, Hal Kronick, Tom Reed, Kim Hester-Williams, and Barbara Morrison for sharing their experiences and opinions with me. Sandra Choron generously helped as well. Everything I write about music owes a debt to Tricia Rose, Rob Walser, Susan McClary, Robin Kelley, and Dan Czitrom. My sister, Mireille Schuck, was there the first time I heard "Willie and the Hand Jive," and her principled work in the world as a teacher and citizen always inspires me. My writing and thinking have been helped greatly by conversations with Chela Sandoval and Diane Fujino inside the NBG at UC, Santa Barbara. Melvin Oliver has been a wonderful interlocutor, ally, and role model throughout my career. Kimberle Crenshaw and Luke Harris help me see how history happens and why culture counts. Two anonymous reviewers for the University of Minnesota Press showed me how to make this a better book, and Adam Brunner and Richard Morrison at the Press did their usual fine job in moving the manuscript through the publication process. Robin Whitaker is the best copy editor I have ever encountered. It has been a delight to work with her again. Barbara Tomlinson's teaching, writing, editing, and integrity inform and enhance everything I do.

This book is dedicated to all the wonderful people I have encountered during the past ten years in the fight for fair housing. Confronting the depth and duration of white supremacy in this society can be depressing, but having the chance to change things by working side by side with serious people of all races who know that there is important work to be done and who think that it is up to us to do it is not depressing at all.

Testimony: In Praise of Johnny Otis

Bob Dylan:

Johnny's career just dazzles the mind. From discovering Esther Phillips and Jackie Wilson, to being a drummer, singer, piano player, bandleader, hit maker, right down to sculpting and painting. He even lost a seat for the California State Assembly. You can't top that. Willie and the hand jive indeed.

Bonnie Raitt:

Johnny Otis is one of the most important figures in the history of R&B and Rock and Roll. Through mentoring and showcasing so many brilliant stars in his legendary live revues and incredible bands, his contributions as writer/player and producer of so many seminal recordings, and his decades of hosting his beloved West Coast radio show, his legacy as Professor Emeritus of R&B will forever remain intact.

Ben Fong-Torres, journalist and author of Not Fade Away:
A Backstage Pass to Twenty Years of Rock & Roll:

It is fitting that Johnny Otis began his musical career as a drummer. A different drummer, of course. In fact, he helped mix the "shave-and-a-haircut/two bits" beat into the early blues and boogie music he was playing, leading years later to the "Bo Diddley beat" that would become a vital part of the rock & roll sound. From there, he became a multi-instrumentalist and vocalist, composer, bandleader, producer, and hit recording artist. He was also a civil rights activist, a preacher, a fine artist, a television host, and a DJ who loved to share his favorite music. Later in life, he returned to the radio, broadcasting from a food market he operated in northern California. All this from a son of Greek immigrants, who made a choice early in life to align himself with the world of African Americans and to travel to the beats of different drums. The original drummers.

Willie Brown, former mayor of San Francisco and speaker of the California State Assembly:

Johnny is the picture of talent and soul. He loves music, people, performing, and giving. You are fortunate if you are ever in his presence (as I have been on numerous occasions), and if this presence includes performances on a Sunday afternoon in the park, or at one of many venues graced by his talent, then you are in for a lifetime treat.

Al Kooper:

Johnny Otis showed me early in my career that there could be no limits if that's what suited someone. Ergo, I have been a songwriter, arranger, bandleader, producer, DJ, journalist, college professor, record company employee, record company owner, and let's not forget short-order cook. Without the influence of Johnny Otis's life, Lord knows what cubbyhole I would have been sandwiched into.

I will never forget the day I spent at his house. I was asking permission to record a duet album with his fifteen-year-old son. There was a moment when words became useless, and Johnny played vibraphone, I played piano, Shuggie played guitar, and one of my other early idols, Don "Sugarcane" Harris, dropped in for a visit and played violin. Four generations smiling and playing the immortal blues together on a sunny afternoon in northern California. It wasn't until the instant musical camaraderie began that the veil dropped: Johnny Otis shook my hand and gave me permission to record his amazing teenaged son. I will treasure that afternoon all my life—a life that was liberated by Johnny Otis and his living biography.

Aaron Neville:

Johnny Otis—he's the coolest! A true pioneer of the music I love.

Mervyn M. Dymally, former U.S. Congressman (D–California):

Johnny Otis is a person for all seasons. He is a multitalented musician, artist, and entertainer, but his talent is not limited to entertainment. I know him very well, personally and professionally. He is a community activist and worked closely with me as a Congressional consultant. History will be very kind to him.

Guitar Shorty:

Johnny Otis means everything to me. He is one of the greatest people I ever worked with, and he was like a father to me. I can't think of enough good things to say about him. He took me to my first big festival in Long Beach and really helped my career get going. He did a lot for me on the road, got me gigs, and helped with my performances. Even today I still remember things he told me. He is such a powerful person, but I never heard him say a bad word about anyone.

Michael Tilson Thomas, music director, San Francisco Symphony; founder and artistic director, New World Symphony; and principal guest conductor of the London Symphony Orchestra:

Johnny Otis has been a model of hip, cool, and charm for generations of musicians of all kinds. It is a pleasure to salute him.

Sugar Pie DeSanto:

In 1955 I won the talent contest at the Ellis Theater in San Francisco. Johnny Otis was in the audience and saw me; he asked me if I wanted to record, and I said yeah. That's when he took me to Los Angeles to record on the Federal label. I recorded "Boom Diddy Wa Wa Baby." I was so short he had to get a Coca-Cola box for me to stand on so I could reach the microphone. Then he said, "I can't use Umpeylia. You're so sweet and cute, why don't we call you Sugar Pie?" That's how he gave me the first part of my stage name. He was a genuinely great guy and he was all about the music. He started me on my career, and he helped start Etta James, Esther Phillips, and Mel Williams, too. He was a pioneer in the music industry.

Joan Baez:

We are lucky to have Johnny Otis, as the world is short on smart, soulful, funny, gifted, walk-the-walk folk. Bless his heart.

Dan Bourgoise, founder and former CEO of Bug Music:

I would love it when I got a phone call from Johnny. He would be calling about some administrative matter having to do with his publishing company, but we would always end up talking about many of the colorful characters that he had done business with over the years. He always had me laughing as I heard how he navigated his musical ship around—and through—the bandits that populated the music industry. I learned a lot from him!

David Ritz, author of Divided Soul: The Life of Marvin Gaye:

Johnny Otis is a major character in the history of our musical culture—unique, brilliant, witty, and wise. Everyone needs to read about Johnny Otis!

Charlie Musselwhite:

First of all, Johnny Otis is my hero. He paved the way for people and music in ways that many people are probably not even aware of. I doubt many musicians today even realize the ENORMOUS influence he has had on them. Echoes of his style of R&B are still heard in today's most modern music.

I have always applauded Johnny's crossing the color line early on. He suffered no fools during his long career committed to excellence in music and keeping it real. He's a legend to all who know the depth of this man. Long live Johnny Otis!

*Portia K. Maultsby, professor of folklore and ethnomusicology
and director, Archives of African American Music and Culture,
Indiana University:*

Johnny Otis is a musical legacy…a trailblazer. He was a bandleader, drummer, pianist, songwriter, talent scout, and producer. And he was instrumental in shaping major developments in rhythm and blues that spread from the West Coast to the East Coast. Among his many innovations was the formation of his traveling revue known as the Johnny Otis Rhythm & Blues Caravan, renamed the Johnny Otis Show. This revue set the stage for the rock 'n' roll touring shows in the 1950s and the Motown and Stax Revues in the 1960s.

The most memorable moment of my nearly thirty-year friendship with Johnny was the featured performance of the Johnny Otis Show during the annual meeting of the Society of Ethnomusicology at Indiana University in 1998. The band was hot and the dance floor in the convention center was packed all night.

Johnny used music as his tool in the struggle for racial equality and to bring recognition to the creativity of African Americans. During the era of segregation, he added color to television in Los Angeles by producing and hosting *The Johnny Otis Show,* which featured African American rhythm and blues singers and instrumentalists. These shows and their radio manifestations, as well as interviews with and photographs of Johnny, are housed in the Archives of African American Music and Culture at Indiana University in Bloomington, Indiana. The Johnny Otis Collection preserves the legacy of this trailblazer and provides a rare insight into his fascinating and multifaceted life and career.

Dan Aykroyd (aka Elwood Blues):

Besides his amazing musical legacy as one of the world's greatest jump swing and RnB entertainers, Johnny Otis might rightly be recognized as one of the nation's premier impressionist painters. Influences of Chagall and Glackens are vividly rendered against a distinctly American backdrop and milieu.

Roy Rogers:

Johnny Otis has played an important and pivotal role in the development of rhythm and blues. What an amazing, inspiring career and broad influence he has had.

Rosie "Angel Baby" Hamlin:

I was just fifteen when my recording of "Angel Baby" became a hit in 1960. At one of my first concert performances Johnny Otis was one of the headliners and the bandleader, and what a band he had! I was starstruck! I was so scared of the big stage that I was literally glued to the floor, my legs wobbled when I tried to walk, and my voice had a tremble. Johnny was rehearsing me, and he saw what I was going through. He got off the piano, walked over to me, and said, "When you walk out onto the stage, you come over to about here, and you don't have to do anything but sing. You can look at the audience but look just over the tops of their heads, and if you can smile that would be great!" He knew if I looked at anyone I would lose my words—I was that frightened.

Johnny had so much class, and he had the ability to turn amateurs into professionals. He was and is a genius writing out charts for every instrument in his orchestra. He was also a first in putting minorities on his TV show at a time in history when that was totally unheard of. Before I ever met him I looked forward to watching his TV show on Friday nights in San Diego.

He has opened doors for many folks in music. I've worked with Johnny and his orchestra at many concerts throughout the years, and I have always felt like family, especially when we went to eat BBQ after!

Alec Palao, Ace Records:

The opportunity to comb Johnny's extensive tape archive in depth and marvel at the riches within was, for this archivist, a rare and singular delight. The gentleman is truly the architect of rhythm and blues.

Lee Hildebrand, freelance writer and contributor to Living Blues
and the San Francisco Chronicle:

Johnny Otis is one of the most extraordinary Americans of our time. He rejected the racist conventions that define so much of life in the United States and cast his lot early with the culture and struggles of the African American community. He went on to make significant contributions to politics, broadcasting, visual arts, and especially music, in which he was a major participant in the birth of rhythm and blues.

Art Neville:

I was living in the Projects when I first heard Johnny Otis. I loved it—it was the baddest thing I'd ever heard. It was cold-blooded, man, I felt like I knew him from the first note.

Elvin Bishop:

Johnny Otis crossed over twenty or thirty years before the music did: very early on he just decided he was culturally Black. I was always impressed by the way he kept finding and helping new artists—many great performers were brought to the attention of the world by Johnny Otis. I first met him when we played on the same show at a casino in Lake Tahoe. I went to visit him at his hotel and found him cooking a big dinner for his band. As we got to know each other, I saw we had a lot in common—fishing, raising our own food, and cooking, both on and off the bandstand. He's a hell of a guy.

Chris Strachwitz, founder of Arhoolie Records:

Johnny Otis is the premier musician and promoter who brought rhythm and blues out of the black ghettos and to the attention of a huge white audience—who later faked their own version of this music and called it Rock & Roll!

For me it started probably back in 1949 or '50 when I would listen to a radio program called *Harlem Matinee* hosted every afternoon from 2 to 4 by DJ Hunter Hancock over LA's KFVD. He called himself "Old HH" and his theme song was "Midnight at the Barrelhouse," an early recording by Johnny Otis and his orchestra. If memory serves me right, the program covered everything "from bebop to blues, from swing to jazz, and from boogie to ballads." I had never heard this kind of music before and was absolutely captivated, mainly by its powerful beat and intensity of singing and rhythm. Although I was primarily taken by the powerful and emotional voices of the blues singers, I also enjoyed the frantic honking antics of the likes of Big Jay McNeely and Joe Houston. Then there were the great rhythmic vocal groups like the Dominos and the Spiders.

Much later I discovered that Johnny Otis was behind the production of many R&B discs that aired over several West Coast radio stations and very democratically entered the house of anyone willing and able to tune in that urban frequency. On many of these records Johnny's unique sounding vibraphone could be heard backing various singers. Then the atom bomb hit with Big Mama Thornton: "You ain't nothing but a hound dog, snooping 'round my door"—what a record! And guess who the accompanying band was? None other than the amazing Johnny Otis, who had the right touch, connections, and arranging skills to create this monster hit. Elvis tried it, too, and sold a lot more records but couldn't match Big Mama, no way!

That's pretty much all I knew about Johnny Otis for many years until he started doing radio programs, first over KPFK in Los Angeles and then KPFA here in Berkeley. It soon became clear that we had a genius on our hands and in our midst—not only a great musician, civil rights advocate, arranger, producer, but visual artist, teacher, author, and manufacturer of apple juice! Johnny became this incredible human being found right among us in northern California. How lucky I was to hang out with him, hear his lectures, and share with him some wonderful presentations. Johnny, always the advocate for the real stuff, the Black musicians who created this remarkable music: he has given his all and shared everything he knew. What a fantastic, unique human being—I am jealous, Johnny, how did you do it all?

John Broven, author of Record Makers and Breakers: Voices of the Independent Rock 'n' Roll Pioneers:

In the early 1970s, Johnny Otis was one of the first to apply the term "national treasure" to then-forgotten R&B heroes such as Louis Jordan, Big Joe Turner, Ivory Joe Hunter, Joe Liggins, and Roy Milton. That accolade has been earned by Johnny Otis, too.

Joel Selvin, journalist, music critic, and author of Ricky Nelson: Idol for a Generation:

Johnny Otis stands at the center of American music, and he knows the secrets of black America like no white man ever did. His life is a lesson to us all.

Notes

Introduction

1. Gerald Horne, *Fire This Time: The Watts Uprising and the 1960s* (New York: Da Capo Press, 1997), 2; Martin Schiesl, "Behind the Shield," in Martin Schiesl and Mark M. Dodge, eds., *City of Promise: Race and Historical Change in Los Angeles* (Claremont, Calif.: Regina Books, 2006), 144.

2. Horne, *Fire This Time,* 82.

3. Preston Love, "An Introduction," in Johnny Otis, *Listen to the Lambs* (New York: W. W. Norton, 1968; reprinted with a foreword by George Lipsitz, Minneapolis: University of Minnesota, 2009), 9. All citations refer to the 1968 edition.

4. Johnny Otis, "Johnny Otis Says Let's Talk," *Los Angeles Sentinel,* May 17, 1962, 6A.

5. Johnny Otis, "Johnny Otis Says Let's Talk," *Los Angeles Sentinel,* June 28, 1962, 6A.

6. Horne, *Fire This Time,* 140.

7. Ibid., 45.

8. NAACP Collection, Library of Congress, box 243 A, folder 3, October 6, 1961, and March 7, 1962.

9. Martin J. Schiesl, "Behind the Badge: The Police and Social Discontent in Los Angeles since 1950," in Norman M. Klein and Martin J. Schiesl, eds., *Twentieth Century Los Angeles: Power, Promotion, and Social Conflict* (Claremont, Calif.: Regina Books, 1990), 64, quoted by Steven L. Isoardi, *The Dark Tree: Jazz and the Community Arts in Los Angeles* (Berkeley: University of California Press, 2006), 70; Horne, *Fire This Time,* 68.

10. Johnny Otis, *Red Beans and Rice and Other Rock 'n' Roll Recipes* (San Francisco: Pomegranate Books, 1997), vi.

11. Johnny Otis, *Upside Your Head! Rhythm and Blues on Central Avenue* (Hanover, N.H.: Wesleyan/University Press of New England, 1993), 3.

12. Maureen Jung and Jack Rhyne, "Live at the 5-4 Ballroom," *Living Blues* 121, June 1995, 35.

13. R. J. Smith, *The Great Black Way: L.A. in the 1940s and the Lost African American Renaissance* (New York: Public Affairs, 2006), 75–78, 89, 91.

14. Otis, *Upside Your Head!* 42–45; Lee Hildebrand, "A Unique American Life," in Johnny Otis, *Colors and Chords* (Rohnert Park, Calif.: Pomegranate Art Press, 1995), 16.

15. Isoardi, *The Dark Tree,* 68; Steve Pezman and C. R. Stecyk, *Dora Lives: The Authorized Story of Miki Dora* (Santa Barbara, Calif.: T. Adler Books, 2005), 48.

16. Barney Hoskyns, *Waiting for the Sun: Strange Days, Weird Scenes, and the Sound of Los Angeles* (New York: St. Martin's, 1996), 59.

17. Mark Ribowski, *He's a Rebel: Phil Spector: Rock 'n' Roll's Legendary Producer* (New York: Da Capo Press, 2007), 10, 24.

18. Hoskyns, *Waiting for the Sun,* 30.

19. Barry Miles, *Zappa: A Biography* (New York: Grove Press, 2005), 42–43.

20. Fred Shuster, "Dave Alvin Remembers the L.A. That Shaped His Musical Life," *Los Angeles Daily News,* reprinted in *Santa Cruz Sentinel,* January 27, 2005.

21. Phil Carson and Roy Buchanan, *Roy Buchanan: American Axe* (San Francisco: Backbeat Books, 2001), 33–34.

22. Otis, *Upside Your Head!* 136; Bob Dylan, *Chronicles* (New York: Simon and Schuster, 2004), 186.

23. Norbert Hess, "You Ole Houn' Dawg," liner notes to *You Ole Houn' Dawg,* 1989, Ace Records CHAD 277.

24. Otis, *Red Beans and Rice,* vii; Galen Gart and Roy C. Ames, *Duke/Peacock: An Illustrated Discography* (Milford, N.H.: Big Nickel Publications, 1990), 63.

25. Hess, "You Ole Houn' Dawg."

26. *The Johnny Otis Show,* Johnny Otis Collection, Archives of African American Music and Culture, Indiana University, Bloomington, Indiana, March 21, 1987, EC 10" 2392; Otis, *Upside Your Head!* 73–78.

27. Douglas Henry Daniels, *Lester Leaps In: The Life and Times of Lester "Pres" Young* (Boston: Beacon Books), 2002.

28. Otis, *Upside Your Head!* 73–78.

29. Daniels, *Lester Leaps In,* 351.

30. Otis, *Listen to the Lambs,* 20.

31. Otis, *Upside Your Head!* 44.

32. Horne, *Fire This Time,* 123.

33. Otis, *Listen to the Lambs,* 193.

34. Malcolm X, "The Ballot or the Bullet," Detroit, Michigan, April 12, 1964, American Rhetoric, Top One Hundred American Speeches, Online Speech Bank, www.americanrhetoric.com.

35. Interview with Nick Veliotes, December 3, 2005, Washington, D.C.

36. Joe Safy, "Johnny Otis' Fifth Decade," *Washington Post,* June 24, 1985, B7.

37. Otis, *Listen to the Lambs,* 107–20; Otis, *Upside Your Head!* 43.

38. Interview with Johnny Otis, December 14, 1986, Altadena, California.

39. Derek Richardson, "R&B's Johnny Otis Back Again," *San Francisco Chronicle,* Datebook Section, June 26, 1983, 45.

40. Johnny Otis, "Johnny Otis Says Let's Talk," *Los Angeles Sentinel,* March 24, 1960, 4A.

41. Otis, *Listen to the Lambs,* 20. According to several others who remember the hand signal a bit differently, one finger extended meant a resident from Watts; two fingers,

a resident from Compton; three fingers, a resident of Willowbrook. See Magnificent Montague, *Burn, Baby! Burn!* with Bob Baker (Urbana: University of Illinois Press, 2003), 131; and Horne, *Fire This Time,* 67.

42. Otis, *Listen to the Lambs,* 21.

43. Ibid.

44. Ibid.

45. Ibid., 198.

46. Ibid.

47. Ibid., 19.

48. Interview with Johnny Otis, December 14, 1986, Altadena, California.

49. Otis, *Listen to the Lambs,* 97.

50. Johnny Otis, "Johnny Otis Says Let's Talk," *Los Angeles Sentinel,* November 17, 1960, 6A.

51. Mary Lovelace O'Neal, "Colors and Chords," in Johnny Otis, *Colors and Chords* (Rohnert Park, Calif.: Pomegranate Art Books, 1995), 24.

52. *The Johnny Otis Show,* Johnny Otis Collection, Archives of African American Music and Culture, Indiana University, August 30, 1982, EC 2534.

53. Hildebrand, "A Unique American Life," 12.

54. Ibid.

55. Ibid.

56. Cedric Johnson, *From Revolutionaries to Race Leaders* (Minneapolis: University of Minnesota Press, 2007), 9.

57. Otis, *Upside Your Head!* 113.

58. Ibid.

59. Interview with Johnny Otis, December 14, 1986, Altadena, California.

60. Otis, *Upside Your Head!* 117–18.

61. Ibid., 50, 81.

62. Ibid., 4.

63. John Arthur Maynard, *Venice West: The Beat Generation in Southern California* (New Brunswick, N.J., and London: Rutgers University Press, 1991), 2.

1. Central Avenue Breakdown

1. April Schultz, *Ethnicity on Parade* (Amherst: University of Massachusetts Press), 1995; John Higham, *Strangers in the Land: Patterns of American Nationalism, 1860–1925* (New Brunswick, N.J.: Rutgers University Press), 2002.

2. David Roediger, *Working toward Whiteness: How America's Immigrants Become White* (New York: Basic Books, 2005), 172.

3. Quoted in Yiota Papadopoulas, "Prejudice and Its Relationship to Acculturation for Greek Immigrants in the United States," in Spyros D. Orfanos, ed., *Reading Greek America: Studies in the Experience of Greeks in the United States* (New York: Pella Publishing Company, 2002), 348.

4. Helen Z. Papanikolas, "The Exiled Greeks," in Helen Z. Papanikolas, ed., *The Peoples of Utah* (Salt Lake City: Utah State Historical Society, 1981), 427–30.

5. David Roediger, *Colored White: Transcending the Racial Past* (Berkeley: University of California Press, 2002), 45–46.

6. Roediger, *Working toward Whiteness,* 59.

7. Ibid., 152.

8. Roediger, *Colored White,* 161; Roediger, *Working toward Whiteness,* 87.

9. Dan Georgakas, *My Detroit: Growing Up Greek and American in Motor City* (New York: Pella Publishing Company, 2006), 13.

10. Otis, *Listen to the Lambs,* 35.

11. Gary Stewart, *Rumba on the River: A History of the Popular Music of the Two Congos* (London: Verso, 2000), 23.

12. Interview with Nick Veliotes, December 3, 2005, Washington, D.C.

13. Ibid.

14. Otis, *Listen to the Lambs,* 36.

15. Jerry Crowe, "Some Overdue Recognition for a Basketball Trailblazer," *Los Angeles Times,* January 29, 2007, D2.

16. Interview with Nick Veliotes, December 3, 2005, Washington, D.C.

17. Interview with Johnny Otis, December 14, 1986, Altadena, California.

18. Interview with Nick Veliotes, December 3, 2005, Washington, D.C.

19. Ibid.

20. Otis, *Listen to the Lambs,* 122.

21. Steven Frangos, "Maria Papagika and the Transformations in Modern Greek Music," in Orfanos, ed., *Reading Greek America,* 223–39.

22. Otis, *Listen to the Lambs,* 42; Hildebrand, "A Unique American Life," 9.

23. Doris G. Worsham, "Revival in R&B Is Also a Revival for Johnny Otis," *Oakland Tribune,* March 10, 1983.

24. Otis, *Listen to the Lambs,* 27.

25. Ibid., 28.

26. Interview with Hal Kronick, December 9, 2005, Berkeley, California.

27. Lizabeth Cohen, *Making a New Deal: Industrial Workers in Chicago, 1919–1939* (Cambridge: Cambridge University Press, 2008).

28. Michael Denning, *The Cultural Front* (New York: Verso, 2000); Cohen, *Making a New Deal.*

29. Robert Warshow, *The Immediate Experience* (Cambridge, Mass.: Harvard University Press, 2001), 25–38.

30. Robert Cantwell, *When We Were Good: The Folk Revival* (Cambridge, Mass.: Harvard University Press, 1997), 182.

31. Denning, *The Cultural Front,* 239.

32. Interview with Hal Kronick, December 9, 2005, Berkeley, California.

33. Denning, *The Cultural Front,* 65, 217, 222, 225, 235, 447. The Greek Norwegian Andrews Sisters' song "Bei Mir Bistu Shein" was originally a Yiddish theater melody popularized by Black vaudevillians Johnnie and George, whose performance of the song at the Apollo Theatre encouraged Sammy Cahn to add the English-language lyrics that dominated the Andrews Sisters' version.

34. Interview with Hal Kronick, December 9, 2005, Berkeley, California.

35. Rick Coleman, *Blue Monday: Fats Domino and the Lost Dawn of Rock 'n' Roll* (New York: Da Capo Press, 2006), 37.

36. Otis, *Listen to the Lambs,* 131.

37. Interview with Nick Veliotes, December 3, 2005, Washington, D.C.

38. Hildebrand, "A Unique American Life," 9.

39. *The Johnny Otis Show,* Johnny Otis Collection, Archives of African American Music and Culture, Indiana University, August 3, 1970, OT 12903 and ATM Reel #2535.

40. Otis, *Listen to the Lambs,* 80. Otis refers to the band as the House Stompers in his 1968 book but as the House Rockers in his 1993 book, *Upside Your Head!* 53–55.

41. Otis, *Upside Your Head!* 39–41; Otis, *Listen to the Lambs,* 47.

42. Otis, *Listen to the Lambs,* 13.

43. Ibid.

44. Interview with Nick Veliotes, December 3, 2005, Washington, D.C; Otis, *Listen to the Lambs,* 13; Otis, *Upside Your Head!* 59.

45. Interview with Johnny Otis, December 14, 1986, Altadena, California.

46. Otis, *Upside Your Head!* 59.

47. Otis, *Listen to the Lambs,* 83. Name changes by entertainers were common in this era. Doris Kappelhoff became Doris Day. Norma Egstrom became Peggy Lee. Arthur Arshawsky became Artie Shaw. Milton Rajonsky became Shorty Rogers. Advertisers and marketers sometimes claimed that it was easier to market memorable "standard" names, but in almost every case, this process entailed ethnic whites taking names that sounded Anglo-Saxon, which indicates that part of the motivation came from a desire to escape discrimination by Anglo-Protestants. Michael Denning takes a different view of this process, claiming that the nationalist New Deal cultural front of the 1930s enabled formerly ostracized ethnic whites to claim roles as redemptive insiders by adopting new names that claimed America for themselves. See his great book *The Cultural Front,* 153. I discuss Otis's relationship to coining new names in chapter 8 of this book.

48. Otis, *Upside Your Head!* 75–77.

49. Love, *A Thousand Honey Creeks Later,* 54.

50. Love, "An Introduction," in Otis, *Listen to the Lambs,* 7–10.

51. Johnny Otis, "Johnny Otis Says Let's Talk," *Los Angeles Sentinel,* November 17, 1960, 6A.

52. Otis, *Upside Your Head!* 137.

53. At least two people in show business have been named Darby Hicks, a Cajun singer and a dancer from Chicago, but *this* Darby Hicks comes from the folklore of the streets—a character who sleeps with other men's wives and girlfriends, something like the "Jody" character in the folklore of U.S. military personnel in the mid-twentieth century. See Jeff Hannusch, "The Legend of Jody Ryder," *Living Blues* 163, May/June 2002, 21–22.

54. Otis, *Upside Your Head!* 137.

55. Love, *A Thousand Honey Creeks Later,* 61–62.

56. Otis, *Listen to the Lambs,* 85; Hildebrand, "A Unique American Life," 10.

57. Otis, *Listen to the Lambs,* 105.

58. Otis, *Upside Your Head!* 24.

59. Interview with Johnny Otis, December 14, 1986, Altadena, California.

60. Roy Porter, *There and Back: The Roy Porter Story* (Baton Rouge: Louisiana State University Press, 1991), 76.

61. Otis, *Colors and Chords,* 97.

62. Otis, *Listen to the Lambs,* 108–9.

63. Ibid., 171.

64. Ibid., 88.

65. *The Johnny Otis Show,* Johnny Otis Collection, Archives of African American Music and Culture, Indiana University, March 12, 1987, EC10" 2392; Hildebrand, "A Unique American Life," 11.

66. René Bloch interview, by Steven L. Isoardi, Central Avenue Sounds Oral History Collection, transcript 1995, Record ID 4230389, UCLA Libraries and Collections, 53.

67. Otis, *Listen to the Lambs,* 86–87; Otis, *Red Beans and Rice,* 64.

68. Daniel Widener, "Perhaps the Japanese Are to Be Thanked? Asia, Asian Americans, and the Construction of Black California," *Positions* 11, no. 1 (Spring 2003): 150.

69. Ted Gioia, *West Coast Jazz: Modern Jazz in California, 1945–1950* (Berkeley: University of California Press, 1998), 352.

70. Otis, *Red Beans and Rice,* 64.

71. Otis, *Listen to the Lambs,* 173.

72. Interview with Johnny Otis, December 14, 1986, Altadena, California.

73. Otis, *Listen to the Lambs,* 115–16.

74. Ibid., 87.

75. *The Johnny Otis Show,* Johnny Otis Collection, Archives of African American Music and Culture, Indiana University, ATM Reel #2526.

76. René Bloch interview, by Steven L. Isoardi, Central Avenue Sounds Oral History Collection, transcript 1995, Record ID 4230389, UCLA Libraries and Collections, 45; Hildebrand, "A Unique American Life," 11; Bruce Robinson, "Preacher Man," *Pacific Sun,* April 9–15, 1997, 14.

77. *The Johnny Otis Show,* Johnny Otis Collection, Archives of African American Music and Culture, Indiana University, June 12, 1989, OT 081.

78. Hildebrand, "A Unique American Life," 11. Otis meant the remark sarcastically, but it contained a truth nonetheless. Unlike many other bandleaders and musicians, he respected and championed the skills of women players and hired not only women singers but also Lady Dee Williams and Clora Bryant (among others) to play instruments in his bands.

2. Double Crossing Blues

1. Cholly Atkins and Jacqui Malone, *Class Act: The Jazz Life of Choreographer Cholly Atkins* (New York: Columbia University Press, 2001), 82.

2. Otis, *Listen to the Lambs,* 167.

3. Ibid., 167–68.

4. Hildebrand, "A Unique American Life," 12; Otis, *Upside Your Head!* 112–13.

5. *The Johnny Otis Show,* Johnny Otis Collection, Archives of African American Music and Culture, Indiana University, August 30, 1982, EC 2534.

6. Peter Guralnick, *Dream Boogie: The Triumph of Sam Cooke* (Boston: Little, Brown, 2005), 333.

7. Otis, *Red Beans and Rice,* vii.

8. Guralnick, *Dream Boogie,* 112.

9. Art Neville, Aaron Neville, Charles Neville, Cyril Neville, and David Ritz, *The Brothers: An Autobiography* (New York: Da Capo, 2000), 68; Guralnick, *Dream Boogie,* 112; Etta James, *Rage to Survive,* with David Ritz (New York: Villard Books, 1995), 164–65.

10. Neville et al., *The Brothers,* 59.

11. Otis, *Upside Your Head!* 13.

12. D. Thomas Moon, "We and Big Joe, Part 2" *Living Blues* 177, March/April 2005, 78.

13. Mark Hoffman and James Segrest, "Moanin' at Midnight: The Life and Times of Howlin' Wolf," *Living Blues* 173, July/August 2004, 94; Ellis Kell, "The Double Shuffle: Sam Lay," *Living Blues* 96, March/April 1991, 31.

14. Otis, *Upside Your Head!* 89–90.

15. Terry Hansen, "Otisology: The Spirit of Johnny Otis," *Goldmine,* April 1, 1994, 20; René Bloch interview, by Steven L. Isoardi, Central Avenue Sounds Oral History Collection, transcript 1995, Record ID 4230389, UCLA Libraries and Collections, 123.

16. *The Johnny Otis Show,* Johnny Otis Collection, Archives of African-American Music and Culture, Indiana University, Bloomington, Indiana, June 18, 1990, EC 2489.

17. Ibid., October 27, 1986, EC 2366.

18. Ibid., ATM Reel #2538 and Reel #2539. The "Blow, Jay, Blow" chant was a device often used by rhythm and blues bands to show off the playing of soloists. See, for example, Huey Smith and the Crowns, "Everybody's Whalin'" on *The Cosimo Matassa Story,* Proper P 1616, 2007.

19. *The Johnny Otis Show,* Johnny Otis Collection, Archives of African American Music and Culture, Indiana University, ATM Reel #2532.

20. Ibid., August 30, 1982, EC 2534.

21. Maureen Jung and Jack Rhyne, "Live at the 5-4 Ballroom," *Living Blues* 121, June 1995, 36.

22. Jeff Hannusch, *I Hear You Knockin': The Sound of New Orleans Rhythm and Blues* (Ville Platte, La.: Swallow Publications, 1985), 292–93.

23. Dr. John (Mac Rebennack), *Under a Hoodoo Moon: The Life of the Night Tripper,* with Jack Rummel (New York: St. Martin's 1994), 71.

24. Jeff Hannusch, *The Soul of New Orleans: A Legacy of Rhythm and Blues* (Ville Platte, La.: Swallow Publications, 2001), 339.

25. Hansen, "Otisology," 17.

26. *The Johnny Otis Show,* Johnny Otis Collection, Archives of African American Music and Culture, Indiana University, October 27, 1986, EC 2366.

27. Ibid.

28. Hansen, "Otisology," 17.

29. Anthony Summers, *Sinatra: The Life* (New York: Vintage, 2006), 39.

30. Hansen, "Otisology," 17.

31. *The Johnny Otis Show,* Johnny Otis Collection, Archives of African American Music and Culture, Indiana University, July 30, 1984, EC 2328, and July 24, 1989, OT 10 105.

32. Otis, *Upside Your Head!* 112.

33. Interview with Tom Reed, January 28, 2006, North Hills, California.

34. Otis, *Listen to the Lambs,* 173; Hildebrand, "A Unique American Life," 12–13.

35. Smith, *The Great Black Way,* 190.

36. Otis, *Listen to the Lambs,* 169.

37. Leonard Feather, "Blues Singer Esther Phillips Dies at 48," *Los Angeles Times* August 8, 1984, A8.

38. *The Johnny Otis Show,* Johnny Otis Collection, Archives of African American Music and Culture, Indiana University, July 24, 1989, OT 10, 103.

39. "Big Little Girl," *Time,* July 17, 1950.

40. James M. Salem, *The Late Great Johnny Ace and the Transition from R&B to Rock 'n' Roll* (Urbana: University of Illinois Press, 1999), 129.

41. Hess, liner notes to *You Ole Houn' Dawg.*

42. Galen Cart and Roy C. Ames, *Duke Peacock Records: An Illustrated History with Discography* (Milford, N.H.: Big Nickel Publications, 1990), 95–96.

43. *The Johnny Otis Show,* Johnny Otis Collection, Archives of African American Music and Culture, Indiana University, July 30, 1984 EC 2328.

44. Hansen, "Otisology," 2; *The Johnny Otis Show,* Johnny Otis Collection, Archives of African American Music and Culture, Indiana University, October 27, 1986, EC 2366.

45. Rick Kennedy and Randy McNutt, *Little Labels—Big Sound: Small Record Companies and the Rise of American Music* (Bloomington: Indiana University Press), 57.

46. Magnificent Montague, *Burn, Baby Burn!* 63–64.

47. Cart and Ames, *Duke Peacock Records,* 51.

48. Dr. John, *Under a Hoodoo Moon,* 78.

49. Salem, *The Late Great Johnny Ace and the Transition from R&B to Rock 'n' Roll,* 195.

50. *The Johnny Otis Show,* Johnny Otis Collection, Archives of African American Music and Culture, Indiana University, September 6, 1982, EC 2536.

51. Ibid.

52. Love, *A Thousand Honey Creeks Later,* 126.

53. Johnny Otis, "Johnny Otis Says Let's Talk," *Los Angeles Sentinel,* September 3, 1960, 4A.

54. Ibid., September 8, 1960, 4A.

55. Jesse Hamlin, "Soulful Sounds in Sebastopol," *San Francisco Chronicle,* December 21, 1993, E3.

56. Jonny Whiteside, "Nervous Man Nervous: Big Jay McNeely in 3D," *LA Weekly,* February 10, 2000, 2, www.laweekly.com/ink/00/11/music-whiteside.php.

57. *The Johnny Otis Show,* Johnny Otis Collection, Archives of African American Music and Culture, Indiana University, ATM Reel #2539.

58. Suzanne Smith, *Dancing in the Street: Motown and the Cultural Politics of Detroit* (Cambridge, Mass.: Harvard University Press, 1999), 149.

59. Ibid., 150.

60. Josh Sides, *L.A. City Limits: African American Los Angeles from the Great Depression to the Present* (Berkeley: University of California Press, 2003), 102–3.

61. Charles Perry, "O, Happy Days! When We Were Very Young," *Los Angeles Times Magazine,* February 4, 1990, 14.

62. Jung and Rhyne, "Live at the 5-4 Ballroom."

63. Horne, *Fire This Time,* 34.

64. John Anthony Brisbin, "Charles Brown," *Living Blues* 118 (December 1994), 21.

65. Michael B. Bakan, "Way Out West on Central: Jazz in The African-American Community of Los Angeles Before 1930," in Jacqueline Cogdell DjeDje and Eddie S. Meadows, *California Soul* (Berkeley: University of California Press, 1998), 30.

66. Hoskyns, *Waiting for the Sun,* 8.

67. Gary Marmonstein, "Central Avenue Jazz: Los Angeles Black Music of the Forties," *Southern California Quarterly* 70 (1988): 418–19.

68. Robert Gordon, *Jazz West Coast* (London: Quartet Books, 1986), 16.

69. Clora Bryant, Buddy Collette, William Green, Steven Isoardi, Jack Kelson, Horace Tapscott, Gerald Wilson, and Marl Young: Central Avenue Sounds Editorial Committee, *Central Avenue Sounds: Jazz in Los Angeles* (Berkeley: University of California Press, 1998), 365.

70. Hoskyns, *Waiting for the Sun,* 8.

71. Eric Avila, *Popular Culture in the Age of White Flight: Fear and Fantasy in Suburban Los Angeles* (Berkeley: University of California Press, 2004), 54.

72. Smith, *The Great Black Way,* 221.

73. Mina Yang, "A Thin Blue Line Down Central Avenue: The LAPD and the Demise of a Musical Hub," *Black Music Research Journal* 22, no. 2 (Autumn 2002): 218, 230.

74. Lynn Spigel, "Installing the Television Set: Popular Discourses on Television and Domestic Space, 1948–1955," *Camera Obscura* 16 (1988): 20; Milton MacKaye, "The Big Brawl: Hollywood vs. Television," *Saturday Evening Post,* January 19, 1952, 71.

75. MacKaye, "The Big Brawl," 17–18.

76. "The Lush New Suburban Market," *Fortune,* November 1953, 128.

77. Records of the Federal Home Loan Bank System, National Archives, Washington, D.C., Records Group 195, box 74, City Survey File, Los Angeles, D-50.

78. Ibid., D-33.

79. Ibid., D-29, D-13.

80. Hildebrand, "A Unique American Life," 15.

3. Willie and the Hand Jive

1. Smith, *The Great Black Way,* 270.

2. Johnny Otis, "Redd Foxx and Slappy White," in Otis, *Colors and Chords,* 76.

3. *The Johnny Otis Show,* Johnny Otis Collection, Archives of African American Music and Culture, Indiana University, ATM Reel #2528.

4. James, *Rage to Survive,* 44–45.

5. *Johnny Otis Show: Vintage 1950s Broadcasts from Los Angeles,* Ace Records, B0000C16NO.

6. Interview with Tom Reed, January 28, 2006, Los Angeles.

7. Ibid.

8. *The Johnny Otis Show*, Johnny Otis Collection, Archives of African American Music and Culture, Indiana University, ATM Reel #2532.

9. Interview with Tom Reed, January 28, 2006, Los Angeles.

10. Johnny Otis, "Johnny Otis Says Let's Talk," *Los Angeles Sentinel*, January 28, 1960, 4A.

11. Hildebrand, "A Unique American Life," 15.

12. See my discussion of television and consumer culture in George Lipsitz, *American Studies in a Moment of Danger* (Minneapolis: University of Minnesota Press, 2001), 248–62.

13. Interview with Johnny Otis, December 14, 1986, Altadena, California.

14. Steven Loza, "The Musical Life of the Mexican/Chicano People in Los Angeles, 1945–1985: A Study in Maintenance, Change, and Adaptation," Ph.D. dissertation, University of California, Los Angeles, 1985, 242–43.

15. Max Nunez, "Pachuco Boogie," *Q-VO* 2, no. 2, June 1980, 65; Loza, "The Musical Life of the Mexican/Chicano People," 214.

16. Loza, "The Musical Life of the Mexican/Chicano People," 310.

17. *The Johnny Otis Show*, Johnny Otis Collection, Archives of African American Music and Culture, Indiana University, June 18, 1990, EC 2489.

18. Susan Kresnicka Wilbur, "The History of Television in Los Angeles: 1931–1952," M.A. thesis, University of Southern California, 1976, 39.

19. Ibid., 43.

20. "Hadda Brooks," *Ebony* 6, April 1951, 101.

21. Interview with Johnny Otis, December 14, 1986, Altadena, California; *The Johnny Otis Show*, Johnny Otis Collection, Archives of African American Music and Culture, Indiana University, June 18, 1990, EC 2489.

22. Interview with Johnny Otis, December 14, 1986, Altadena, California.

23. Steven Loza, *Barrio Rhythm* (Urbana: University of Illinois Press, 1993), 81.

24. "Pop Beat," *Los Angeles Times*, February 4, 1989, part 5, 6.

25. Interview with Johnny Otis, December 14, 1986, Altadena, California.

26. David Reyes and Tom Waldman, *Land of a Thousand Dances: Chicano Rock 'n' Roll from Southern California* (Albuquerque: University of New Mexico Press, 1998), 17.

27. Interview with Johnny Otis, December 14, 1986, Altadena, California.

28. *The Johnny Otis Show*, Johnny Otis Collection, Archives of African American Music and Culture, Indiana University, ATM Reel #2693; James, *Rage to Survive*, 46.

29. *The Johnny Otis Show*, Johnny Otis Collection, Archives of African American Music and Culture, Indiana University, ATM Reel #2693.

30. James, *Rage to Survive*, 46–52; *The Johnny Otis Show*, Johnny Otis Collection, Archives of African American Music and Culture, Indiana University, ATM Reel #2693.

31. James, *Rage to Survive*, 46.

32. Ibid., 47.

33. Mickey Katz, *Papa, Play for Me: The Autobiography of Mickey Katz* (Middletown, Conn.: Wesleyan University Press), 2002.

34. Robinson, "Preacher Man," 15.

35. Interview with Johnny Otis, December 14, 1986, Altadena, California.

36. Robinson, "Preacher Man," 26.

37. Interview with Johnny Otis, December 14, 1986, Altadena, California.

38. Guralnick, *Dream Boogie,* 327.

39. "Were His Tires Slashed by Little Rock Vandals?" *Sepia,* June 1960, 51.

40. Johnny Otis, "Johnny Otis Says Let's Talk," *Los Angeles Sentinel,* March 24, 1960, 4A.

41. Johnny Otis, "Johnny Otis Says Let's Talk," *Los Angeles Sentinel,* August 3, 1961, 6A.

42. Otis, *Listen to the Lambs,* 239.

43. Hildebrand, "A Unique American Life," 16.

44. Mervyn Dymally, "Epilogue: Voter Rights Revisited," in Bud Schultz and Ruth Schultz, *The Price of Dissent: Testimonies to Political Repression in America* (Berkeley: University of California Press, 2001), 254–58; Mervyn M. Dymally, Oral History Interview, conducted 1996 and 1997 by Elston H. Carr, UCLA Oral History Program and California State Archives, State Government Oral History Program, vol. 1, pt. 1, 9, 11, 35, 128.

45. O'Neal, "Colors and Chords," 23.

46. Otis, *Upside Your Head!* 42–45.

47. Hildebrand, "A Unique American Life," 16.

48. *Los Angeles Sentinel,* August 28, 1968, reprinted in Tom Reed, *The Black Music History of Los Angeles: Its Roots: A Classical Pictorial History of Black Music in Los Angeles from the 1920s–1970* (Los Angeles: Black Accent on LA Press, 2000), 465.

49. Interview with Tom Reed, January 28, 2006, North Hills, California.

50. Reed, *The Black Music History of Los Angeles and Its Roots,* 285.

51. Otis, *Red Beans and Rice,* 38.

52. Horne, *Fire This Time,* 70, 99, 65.

53. Ibid., 2.

54. Ibid., 38.

55. Ibid., 67.

56. Richard Dedeaux, "I Remember Watts," on Watts Prophets, *When the 90s Came,* Payday/FFRR 422 828 880–2.

57. Otis, *Listen to the Lambs,* 247–48.

4. Listen to the Lambs

1. Otis, *Listen to the Lambs,* 18.

2. Cedric Johnson, *From Revolutionaries to Race Leaders* (Minneapolis: University of Minnesota Press, 2007), 10.

3. Otis, *Listen to the Lambs,* 91.

4. Ibid., 131.

5. Ibid.

6. Ibid., 22.

7. I take this phrase and analysis of the insurrection from Gerald Horne's extraordinary book *Fire This Time,* 128.

8. Otis, *Listen to the Lambs,* 78.

9. Ibid., 79.

10. Ibid.

11. Ibid., 52–62.

12. Ibid., 76.

13. Ibid., 67.

14. Richard Wright, *Native Son* (New York: Harper Collins, 1998), 440.

15. Otis, *Listen to the Lambs,* 239.

16. Ibid., 97.

17. Ibid., 137.

18. Miya Iwataki, "Congressman Mervyn M. Dymally—Unsung Hero," http://www.ncrr-la.org/NCRR_archives/dymally/dymally.htm.

19. Locke quoted in David Luis-Brown, *Waves of Decolonization: Discourses of Race and Hemispheric Citizenship in Cuba, Mexico, and the United States* (Durham, N.C.: Duke University Press, 2008), 153.

20. Theophus Smith, *Conjuring Culture: Biblical Formations of Black America* (New York: Oxford University Press, 1994), 252.

21. Otis, *Listen to the Lambs,* 129–30.

22. Ibid., 129.

23. Ibid., 135.

24. Charles Hamilton and Stokely Carmichael, *Black Power* (New York: Vintage, 1992), 3, 47.

25. Ibid., 44.

26. Ibid., 41.

27. Ibid., 53.

28. Martin Luther King Jr., *Where Do We Go from Here: Chaos or Community?* in James M. Washington, ed., *A Testament of Hope: The Essential Writings and Speeches of Martin Luther King, Jr.* (New York: HarperCollins, 1986), 568.

29. Ibid.

30. Otis, *Listen to the Lambs,* 254.

31. My particular use of the terms *bloodlines* and *bloodshed* comes from Robin D. G. Kelley. The phrase about people lying in graves as unmarked as their place in history comes from the opening of Sidney Poitier's great 1972 film, *Buck and the Preacher.*

5. All Night Long

1. Hansen, "Otisology," 24.

2. Otis, *Upside Your Head!* 62.

3. Ibid., 61.

4. *The Johnny Otis Show,* broadcast July 30, 1984.

5. *The Johnny Otis Show,* Johnny Otis Collection, Archives of African American Music and Culture, Indiana University, EC 2489.

6. Hildebrand, "A Unique American Life," 17.

7. See Lawrence Levine, *Black Culture, Black Consciousness* (New York: Oxford University Press, 1977).

8. Keneth Kinnamon and Michel Fabre, eds., *Conversations with Richard Wright* (Jackson: University Press of Mississippi, 1993), 243.

9. *The Johnny Otis Show*, broadcast July 30, 1984.

10. Otis, *Upside Your Head!* 89.

11. David Serlin, *Replaceable You: Engineering the Body in Postwar America* (Chicago: University of Chicago Press, 2004), 1, 114.

12. Laura Love, *You Ain't Got No Easter Clothes* (New York: Hyperion Books, 2004), 213.

13. Ibid.

14. Anthony Summers and Robbyn Swan, *Sinatra: The Life* (New York: Vintage, 2006), 52.

15. Ibid., 89.

16. Albert Goldman, *Elvis* (New York: McGraw-Hill, 1981), 338.

17. Summers and Swan, *Sinatra,* 85.

18. Jerry Butler, *Only the Strong Survive,* with Earl Smith (Bloomington: Indiana University Press, 2000), 61.

19. Guralnick, *Dream Boogie,* 532.

20. Sherrie Tucker, *Swing Shift: All-Girl Bands of the 1940s* (Durham, N.C.: Duke University Press, 2000), 323.

21. Bil Carpenter, "Big Mama: 200 Pounds of Boogaloo," *Living Blues* 106, November/December 1992, 29.

22. James, *Rage to Survive,* 45, 240.

23. Smith, *The Great Black Way,* 90.

24. Ibid., 218–19.

25. John Anthony Brisbin, "Charles Brown," *Living Blues* 118, December 1994, 29.

26. Hannusch, *I Hear You Knockin',* 48.

27. Johnny Otis related this story to me in a personal conversation backstage at the Club Ashkenaz, in Berkeley, on September 10, 2001.

28. Johnny Otis, "Johnny Otis Says Let's Talk," *Los Angeles Sentinel,* March 24, 1960, A4.

29. Stuart Goldman, "R&B Pioneer Johnny Otis: He Plays God's Music Now," *Los Angeles Times,* October 7, 1979, N3. See also Hildebrand, "A Unique American Life," 18.

30. Guralnick, *Dream Boogie,* 139.

31. Johnny Otis, "Johnny Otis Says Let's Talk," *Los Angeles Sentinel,* March 24, 1960, A4.

32. Kristina Lindgren, "Pioneer Rocker Plays Political Tune in Backing Black Rights," *Los Angeles Times,* May 3, 1981, D1.

33. Miya Iwataki, "Congressman Mervyn M. Dymally—Unsung Hero," http://www.ncrr-la.org/NCRR_archives/dymally/dymally.htm.

34. Hildebrand, "A Unique American Life," 18.

35. Josh Sides, *L.A. City Limits: African American Los Angeles from the Great Depression to the Present* (Berkeley: University of California Press, 2003), 33, 51.

36. Horace Boyer, *The Golden Age of Gospel* (Urbana: University of Illinois Press, 2000), 9.

37. Douglas Flamming, *Bound for Freedom: Black Los Angeles in Jim Crow America* (Berkeley: University of California Press, 2005), 115.

38. Cheryl J. Sanders, *Saints in Exile: The Holiness-Pentecostal Experience in African American Religion and Culture* (New York: Oxford University Press, 1996), 29.

39. Ibid., 32.

40. Harvey Cox, *Fire from Heaven: The Rise of Pentecostal Spirituality and the Reshaping of Religion in the 21st Century* (New York: Da Capo, 2001), 82, 95.

41. Robinson, "Preacher Man," 15.

42. Bob Claypool, "'Godfather of R&B' Puts That Ol' Time Feelin' Back in Music," *Houston Post,* February 25, 1983, 12E.

43. Ibid.

44. Otis, *Upside Your Head!* 125–28; *The Johnny Otis Show,* Johnny Otis Collection, Archives of African American Music and Culture, Indiana University, ATM Reel #2528–29.

45. Interview with Kim Hester-Williams, February 4, 2006, Berkeley, California.

46. Otis, *Upside Your Head!* 128.

47. Interview with Kim Hester-Williams, February 4, 2006, Berkeley, California.

48. Letter from Kim Hester-Williams to George Lipsitz, February 10, 2006.

49. Steven Dougherty, "Amen Corner Full for Big Mama Thornton," *Los Angeles Herald Examiner,* August 1, 1984, A3; Carpenter, "Big Mama: 200 Pounds of Boogaloo," 32.

50. Interview with Johnny Otis, December 14, 1986, Altadena, California.

51. Derek Richardson, "R&B's Johnny Otis Back Again," *San Francisco Chronicle,* Datebook Section, June 26, 1983, 45.

6. Play Misty for Me

1. Gene Connors hails from Birmingham, where his mother was a gospel singer in Dorothy Love Coates's Harmonettes.

2. Hildebrand, "A Unique American Life," 17. Leonard Feather, liner notes to *The Johnny Otis Show Live at Monterey! The Historic Rhythm and Blues Extravaganza that Rocked the 1970 Monterey Jazz Festival,* Epic/Legacy EK53628, 1993.

3. Brisbin, "Charles Brown," 28.

4. Love, *A Thousand Honey Creeks Later,* 243–44.

5. John Broven, *Rhythm and Blues in New Orleans* (Gretna, La.: Pelican Publishing, 1978), 24.

6. Hildebrand, "A Unique American Life," 17.

7. Greg Cahill, "Blues Deluxe: Guitarist Shuggie Otis Steps Centerstage," *Sonoma County Independent,* December 14, 1995, www.metroactive.com/papers/sonoma/12.14.95/blues-9550.html. This is the same Ethel Fort whose testimony about the Watts Riots appears in *Listen to the Lambs.*

8. Cahill, "Blues Deluxe."

9. Hildebrand, "A Unique American Life," 17.

10. Otis, *Upside Your Head!* 11.

11. Cahill, "Blues Deluxe."

12. Interview with Johnny Otis, December 14, 1986, Altadena, California.

13. *The Johnny Otis Show,* Johnny Otis Collection, Archives of African American Music and Culture, Indiana University, June 4, 1984, EC 10 2319.

14. Interview with Johnny Otis, December 14, 1986, Altadena, California.

15. *The Johnny Otis Show,* Johnny Otis Collection, Archives of African American Music and Culture, Indiana University, October 18, 1982, EC 2528.

16. Ibid., EC 10 2319.

17. Ibid., June 18, 1980, EC 2489.

18. Ibid., August 30, 1982, EC 2534.

19. Ibid., October 18, 1982, EC 2528, and August 30, 1982, EC 2534.

20. Ibid., ATM Reel #2528.

21. Ibid., ATM Reel #2534, and August 3, 1970, OT 12903, and September 21, 1970, OT 12904.

22. Ibid., ATM Reel #2534.

23. Ibid.

24. Ibid., September 6, 1982, EC 2536.

25. Ibid., ATM Reel #2532, and September 6, 1982, EC 2536.

26. Ibid., ATM Reel #2539.

27. Ibid.

28. Ibid.

29. Ibid., September 6, 1982, EC 2536.

30. Ibid., June 18, 1990, EC 2484.

31. Ibid., July 30, 1984, EC 2328.

32. Ibid., June 4, 1984, EC 10 2319.

33. Ibid., August 30, 1982, EC 2534 and EC 2535.

34. Ibid., ATM Reel #2535, and August 30, 1982, EC 2534.

35. Hannusch, *I Hear You Knockin',* 222.

36. *The Johnny Otis Show,* Johnny Otis Collection, Archives of African American Music and Culture, Indiana University, ATM Reel #2534, and August 30, 1982, EC 2534.

37. Ibid., September 6, 1982, EC 2537.

38. Ibid., EC 2536.

39. Ibid., June 4, 1984, EC 10 2319.

40. Peggy Murphy, "Zaven: True Blues Brother from Jerusalem," *Watts Sun Times,* October 29, 1980, 8.

41. *The Johnny Otis Show,* Johnny Otis Collection, Archives of African American Music and Culture, Indiana University, July 30, 1984, EC 2328.

42. Ibid., ATM Reel #2534, and August 30, 1982, EC 2534.

43. Ibid., March 2, 1987, EC 10 2392.

44. Ibid., ATM Reel #2534, and August 30, 1982, EC 2534.

45. Robinson, "Preacher Man," 15.

46. Helen Oakley Dance, *Stormy Monday: The T-Bone Walker Story* (New York: Da Capo, 1990), 187. Otis thought Hite was a nice man, and he was impressed by Hite's efforts to get Son House back into a recording studio, to persuade his label to sign Albert Collins, and to make music himself with John Lee Hooker. Yet he felt that Hite had over-looked something important when his band secured enormous sales of their cover versions

of classic blues songs. "Whites mouth the blues and do a good job, but they don't *create,*" Otis maintained. "The blues is created by Blacks. Why can't we quit looking for a white hope in every damned thing? Can't the Black man have any single game of his own?" Ibid.

47. Ibid.

7. The Watts Breakaway

1. Lawrence Christon, "Johnny Otis: 40 Years of Preaching R&B Sermons," *Los Angeles Times,* April 3, 1985, E1.

2. O'Neal, "Colors and Chords," 23.

3. Otis, *Upside Your Head!* 132–36.

4. O'Neal, "Colors and Chords," 24.

5. Ibid.

6. Ibid., 26.

7. Hildebrand, "A Unique American Life," 8.

8. Samella Lewis, *African American Art and Artists* (Berkeley: University of California Press, 2003), 198.

9. Sarah Schrank, *Art and the City: Civic Imagination and Cultural Authority in Los Angeles* (Philadelphia: University of Pennsylvania Press, 2008), 134–35.

10. John Outterbridge, foreword, in Otis, *Colors and Chords,* 4.

11. Lewis, *African American Art and Artists,* 299–301.

12. O'Neal, "Colors and Chords," 23.

13. Hamlin, "Soulful Sounds in Sebastopol."

14. *The Johnny Otis Show,* Johnny Otis Collection, Archives of African American Music and Culture, Indiana University, ATM Reel #2529.

15. Jung and Rhyne, "Live at the 5–4 Ballroom," 39.

16. Interview with Brad and Brooke Pierce, February 11, 2006, Canoga Park, California.

17. Ibid.

18. The Johnny Otis Show, *Good Lovin' Blues,* Ace Records B000008J60.

19. Lee Hildebrand, "Breaking Out: Jackie Payne," *Living Blues* 170, November/December 2003, 20.

20. Interview with Brad and Brooke Pierce, February 11, 2006, Canoga Park, California.

21. Ibid.

22. Ibid.

23. Ibid.

24. Ibid.

25. E-mail from Barbara Morrison to George Lipsitz, August 20, 2007.

26. Ibid.

27. Ibid.

28. Ibid.

29. Hamlin, "Soulful Sounds in Sebastopol."

30. Schiesl, "Behind the Shield," 159.

31. Horne, *Fire This Time,* 355–56.

32. Otis, *Upside Your Head!* 148.

33. Ibid., 163.

34. Ibid., 4, 21.

35. Ibid., 163.

36. Ibid., 164.

37. Interview with Carlos Zialcita, August 31, 2004, Berkeley, California.

38. Ibid.

39. Ibid.

40. Ibid.

41. Ibid.

42. Lee Hildebrand, "Sugar Pie DeSanto," *Living Blues* 186, September/October 2006, 34.

43. James Porter, "Sugar Is Sweet," *Roctober* 24 (1999).

44. Hildebrand, "Sugar Pie DeSanto," 34, 35.

45. Porter, "Sugar Is Sweet."

46. Hildebrand, "Sugar Pie DeSanto," 37.

47. Interview with Carlos Zialcita, August 31, 2004, Berkeley, California.

48. Ibid.

49. Ibid.

50. Ibid.

8. Midnight at the Barrelhouse

1. Robert Farris Thompson, *The Flash of the Spirit* (New York: Vintage, 1983), 19.

2. Smith, *Conjuring Culture;* Thompson, *The Flash of the Spirit.*

3. Moris Moriset is president of the Haitian *rara* group, Rara Ti-Malis Kache. He is quoted by Elizabeth McAlister in the epigraph of her very important book, *Rara! Vodou, Power, and Performance in Haiti and Its Diaspora* (Berkeley: University of California Press, 2002).

4. Smith, *Conjuring Culture,* 208–9.

5. George P. Rawick, *From Sundown to Sunup* (Westport, Conn.: Greenwood Press, 1972), 30–52.

6. Smith, *Conjuring Culture,* 209–12.

7. Robert Farris Thompson, "Big Hearted Power," in Grey Gundaker, ed., *Keep Your Head to the Sky: Interpreting African American Home Ground* (Charlottesville: University Press of Virginia, 1998), 43–44.

8. Otis, *Upside Your Head!* 55.

9. Hildebrand, "An Unusual American Life," 20.

10. *The Johnny Otis Show,* Johnny Otis Collection, Archives of African American Music and Culture, Indiana University, July 24, 1989, OT 10 106.

11. Ibid., June 18, 1990, EC 2489.

12. Otis, *Upside Your Head!* 112.

13. Interview with Brad Pierce, February 11, 2006, Canoga Park, California.

14. Otis, *Listen to the Lambs,* 32–50.

15. Ibid., 36.

16. Ibid., 116.

17. Otis, *Upside Your Head!* 44.

18. J. Alvin Kugelmass, "Name-Changing—and What It Gets You: Twenty-Five Who Did It," *Commentary* 14 (August 1952): 145.

19. Michael Denning, *The Cultural Front* (New York: Verso, 2000), 153.

20. Kimberly W. Benston, "'I Yam What I Am': Naming and Unnaming in Afro-American Literature," *African American Review* 16, no. 1 (Spring 1982): 3.

21. David Luis-Brown, *Waves of Decolonization: Discourses of Race and Hemispheric Citizenship in Cuba, Mexico, and the United States* (Durham, N.C.: Duke University Press, 2008), 159.

22. Otis, *Listen to the Lambs,* 84–85, 219.

23. Charles Payne, *I've Got the Light of Freedom: The Organizing Tradition and the Mississippi Freedom Struggle* (Berkeley: University of California Press, 1995), 389; Nikhil Pal Singh, *Black Is a Country: Race and the Unfinished Struggle for Democracy* (Cambridge, Mass.: Harvard University Press, 2005), 205.

24. King Jr., "Where Do We Go from Here: Chaos or Community?" 561.

25. Otis, *Listen to the Lambs,* 226.

26. Martin Luther King Jr., *Strength to Love* (Philadelphia: Fortress Press, 1981), 13.

27. Ibid., 15, 17, 22.

28. Ibid., 31–38.

29. Ibid., 97–106.

30. Martin Luther King Jr., "The Drum Major Instinct," in Washington, ed., *A Testament of Hope,* 259–67.

31. Martin Luther King Jr., "A Time to Break Silence," in Washington, ed., *A Testament of Hope,* 242.

32. King Jr., *Strength to Love,* 77–78.

33. Ibid., 58–59, 75.

34. Ibid., 66.

35. Ibid., 67.

36. Ibid., 68.

37. Interview with Johnny Otis, December 14, 1986, Altadena, California.

38. Interview with Hal Kronick, December 9, 2005, Berkeley, California.

39. Ibid.

40. Hisaye Yamamoto, *Seventeen Syllables* (New Brunswick, N.J.: Rutgers University Press, 2001), 150–57.

41. O'Neal, "Colors and Chords," 24.

42. Interview with Johnny Otis, December 14, 1986, Altadena, California.

43. O'Neal, "Colors and Chords," 24.

44. Mezz Mezzrow and Bernard Wolfe, *Really the Blues* (New York: Citadel Underground, 1990).

45. Otis, *Upside Your Head!* 160.

46. Claire Jean Kim, *Bitter Fruit: The Politics of Black–Korean Conflict in New York City* (New Haven, Conn.: Yale University Press, 2000), 11.

47. See, for example, Coleman, *Blue Monday;* and Brian Ward, *Just My Soul Responding: Rhythm and Blues, Black Consciousness and Race Relations* (Berkeley: University of California Press, 1998).

48. Love, *A Thousand Honey Creeks Later;* Otis, *Upside Your Head!*

49. Toni Morrison, *Beloved* (New York: New American Library, 1987), 275.

Index

George Lipsitz is professor of black studies and sociology at the University of California, Santa Barbara. He wrote the foreword for a recent republication of Johnny Otis's *Listen to the Lambs,* and he is the author of *Footsteps in the Dark: The Hidden Histories of Popular Music; Time Passages: Collective Memory and American Popular Culture;* and *American Studies in a Moment of Danger,* all published by the University of Minnesota Press.